The Measure of Injury

The Measure of Injury

Race, Gender, and Tort Law

Martha Chamallas and
Jennifer B. Wriggins

NEW YORK UNIVERSITY PRESS
New York and London

NEW YORK UNIVERSITY PRESS
New York and London
www.nyupress.org

Library of Congress Cataloging-in-Publication Data

Chamallas, Martha.
The measure of injury : race, gender, and tort law /
Martha Chamallas and Jennifer B. Wriggins.
p. cm.
Includes bibliographical references and index.
ISBN-13: 978-0-8147-1676-2 (cl : alk. paper)
ISBN-10: 0-8147-1676-8 (cl : alk. paper)
1. Personal injuries—United States. 2. Torts—United States.
3. Race discrimination—Law and legislation—United States.
4. Sex discrimination—Law and legislation—United States.
I. Wriggins, Jennifer B. II. Title.
KF1257.C43 2010
346.7303—dc22 2009049623

New York University Press books are printed on acid-free paper,
and their binding materials are chosen for strength and durability.
We strive to use environmentally responsible suppliers and materials
to the greatest extent possible in publishing our books.

Manufactured in the United States of America
10 9 8 7 6 5 4 3 2 1

In memory of my mother, Lisa Chamallas

MC

To Mary, Jean, and Sarah

JW

Contents

Acknowledgments ix

Introduction 1

1 Theoretical Frames 13

2 Historical Frames 35

3 Intentional Torts 63

4 Negligence 89

5 Causation 119

6 Damages 155

Conclusion 183

Notes 191

Index 223

About the Authors 228

Acknowledgments

For both of us, this book represents the culmination of decades-long research on race, gender, and tort law. During this time, we have received invaluable help from colleagues and students too numerous to mention and have been inspired and influenced by scholars and friends across the country and overseas. In the more than three years since we started collaborating on this book, each of us has built up special debts of gratitude.

Martha wishes to thank her colleagues at the Moritz College of Law, The Ohio State University, for the support they have given her and for the opportunity to showcase early versions of two chapters of this book as part of her University Distinguished Lecture. She also thanks the faculty of the Suffolk Law School for their contributions during her semester as a visiting professor. Over the years, she benefited greatly from the insights, criticisms, and suggestions made by participants at workshops and classes at the University of Denver-Sturm College of Law, University of California at Davis, Wake Forest University, University of Cincinnati, Mississippi College, Widener University, Washington University, New York University, Harvard University, and Columbia University law schools. Most especially, she is grateful to her splendid group of research assistants: Brett Taylor, Amanda Klase, Ben Rose, Melissa Gilbert, Barbara Schwabauer, and Katie Johnson. And she sends a special note of appreciation to Peter Shane and Beth Shane for their personal and professional wisdom and encouragement.

Jenny wishes to thank her colleagues at the University of Maine School of Law, particularly Deans Donald N. Zillman, Colleen Khoury, and Peter Pitegoff, for providing support, challenge, and encouragement over the years. She also appreciates the input from participants in faculty workshops and classes at Boston University School of Law, Harvard Law School, Northeastern University School of Law, the Moritz College of Law, The Ohio State University, Suffolk University School of Law, and the University of Denver-Sturm College of Law, as well as from participants in the Insurance and Social Policy Study group organized by Tom Baker and the University of Connecticut School of

Law. She is grateful to the University of Southern Maine (USM) for its support and for the opportunity to present an early version of some of these ideas as the 2007 USM Trustee Professor Lecturer. She thanks her torts students who have raised many questions that required research to begin to answer, particularly Wil Smith. She is forever indebted to her wonderful research assistants, Marya Baron, Zachary Brandmeir, Joy Britting, Dennis Carillo, David Goldman, Erin Krause, Katharine I. Rand, Josh Scott, and Rebekah Smith. The law librarians at the Garbrecht Law Library at the University of Maine School of Law have been essential to this book, and Jenny is deeply grateful for their help. They include Christine Hepler, Maureen Quinlan, Sherry McCall, Greg Stowe, and Julie Welch. Administrative staff, including Frances Dee Smith, Joy Mercier, Jeremy LeStage, Jenni Hebert, Katie Boone, and Tara Artinyan, also provided skilled and indispensable assistance. She also thanks her friends and family members for all their help, particularly her siblings Chris Wriggins and Diana Cundy, and her friends George Chauncey, Ron Gregg, Sadhbh Neilan, and Traci West. She also appreciates the support of her parents, Howard Wriggins, who passed away as this book was being written, and Sally Wriggins, as well as that of Mary L. Bonauto, Jean Bonauto Wriggins, and Sarah Bonauto Wriggins.

Finally, we both thank Debbie Gershenowitz, our terrific editor, for her valuable help and patience on this project.

Portions of Chapter 2 originated in Martha Chamallas with Linda K. Kerber, "Women, Mothers and the Law of Fright: A History," 88 Mich. L. Rev. 601 (1990); Jennifer B. Wriggins, "Toward a Feminist Revision of Torts," 13 Am. U. J. Gender Soc. Pol'y & L. 139 (2005); and Jennifer B. Wriggins, "Torts, Race, and the Value of Injury, 1900–1949," 49 Howard L.J. 99 (2005). Earlier versions of portions of chapter 3 appeared in Martha Chamallas, "Discrimination and Outrage: The Migration from Civil Rights to Tort Law," 48 Wm. & Mary L. Rev. 1 (2007); Martha Chamallas, "Shifting Sands of Federalism: Civil Rights and Tort Claims in the Employment Context," 41 Wake Forest L. Rev. 697 (2006); Martha Chamallas, "Discrimination and Outrage," in Fault Lines: Tort Law as Cultural Practice (David Engel and Michael McCann eds., Stan. Law Books 2009); and Jennifer B. Wriggins, "Domestic Violence Torts," 75 So. Cal. L. Rev. 121 (2001). An earlier version of portions of chapter 4 appeared in Martha Chamallas, "Unpacking Emotional Distress: Sexual Exploitation, Reproductive Harm, and Fundamental Rights," 44 Wake Forest L. Rev. 1109 (2009). Parts of chapter 5 derived from Jennifer Wriggins, "Genetics, IQ, Determinism, and Torts: The Example of Discovery in Lead Exposure Litigation," 77 B.U. L. Rev. 1025 (1997). An earlier version of portions of chapter 6 appeared in Martha Chamallas, "Civil Rights in Ordinary Torts Cases: Race, Gender and the Calculation of Economic Loss," 38 Loy. (L.A.) L. Rev. 1435 (2005); Jennifer B. Wriggins, "Damages in Tort Litigation: Thoughts on Race and Remedies, 1865-2007," 27 Rev. of Lit. 37 (2007); and Jennifer B. Wriggins, "Whiteness, Equal Treatment, and the Valuation of Injury in Torts, 1900–1949" in Fault Lines: Tort Law as Cultural Practice (David Engel and Michael McCann eds., Stan. Law Books 2009).

Introduction

Despite its social importance, the topic of the significance of race and gender in the law of torts has not received sustained attention largely because, on its surface, the world of torts appears divided between those who suffer injury and those who inflict injury, categories that are race and gender neutral. To be sure, there is a vague awareness that particular social groups are more likely to sustain certain types of injuries, for example, that women are disproportionately hurt by domestic violence and that African American children are at greater risk than white children of suffering injury from exposure to lead paint. However, the conventional wisdom is that the legal rules, concepts, and structures for liability no longer take account of the race or gender of the parties.

This book contests that conventional wisdom and explores how the shape of contemporary U.S. tort law—from the types of injuries recognized, to judgments about causation, to the valuation of injuries—has been affected by the social identity of the parties and cultural views on gender and race. At a time when formal doctrine is neutral on its face and rights and liabilities are stated in universal terms, considerations of race and gender most often work their way into tort law in complex, subtle ways. This book thus pays close attention to the social construction of harms, unconscious cognitive bias that affects legal reasoning, and the tacit measures by which the law places a dollar value on human suffering. We examine the basic building blocks of tort liability—the concepts of intent, negligence, causation, and damages—for evidence of hidden race and gender bias, and we identify the gender and race implications of deep-seated assumptions that mark out the boundaries of the field.

The story we tell is a complex one. Not all tort rules disadvantage women and racial minorities, and it is important to recognize that tort law has been a site for promoting equality as well as for perpetuating hierarchies. Particularly in the past two decades, certain principles and concepts first enunciated in statutory civil rights litigation have migrated into tort law to produce a more egalitarian body of cases. However, when viewed through a wider cultural lens, the basic structure of contemporary tort law still tends to reflect and reinforce the social marginalization of women and racial minorities and to place a lower value on their lives, activities, and potential. We trace this thread of devaluation throughout tort law by dissecting the doctrines that can pose insuperable—but most often partial—barriers to the recovery of damages in contexts which specially affect women and racial minorities.

The Measure of Injury offers a critical re-examination of the "proper" domain of tort law, focusing on which injuries have been placed at the "core" of tort law and which harms have been relegated to the margins. The most current revision of the prestigious American Law Institute's Restatement of Torts (Third) is built around the dual premises that accidental injury lies at the core of tort law and that physical injury, rather than emotional harm or injuries to relationships, is of paramount concern. We question these foundational assumptions on both descriptive and normative grounds. We argue that the privileging of accidental injury is possible only because massive injuries caused by domestic violence and sexual exploitation have fallen outside the realm of compensable harms. In theory, the protection the law offers against intentional harm is certainly capable of capturing injuries suffered by victims of domestic violence and discriminatory workplace harassment. In practice, however, tort law has been a poor vehicle for compensation for these victims and does little to deter even the most blatant forms of aggression and abuse.

Similarly, we contend that the privileged status of physical harm over emotional and relational injury found in contemporary tort law is sustained by dubious assumptions about the greater seriousness and importance of this type of injury in the lives of ordinary people. This book addresses the conceptual weakness of the physical/emotional distinction that pervades the law of torts. We explain how certain injuries—often related to reproduction and motherhood—have been socially constructed as "emotional," rather than "physical," with significant implications for the prospects of recovery. In a similar vein, we analyze the recent trend toward eliminating or curtailing noneconomic damages that has emerged as a corollary to the privileging of physical harm. This recent effort has created a hierarchy of damages that ranks economic damages over noneconomic damages and casts doubt on the legitimacy and centrality of many kinds of intangible losses suffered by seriously injured tort victims. We detail how widespread tort reforms, such as the placement of caps on recovery of noneconomic damages, have had serious negative consequences for female and minority plaintiffs. Overall, we explain how the marginalizing of emotional harm and noneconomic injury has worked to the systematic disadvantage of women and minority plaintiffs, who may find that the most serious recurring injuries in their lives are not compensable in tort.

One of the principal objectives of this book is to connect the current emphasis on negligence, physical harms, and economic damages to gender and race bias, broadly conceived. The book catalogues a variety of mechanisms—in contemporary law and historically—through which racial and gender hierarchies have been sustained and reproduced. In several contexts, old forms of bias have resurfaced in updated forms. In their new guises, the rules for recovery are often softer and less exclusionary but nonetheless operate to perpetuate disparities linked to race and gender. In the realm of intentional torts, for example, the old doctrine of interspousal immunity prevented wives from holding abusive husbands accountable for domestic violence that would otherwise be actionable in tort as battery, assault, or false imprisonment. Today, the obstacles to recovery for domestic violence torts are less total but also less visible. Contemporary claims of domestic violence victims have been stymied by short statutes of limitations, the imposition of technical procedural rules that steer cases into family court, and a system of insurance that denies coverage for women abused in their homes. As a result, tort claims for domestic violence are still exceedingly rare and are regarded as exceptional and problematic.

A similar trajectory can be seen with respect to tort claims for injuries caused by workplace harassment. Prior to the 1980s, racial and sexual harassment were unacknowledged as legal harms and were generally dismissed as harmless teasing, flirtation, or hazing. Largely because of the development of the concept of the "hostile environment," workplace harassment has now been converted to a legal harm. Nevertheless, tort claims of harassment victims are often defeated by special judge-made rules of preemption and heavy threshold requirements of proof that cordon off these suits from the domain of torts, leaving only statutory civil rights remedies as a possible means of recovery. This sharp separation of civil rights law from torts lessens the amount of recovery for harassment victims; it also sends the message that tort law has no room for promoting race and gender equity and that public policy should not affect the contours of tort doctrine.

With respect to negligence claims, we trace how gender-linked limitations on recovery have been part of the ongoing struggle by which each jurisdiction determines the scope of duties owed by tort defendants. Under the general rubric of recovery for negligent infliction of emotional distress, courts routinely confront gender-inflected issues of sexual exploitation, reproduction, and parent/child relationships. The barriers to recovery in such emotional distress cases have increasingly been liberalized, as courts chip away at the old common law doctrine that denied all legal protection for mental disturbance. In this chaotic area of law, however, courts continue to impose a host of limiting doctrines—from refusing to recognize "stand-alone" claims for emotional distress to insistence on the existence of a contractual relationship between the parties—that are designed to make recovery more difficult than in "ordinary" cases of negligence, such as automobile accidents or slip-and-fall cases. Following a pattern characteristic of contemporary forms of bias, the gender dynamic in these cases does not favor individual male plaintiffs over similarly situated female plaintiffs but instead operates to disfavor the type of claim that women plaintiffs are likely to bring, placing them at a considerable structural disadvantage.

In addition to focusing on how tort law selects injuries for legal recognition, the book explores how cultural attitudes on race and gender affect legal judgments about causation. Employing the language of both traditional tort theory and social and cognitive psychology, we explain how seemingly simple judgments of cause and effect can mask more complex, controversial assessments of blame and responsibility. Our critique of the legal doctrine of causation argues that the quasi-scientific inquiry into "cause-in-fact" ought to be recast as an active mental process of "causal attribution." Once this turn is made, it is easier to appreciate how prevailing gender and race stereotypes, race- and gender-based schemas, and other common cognitive "shortcuts" infect causal judgments and bias decision making.

In certain types of cases, the gender and race of the victims are so salient that they deflect attention from the negligent actions of the defendant, making it seem more likely that the plaintiff is solely responsible for the adverse outcome. The book discusses how issues of causation have been deployed in "wrongful birth" and lead paint cases to both expand and limit claims for marginalized groups. In the context of wrongful birth—a cause of action almost unthinkable prior to *Roe v. Wade*—changing cultural attitudes about reproduction and gender gradually led many courts to shift causal responsibility for an infant's genetic defects away from the pregnant woman and onto the physician who negligently failed to inform her of available reproductive options. We trace how, over time, the causation issue has been framed differently, pointing to dramatically different results. In contrast, in lead paint cases, landlords and housing authorities that negligently failed to abate toxic hazards have sometimes succeeded in their attempts to claim that a minority child's cognitive impairment was traceable to preexisting conditions rather than to exposure to lead paint. We discuss how a court's willingness to ascribe cause to "internal" factors, such as genetics and family background, may be linked to the racial identities of the plaintiffs, particularly in multiple-cause cases where a combination of factors contributed to an adverse outcome. Through these examples, we tease out the cultural dimensions of causal attribution and its dependence on norms and expectations linked to gender and race.

Finally, because the law of damages is so central to tort recovery, *The Measure of Injury* concludes with an in-depth analysis of the methods and processes of the valuation of injury. In the realm of torts, court and juries not only determine liability but are required to measure injuries, as well. Not unlike sentences meted out in criminal cases, tort measurements of lost earnings potential, pain and suffering, and other types of damages can be affected by negative attitudes toward social groups and are not immune from conscious and unconscious gender and race bias. In our sections on economic and noneconomic damages, we focus on the practical effects on women and minorities of statistical tables widely used to predict future economic losses and on the recent cutbacks in awards of noneconomic damages. We also highlight the expressive importance of tort damages as a signal of the social worth of plaintiffs and a societal measure of their suffering.

Our examination of the practices relating to the calculation of lost future earning capacity provides a dramatic illustration of how basic racial and gender hierarchies can be replicated by using low-visibility methods of computation that continue to be based explicitly on the race and gender of the plaintiffs. We discuss how courts and experts in both the United States and Canada have routinely relied on gender- and race-based tables to determine how many years severely injured plaintiffs would have worked if they had not been injured and the amount they would have earned in their lifetimes. This statistical practice tends to yield significantly higher awards for white men than for women of all races and minority men and is reminiscent of the segregationist practices of courts in the Deep South, which pegged tort recoveries of black plaintiffs to prior awards for other black plaintiffs. We also analyze two important recent rulings—by the Special Master of the September 11 Victim Compensation Fund and by Federal District Judge Jack Weinstein in the high-profile Staten Island ferry crash case—that reject such gender- and race-based calculations and devise more egalitarian methods for valuing injuries.

Our discussion of tort damages takes up the contentious debate over the legitimacy of awarding plaintiffs money damages for intangible, noneconomic losses. We critique the recent legislative assault on noneconomic damages brought about by the enactment of caps on this portion of a plaintiff's damage award, stressing the unequal effects such caps have on persons whose injuries defy monetization and who are unable to prove the value of their loss in market-based terms. We argue that the case for imposing such caps is flawed and based on a false dichotomy between the economic and the noneconomic aspects of a plaintiff's injuries. Much like the physical/emotional distinction that denies recognition for certain types of injury, this dichotomy has had the effect of discouraging inquiry into the specifics of plaintiffs' injuries and minimizing the seriousness of those injuries. Denying full recovery for noneconomic harm disparately affects a class of largely female plaintiffs, including those with serious injuries and those who allege sexualized and reproductive harm, as well as elderly plaintiffs in nursing homes. In addition to these gendered effects, we cite evidence that caps on noneconomic damages negatively affect minority plaintiffs, whose cases are more likely to be rejected by prospective attorneys because they will not yield sufficient economic damages to make the lawsuits worth pursuing. The net result of these reforms is to reinforce gender and race disparities and to blunt the more egalitarian effects of jury awards at a moment in history when juries represent the most diverse site of decision making in the torts system.

Most of this book is devoted to describing and deconstructing contemporary tort law. We identify both doctrinal and structural obstacles to gender and race equity and isolate various mechanisms that reproduce disadvantage and disparities. At points, our description is detailed and traditional, focusing in on specific rules, such as the preemption of tort claims for workplace harassment, that are clearly embedded in gendered and racialized contexts. At other points, our description of cognitive biases, tacit hierarchies, and dichotomies that pervade the law is more interpretive and critical; it functions as argument as well as simple description. The connection we draw between the low value placed on emotional harm and the legal treatment of reproductive harms, for example, is meant simultaneously to explain the gender implications of an intricate legal doctrine and to critique the inadequate protection provided to women for a serious injury for which there is no clear male analogue.

Throughout the book, we move from deconstruction to reconstruction and offer some proposals for changes we see as desirable. Our advice on reforming tort law is limited and highly contextual. We suggest both large and small reforms that could push tort law in a more egalitarian and more just direction. Matching our critique, some of our proposals are very specific and pointed, including our proposal for rejecting gender- and race-based tables in favor of more inclusive, neutral computations to measure damage awards. Other prescriptions are pitched at a higher level of generality, such as our advocacy for allowing principles of human and civil rights to migrate into tort law in order to update and transform tort concepts of outrageousness and dignitary harm. Many times, we simply urge that the gender and racial contexts of tort cases be made more visible, even if it means little more than labeling a case one of "harassment," "sexual exploitation," or "reproductive harm," rather than only intentional or negligent infliction of emotional distress.

The approach to tort law we employ in this book differs from the dominant intellectual approach in the United States, which draws heavily from the "law and economics" school, with its emphasis on the efficiency of tort rules. Instead, our critical approach to tort law is not tied to any one school of thought but is influenced by a diverse body of scholarship, within and outside the discipline of law. Throughout the book, we draw upon what is now regarded as "traditional" legal scholarship, particularly theories of equality and civil rights principles developed in constitutional law and statutory antidiscrimination fields, such as employment discrimination law.

Many of our normative commitments and methodologies have been borrowed from the vast multidisciplinary feminist literature that has filtered into law, humanities, and social sciences. With respect to feminist theories, we lean extensively on several of the major perspectives within feminist legal thought—on liberal feminism, with its emphasis on formal equality and equal opportunity, on cultural feminism, with its revaluation of traditionally feminine activities and traits, and on radical feminism, with its condemnation of sexual exploitation and abuse. In attempting to intertwine the major themes of race and gender, we share the viewpoint of postessentialist and critical race feminist writers who have maintained that systems of subordination are interlocking and interdependent and who have insisted that the specific situation of racialized subgroups of women and men may differ radically from those in the mainstream.

Our perspective on race and tort law is informed by an antiracist and critical race literature that regards race as a persistent and central feature in American culture. From this literature we take up one of the prominent themes of this book, namely that slavery and segregation have left an imprint on tort rules and structures and that white racial privilege still affects the recognition and valuation of injury. It is our contention that race also matters in everyday judgments of cause and effect and assessments of responsibility for injury. In our white-dominated society, the lingering cognitive association of blackness with inferiority and with the lack of value can distort legal judgments, devaluing and sometimes erasing the pain and suffering of people of color.

Finally, another particularly important influence that informs our perspective on tort law comes from social and cognitive psychology. We apply insights from that field to help us understand how the decisions of legal actors might be affected by race and gender, even when such actors are unaware of any bias and have no conscious desire to advantage or disadvantage a particular social group. As they operate in institutional contexts, common forms of cognitive bias—particularly habits of thought that make it harder to imagine different outcomes—can affect expectations about what is normal and reasonable and therefore ultimately impact legal liability. The psychological perspective has special relevance to the law because it provides a crucial mediating link between cultural attitudes and decisions made within legal frameworks and institutions.

As with much of the critical literature of the past three decades, this book pays particular attention to the multiple ways power and privilege play out in specific social contexts and to the social construction of legal meanings. In this respect, we regard tort law as a particularly appropriate site for investigating differing "common sense" understandings of such fundamental constructs as dignity, reasonableness, cause, and injury.

On a final note, we wish to underscore one special feature of tort law as a site for progressive reform—its capacity to express and reinforce universal norms and principles. Thus, although this book analyzes the significance of race and gender in tort law—and thus falls under the genre of identity-based scholarship—we are well aware that for many persons the appeal of tort law is that it is not closely tied to identity politics. Interestingly, the migration of civil rights concepts into tort law has the capacity to universalize claims of equal treatment and equal justice beyond traditionally protected groups of plaintiffs, such as women and racial minorities. In this respect, progressive changes in tort law may sometimes disrupt binary categories (such as black or white or male or female) by allowing recovery to plaintiffs whose injuries do not fit the familiar script of gender- or race-based injury.

Organization of the Book

The organization of this book tracks the major demarcation lines in tort law, with chapters on intentional torts, negligence, causation, and damages. For each of these chapters, we have selected topics which best expose the workings of race and gender in those substantive areas. The four substantive law chapters are preceded by two chapters on tort theory and history. In these framework chapters, we situate our approach to tort law within the larger theoretical landscape and discuss important historical themes related to race and gender that are recapitulated in contemporary cases.

Chapter 1 introduces our critical approach to tort law and distinguishes our approach from the two tort theories that currently dominate the field, law and economics and corrective justice. We explain how our approach is influenced by a strong Legal Realist tradition in tort law and by the impact of the Restatement of Torts, including the Restatement of Torts (Third) that is currently under way. We discuss the body of feminist and critical race scholarship that provides the main ingredients for our approach, as well as existing critical torts scholarship focused on gender and race. We conclude chapter 1 by aligning ourselves with "pluralist" scholars who regard the quest for a unified theory of torts as futile and undesirable and applaud tort law's historical capacity to transform itself by absorbing concepts, principles, and norms from other areas of law.

Chapter 2 presents some of the major themes of the book through an examination of two groups of early cases that clearly show the impact of gender and race on the outcome of tort litigation. After a brief discussion of the importance of the institutions of slavery and coverture on the rights of tort plaintiffs, we examine a line of "nervous-shock" cases brought by female plaintiffs at the turn of the 20th century. We trace the development of the "impact" rule that served in many states to defeat recovery for women who suffered miscarriages and stillbirths as a result of shock and fright caused by defendants' negligence. In these nervous-shock cases, we witness courts struggle with the proper classification of injuries cognitively associated with women and the emergence of a dichotomy between physical and emotional harm that continues to pervade the law of torts. Chapter 2 also introduces the concepts of racial devaluation and white racial privilege through an examination of segregation-era cases in which courts took note of the race of the parties and indicated the effect of race on their judgments about liability and damages. We discuss the positive value some courts placed on whiteness and the rights conferred on white plaintiffs to receive compensation when they complained of "insults" from racial minorities. The chapter concludes with an examination of suits brought by African Americans in which their injuries were minimized or devalued by judges who treated their claims less favorably than those of similarly situated whites.

In chapter 3, devoted to intentional torts, we criticize the marginal status that intentional torts currently occupies in contemporary tort law and analyze the slim protection tort law provides for two undertheorized claims of particular importance to women and racial minorities—claims for domestic violence and for workplace harassment. Our examination focuses principally on the tort of intentional infliction of emotional distress, the relatively new cause of action that allows plaintiffs to recover for "outrageous" conduct that produces severe emotional injury. We explore several doctrinal and structural barriers to recovery for these harms, ranging from lack of insurance coverage, to procedural joinder rules, to preemption of tort claims, all of which have the effect of steering domestic violence and harassment claims away from torts and into other areas of the law, such as family law and statutory civil rights law. We criticize this constricting of the domain of tort law because it often leads to lower and inadequate compensation of victims, threatens to stunt development of general tort principles, and sends a dismissive message that these widespread harms do not measure up as injuries worthy of universal protection under tort law.

We address the tort of negligent infliction of emotional distress in chapter 4. The chapter analyzes a growing body of contemporary negligent infliction cases that implicate plaintiffs' interests in sexual integrity and autonomy and in reproductive choice and health. We also discuss "bystander" suits involving claims of parents and other family members who suffer shock and distress from witnessing the death or injury of their children or other intimate family members. The chapter traces several special limitations on recovery imposed by the courts and criticizes judicial efforts to contain liability in emotional distress cases by means of "neutral" rules that do not depend on context. We argue that courts in torts cases should be sensitive to context and should place a high priority on protecting plaintiffs' sexual, reproductive, and intimate familial relationships against negligent injury, analogous to their protection as fundamental interests under the U.S. Constitution.

Chapter 5 examines the legal requirement of cause-in-fact and its relation to the psychological process of causation attribution. We discuss how gender and race stereotypes and other cultural attitudes linked to gender and race may affect judgments about cause and effect in tort litigation. We use two case studies—"wrongful birth" cases and lead paint cases—to analyze cultural shifts in the understanding of causation and to highlight the danger of race and gender bias in "multiple cause" cases when courts and juries must decide whether injury was produced in part by an external or situational force, rather than stemming exclusively from an internal or dispositional source, such as a minority child's genetic makeup or family environment.

Chapter 6 explores how considerations of race and gender have affected the amount of damages awarded to plaintiffs in personal injury cases. We critique the use of race-based and gender-based tables and statistics in computing loss of future earning capacity, arguing that such estimations are neither accurate nor equitable. With respect to noneconomic damages for pain and suffering and other intangible losses, we analyze the disproportionate impact legislative caps on such damages have had on women and racial minorities and argue that noneconomic losses should be treated on a par with economic losses.

The book concludes with a summary of the various pathways through which considerations of race and gender find their way into tort law. We offer three general prescriptions for progressive change designed to make the law more equitable and more responsive to the interests of women and minorities.

1

Theoretical Frames

Few look upon tort law as a field of intellectual inquiry rich in theory. Instead, most students and practitioners approach torts as an inherently practical enterprise, with little thought to the theories that purport to explain or justify the rules and practices of this particular system of compensation for injury. Similarly, the torts curriculum in law schools tends to be practice-oriented. The typical first-year course in torts rarely gets beyond articulating the basic objectives behind the torts system—the twin goals of compensation and deterrence, with perhaps mention of a subsidiary goal of reinforcement of social norms.[1] There is little time for exploring "big-picture" theoretical questions or examining the scholarship of tort theorists.

In academia, however, the theoretical currents are much stronger than they were a generation ago.[2] Tort theory has now emerged as a recognizable—if still small—genre of scholarship that gives some meaning and organization to various arguments and proposals for change in courtrooms, legislatures, and the wider community. Even though many tort scholars still do not feel the need to situate their work within a larger theoretical framework, we find value in being explicit about starting points and assumptions and attempting to acknowledge intellectual debts.

In this book, we describe our approach to tort law as a "critical" approach, signaling our kinship with the broader intellectual forces of feminist theory, critical race theory, and critical theory more generally. We do so with some reluctance. Like most scholars, we are aware of the hazards of labels and are more interested in clarifying our approach than in aligning ourselves with any particular school of thought.[3] To that end, this chapter sets out a theoretical frame for the rest of the book: it locates our approach within the larger theoretical landscape, articulates our major theoretical influences and commitments, and surveys the existing body of critical torts scholarship that serves as part of the foundation for our work.

Such a critical approach to tort law is still quite rare in the torts literature. One reason it is unfamiliar to many students of tort theory is that it does not fall within either of the two tort theories that currently dominate the field. Moreover, the critical torts scholarship that exists often gets categorized exclusively as critical theory, without also penetrating the contours of tort theory.[4] Before describing our critical torts approach in more depth, we first present a shorthand sketch of the two most visible tort theories in contemporary torts scholarship—"law and economics" and "corrective justice." Our brief description does not attempt to delineate the varieties of distinct approaches that arguably fall within the two camps[5] but serves only as background and contrast to our critical theoretical stance.

There is little dispute that, since its emergence in the late 1960s and early 1970s, law and economics has been the "dominant theoretical paradigm for understanding and assessing law and policy."[6] It has left its imprint upon torts in large part through the influential writings of Judge Richard Posner and Ronald Coase,[7] two of the founders of the Chicago school of law and economics. The other visible approach in tort theory—"corrective justice"—grew up partly as a response to law and economics at roughly the same time. As the main competing theory in torts scholarship, it tends to be positioned opposite to, and subordinate to, law and economics.

Scholars generally regard law and economics as an instrumental approach that views tort law as aimed at the paramount goal of "efficiency," as that term is understood in the discipline of economics. As explained in a leading text, law and economics sees tort law as "a system of rules designed to maximize wealth so as to minimize the costs associated with engaging in daily activities."[8] It is noteworthy that, in the lexicon of law and economics, the notion of "harm" is transformed into one of "costs." Law and economics scholars are preoccupied with ascertaining the cost-justified level of accidents, a goal distinct from that of promoting safety more generally[9] and one that seeks to deter only "inefficient" accidents that impose greater costs than the costs expended to avoid them. In this process, law and economics scholars usually steer clear of notions of morality in explaining or justifying human behavior, preferring to rely on "rational choice" models that presume all actors are equal, rational agents who express their preferences through uncoerced, consensual behavior.

Corrective justice theory, on the other hand, rests on a noninstrumental account of law that fixes on the law's role in "correcting" harm done by a particular actor (the defendant) to another person (the plaintiff) and explaining the normative basis behind the defendant's duty of repair.[10] It has its roots in moral theory, stretching back to Aristotle, who first drew a distinction between corrective justice and distributive justice.[11] Corrective justice theorists employ a morally laden language of wrongs and wrongful conduct and generally seek to ground the defendant's duty in the relationship between defendant's conduct and plaintiff's harm. In contrast to law and economics, corrective justice theorists do not believe that tort law, properly understood, deals or should deal with "macro" issues, such as maximizing wealth. Their writings emphasize the particular structure of the torts system, which requires payment only from the offender, even when efficient results would be promoted by compensation from another source. Most important, from a corrective justice viewpoint, compensation to the victim is central to tort law. Law and economics, in marked contrast, views deterrence as the primary function of tort law and regards compensation merely as a means of achieving the optimal level of deterrence of accidents.

Despite their placement on opposite ends of the theoretical pole, law and economics and corrective justice share one important core feature: they each give pride of place to the negligence principle and center accidents in their account of tort law. For the most part, law and economics considers intentional torts to be a peripheral matter, perhaps better left to the criminal law.[12] Even corrective justice theory, despite its language of morality, also has little to say about intentional torts, treating the subject largely as a closed matter of little relevance to tort theory or contemporary tort law.

If we look through a larger intellectual lens, it may seem odd that, at the beginning of the 21st century, law and economics and corrective justice are thought to be the two competing paradigms in torts scholarship. They certainly do not represent opposite ends of the political spectrum. Although there are scholars of every political stripe within the umbrella of law and economics, the movement is commonly associated with the right wing in academia and has been heavily dominated by conservative thinkers. Corrective justice, in contrast, has no discernible political orientation.

In academia today, law and economics is a powerhouse affecting many areas of law and public policy. It qualifies as an intellectual movement, complete with summer camps for aspiring scholars, schools for judges, think tanks and well-funded opportunities for scholarship and career advancement.[13] Corrective justice, on the other hand, is simply too small in scope to be considered a movement. It is mainly limited to tort theory and is still relatively unknown outside its particular confines.

What is striking about the conventional description of tort theory is the absence of critical theory, the other intellectual powerhouse and movement that is so firmly established outside the legal academy. Critical theory has had a strong presence in legal scholarship since its beginnings in the Critical Legal Studies movement in the early 1980s.[14] Critical Legal Studies, feminism, and critical race theory groups have hosted their own summer camps, inspired innumerable academic conferences, and have been remarkably generative in producing scholars and offshoot groups with a steady stream of new adherents.[15]

Like adherents of law and economics, critical legal theorists draw their sustenance primarily from intellectual currents outside the law. Rather than being tied to one particular discipline, however, critical legal scholars draw heavily from the interdisciplinary scholarship coming out of interdisciplinary programs, such as women's studies, black studies, and cultural studies, as well as from English, history, comparative literature, and other "traditional" departments that are now thoroughly saturated with varieties of critical theory. Particularly outside legal circles, the rise of critical theory has been prominently linked to that giant of intellectual trends "postmodernism," with its emphasis on the social construction of the self, the importance of discourse in the construction of individual identity and power in society, and the rejection of liberal concepts of objectivity, neutrality, and universal truth.[16] Putting aside for the moment the harsh divisions among scholars who employ some version of critical theory,[17] there can be little doubt that it is an intellectual movement of the left. Its invisibility from tort theory creates the misimpression that left-leaning theories and discourses have no value for tort law and that the only choice is between efficiency and Aristotelian moral philosophy.

In this book, we address this omission by connecting critical theory to tort law. Unlike the dominant tort theories—which pay virtually no attention to race and gender—the significance of race and gender is a highly developed topic in critical theory, as evidenced by the proliferation of critical approaches that emphasize one or more "outsider" identity, such as critical race theory or Lat Crit theory.[18] The gender and racial lens of this book thus borrows heavily from critical theory's appreciation for the social construction of personal identity, attentiveness to relations of power among legal actors, and critical interpretive analysis in dissecting legal discourse and legal categories.

That being said, our point of departure for this book are not the writings of Foucault or Derrida but rather the approach taken by the Third Restatement of Torts—the closest thing we have at the moment to the "the torts establishment." As the most prominent law reform project in torts, the Third Restatement builds on the influential tradition of notables, such as William Prosser and Frances Bohlen, who served as reporters for the Second and First Restatement of Torts.[19] We draw upon and criticize this tradition in several chapters of this book. Like the Restatement, moreover, much of what is contained in this book is grounded in traditional torts scholarship, still largely a doctrinal discourse that has not yet been taken over by either law and economics or corrective justice theory.

In his 2003 article mapping tort theories in the 20th century, John Goldberg has astutely noted that the scholarly underpinnings of the Torts Restatement should not be left out of the picture when describing the universe of tort theory.[20] In Goldberg's view, there is an implicit theory that animates the approach of the Third Restatement of Torts, despite the widely held notion that the Restatement project is atheoretical and that many of its most influential scholars—Robert Rabin, (the late) Gary Schwartz, Michael Green, and William Powers, to name only a few—are basically pragmatists engaged in "purposive analysis" and not much involved in theory. Goldberg's point is that the scholars in this camp have not been called upon to make their theory explicit largely because they are the establishment.[21]

Goldberg traces a narrative behind the Third Restatement that starts from an assumption that courts in our modern society have a lawmaking, policymaking function and that, similar to the ways administrative agencies function, judges and jurors in tort cases inevitably legislate on matters of social policy. In this respect, the Restatement-type scholars are the inheritors of a Legal Realist tradition that looked beyond the adjudication of individual private disputes to glimpse the regulatory power of tort law or, in Goldberg's words, to transform tort law "from private to 'public' law, whereby it functioned to achieve collective, not corrective, justice."[22]

The next frame in Goldberg's narrative is in our view crucial: he asserts that because of the "nature of the compensatory remedy," Restatement-type scholars believe that tort law should promote only a "discrete set of policy objectives" and that it is "inherently capable of promoting only two goals: deterrence of antisocial conduct and compensation for those who have been injured."[23] He thus labels the implicit theory embraced by Restatement-type scholars as "compensation-deterrence" theory and calls the oft-cited proposition that "the function of tort law is compensate and deter" the "baseline proposition" of that theory. According to "compensation-deterrence" theory as described by Goldberg, there is little or no space for other social policy objectives—such as social justice, redistribution of income, or gender or race equity—that cannot be directly poured into the compensation/deterrence mold.

The rest of Goldberg's narrative traces out the trajectory of contemporary tort law as envisioned by Restatement-type scholars. Similar to the other tort theories, the implicit theory of the Restatement situates negligence cases at the core of the enterprise and treats the fault principle as "the natural expression" of tort law. Unlike the other competing theoretical approaches, however, the Restatement-type theory projects tort law as "moving inexorably toward full implementation of the fault principle" and as gradually shedding arbitrary limitations on liability, such as limited duty rules, immunities, and categorical bans on recovery for emotional and economic harm.[24] The expansionist tendencies of this approach are said to be kept in check, however, by a willingness to curb liability in the name of "administrability, fairness and legitimacy."[25] It is at this point that fears of a flood of litigation, disproportionate liability, and frivolous lawsuits come into play to place limits on recovery and justify the denial of protection to some victims of unreasonable conduct.

In articulating the Restatement-type theory, Goldberg separates the interpretive aspect of a theory from the prescriptive aspect of a theory and goes on to categorize various scholars as either interpretive or prescriptive. According to Goldberg, a tort theory is interpretive if it "purports to make sense of the tort law that we have" and prescriptive if it "offers an account of what tort law *ought* to look like."[26] Here is where we part company with Goldberg. We do not believe that such a strict separation of interpretation and prescription is possible.[27] For critical scholars like ourselves, the interpretive/prescriptive dichotomy is inherently unstable, primarily because we believe that the human process of "interpreting" and "describing" the law cannot free itself from normative considerations of what ought to be. From our perspective, an assertion of common sense (or the claim that an interpretation "makes sense" under the current law) is not simply a discoverable fact but also a claim to authority that simultaneously describes reality and constructs reality.

The Restatement project is itself a good example of just such a descriptive/prescriptive endeavor. While purporting merely to restate principles of law already laid down by the courts, the Restatement has been hugely influential in shaping the future direction of tort law.[28] Even when the Restatement explicitly ventures "no opinion" on a particular aspect of doctrine—for example, in the commentary explaining the boundaries of its blackletter rules—it cannot be taken at face value.[29] Instead, such a disclaimer may be implicitly expressing the normative judgment that the matter is not of sufficient importance to justify taking a position.[30] Additionally, the descriptive/prescriptive dichotomy—like so many dualities in law and legal discourse—not only sets up contrasting terms but implicitly privileges one side of the dichotomy,[31] that is, descriptive over prescriptive analyses. Particularly in the inherently conservative field of law, a "descriptive" theory that could "make sense" of the law as it currently exists has a great advantage over a "prescriptive" theory that argues for major changes and acknowledges that it is substantially rewriting the law. That is why arguments for change are often couched in terms of perfecting the current scheme, recognizing that we are operating in a common law system that honors precedent. Thus, it is not surprising that unmasking assertions of "fact" as "argument" is a well-known move in critical theory.

Therefore, we approach the implicit theory behind the Third Restatement as part description, part prescription and are most interested in determining how much of it we embrace and use in crafting our own stance toward tort law. We regard the Restatement philosophy as our point of departure because we agree with many of its basic tenets and assumptions and are influenced by a torts tradition with deep roots in Legal Realism.[32] Like the Restatement-type theorists, we reject legal formalism and recognize the public law aspects of tort law. In an essay entitled *How Does Law Matter?* Milton Regan described the legacy of Legal Realism as displacing the legal formalism of a prior era that had "asserted that the correct outcome in a legal dispute is determined by reasoning deductively from a set of core legal principles." In its wake, Realists substituted a vision of law as connected to the "practical world" in which law was used "to meet human needs and concerns."[33] By highlighting "the inevitable role of discretion in legal interpretation," Realists opened up discussion about "the value choices" made in adjudication as well as the "social consequences of legal decisions."

This Realist legacy is evident in the new Restatement. Like the work of many Realist scholars, the Restatement commentary teases out the policy and discretion-laden dimensions of topics—such as causation-in-fact—that are still approached by many courts as matters of objective fact and reason. In chapter 5, for example, we discuss how the Restatement commentary relies on the scholarship of David Robertson, a student of prominent Legal Realist, Wex S. Malone, to explain the importance of "framing" in resolving disputes about factual causation. While still embracing the venerable "but-for" test for causation, the Restatement commentary acknowledges that the "but-for" test leaves ample room for the infusion of values and biases in everyday judgments about causation. Additionally, at several points—most notably in the sections on emotional distress—the Restatement disavows arbitrary limitations on recovery, displaying a Realist impatience with outmoded doctrines that cannot be justified on contemporary policy grounds.[34] By the same token, however, the Restatement also places a high premium on the administrability or workability of legal rules within the current jury system for adjudicating tort cases. Reminiscent of the writings of Leon Green and other major Realist scholars, the new Restatement makes many concessions in the name of "judicial administration" and is apt to explain its (and the courts') reluctance to impose negligence liability in certain contexts in such terms.[35]

Our critical approach to torts takes much of this Realist legacy for granted. We start from an assumption that tort rules ought to be evaluated by their "real world" success, however measured, rather than by some measure of internal logic or consistency. We also have little patience for arbitrary limits on recovery when there is demonstrable harm caused by unreasonable conduct. And we agree that rules must be both just and workable, even if we express skepticism about claims that particular rules would be too difficult to administer or give guidance to a jury.

However, this book is also highly critical of the Restatement approach and the implicit tort theory that underlies it. We believe that John Goldberg is right to characterize the Restatement approach as aimed at "the deterrence of antisocial behavior" and at providing "compensation for those who have been injured." In this book, we analyze the scope and meaning of those two broad objectives. In various sectors of tort law, we argue for changes in the way defendants' conduct is evaluated and compensation is measured. In particular, we make the case for expanding the idea of "antisocial behavior" to take full account of evolving civil rights notions of racial and sexual discrimination and harassment. With respect to compensation, we criticize current methods for measuring compensation and look for ways to ensure that compensation is distributed equitably among tort plaintiffs and not inequitably along racial and gender lines.

More generally, we are not always content with liberalizing current rules or tinkering with established doctrine. We argue for a change in the "deep structures" of tort law because we believe that they reflect and reinforce the social subordination of women and racial minorities. In this book, we question the "centering" of negligence and physical injury in tort law. Our approach attempts to push intentional torts and emotional injuries out from the margins of tort law and imagines what tort doctrine might look like if sexual and racial violence and exploitation and "intangible" harms related to reproduction and intimate relationships were taken more seriously. Our project also requires a rethinking of conventional boundaries, particularly between torts and family law and between torts and statutory civil rights law. Such a reordering is necessary to capture and compensate for recurring injuries experienced disproportionately by marginalized groups, such as domestic violence, workplace harassment, sexual exploitation and reproductive injuries.

In this book, we depart from the more traditional, Restatement-type approach in our claim that the current tort system of compensation is inequitable and that current limitations on liability are not just a matter of administrability or manageability. For example, in chapters 2 and 4, we discuss how the historic reluctance to provide compensation for emotional harm—and the tendency to characterize injuries associated with women as "emotional"—cannot be explained or justified solely by the difficulty of measuring intangible injuries or finding a logical stopping point for liability. Instead, we assert that the failure to compensate is related in part to the race and gender of the victims and to the difficulty of comprehending injuries that do not have an analogue in the lives of privileged white men. We search beyond traditional legal sources and rely on critical theory and cognitive psychology to show how injuries of women and minorities can be devalued by failing to recognize or minimizing their suffering, for example, by characterizing a woman's miscarriage solely as an emotional injury or by measuring damages using group-based statistics that undervalue the potential of women and minorities. Particularly with respect to causation, we use cognitive psychology, with its insights into the "irrationalities" of human decision making, to tease out hidden race and gender bias.

Ingredients of Critical Approach

The main ingredients of our critical approach come from feminist theory and critical race theory. From feminist theory, we borrow technique and substance. Throughout the book, we use many of the methods common to feminist legal analysis, and our approach incorporates several prominent themes associated with diverse schools of feminist thought.

Perhaps most fundamental is the importance and attention we attach to gender in analyzing the meaning of and effect of current tort doctrines and in evaluating possible reforms. Despite the continuing significance of gender in our culture, legal scholarship and legal analysis still often proceed in a gender-blind fashion, neglecting to question the gendered origins of a particular rule, the gender implications or consequences of a particular doctrine, or what changes would have to be made to avoid or ameliorate gender disadvantage. Thus, a key feminist move has been to "ask the woman question,"[36] a basic method that encourages posing these gendered inquiries, even when a particular area of law, such as tort law, seems far removed from conventional women's concerns, gender equity, or social justice more generally.

In the nearly thirty years that contemporary feminists have theorized in this fashion about the law, they have sought to answer such gender-linked questions through gaining an understanding of women's lived experiences,[37] in addition to resorting to familiar empirical methods, such as collecting relevant statistics comparing men and women. Such a grounding in "women's experience" is thought to be of critical importance because it has the capacity to uncover areas of exclusion and neglect.[38] Thus, this book hones in on those neglected areas of tort law, such as protection against sexual harassment and sexual exploitation, recovery for reproductive harms, and the valuing of intangible injury that loom large in women's lives but play only a marginal role in the field.

In contrast to other approaches, such as law and economics, which implicitly take the perspective of the legislator or judge, our emphasis on women's experiences is designed to incorporate the "victim's perspective"[39] into our legal analysis and to focus attention on "the position of the governed," on those who are subjected to the law.[40] It is this inclination to address "governed individuals" that distinguishes a critical legal approach, such as ours, from an approach, such as law and economics, that is directed toward policymakers, even though both approaches are instrumentalist and rely on interdisciplinary sources.

Although most of this book focuses on contemporary law, at points we employ a broader historical lens to evaluate changes in the treatment of women under the law. One recurring move in critical feminist scholarship is to look behind claims of progress to uncover important continuities in women's subordinate status. The point is often made that change is not inherently progressive and that even substantial shifts in prevailing legal rules and rhetoric may not alter a basic pattern of male dominance.[41] We document this reproduction of hierarchy—in altered or updated forms—in several areas of tort law. Thus, for example, in chapter 3, we explain that the older case law refused to allow recovery for intentionally caused severe emotional distress if unaccompanied by physical injury. This meant that there was no redress in sexual exploitation or harassment cases that did not amount to a technical battery or assault. While the newer intentional tort doctrine purports to afford recovery for serious emotional injuries, many jurisdictions nevertheless continue to rule for defendants in such cases. The major difference is that the newer case law is more procedural in tone, employing doctrines such as preemption or requiring high thresholds of proof to cut off or curb liability.

A similar phenomenon can be seen in cases of domestic violence: older cases barred recovery outright through the doctrine of interspousal immunity; newer cases recognize that domestic violence may qualify for tort liability, but recoveries are still rare because of special procedural barriers and provisions in liability insurance policies that exclude coverage for suits brought by one family member against another.[42]

Our reliance on feminist methods in detecting patterns of women's experiences should not be taken to suggest that we believe there is a reliable method for tapping into all such experiences or that all women have similar experiences. Rather, in attempting to understand the experiences of marginalized groups, feminist and other critical scholars have long had to grapple with the intersecting and interlocking nature of systems of oppression, and some have tried to avoid the essentialist error of overgeneralizing from the experience of one subgroup of women.[43] In this book, we have consciously used an intersectional approach, highlighting both the race and gender dimensions of tort doctrines and tracing out some of the overlapping, as well as distinctive, racial and gender effects. For example, in our discussion of damages in chapter 6, we explain how the use of gender-based and race-based tables disadvantages women of all races and minority men. In this corner of tort law, the mechanisms by which gender and race bias infiltrate the law are similar and overlapping. In contrast, in our analysis, in chapter 4, of negligence claims involving women's reproductive interests, we show how the claims of African American women in forced sterilization cases differ significantly from the claims of (mostly) white women who seek to recover for harm caused by miscarriages and stillbirths. We recognize, however, that even this simultaneous focus on race and gender is still partial and preliminary; in this project we have not wrestled with other important dimensions of personal identity, such as sexual orientation, disability, and social class, and, for the most part, have concentrated on analyzing published legal decisions, augmented by research done by others that helps place the decisions in social context. Nevertheless, the racial and gender lens through which we view tort law, partial as it is, allows us to give expression to a range of arguments and perspectives that are worthy of serious consideration but that rarely surface in mainstream discussions in the field.

Another related move we borrow from feminist theory is our broad conception of gender bias and our interrogation of seemingly neutral standards and practices for implicit gender bias. In this book, we use the term "gender bias" to capture a wide spectrum of practices and habits of mind that have proven to be effective, historically and in the present, in producing and reproducing the subordination of women. Our definition includes intentional disparate treatment of men and women—the familiar concept of equality so well established in U.S. constitutional discourse—which requires that women who are similarly situated to men receive the same or identical treatment.[44] Thus, our critique of the use of gender-based earnings tables in chapter 6 is premised on such a formal equality notion and posits that the future earnings potential of injured women should not be discounted solely because such plaintiffs are women.

Our conception of bias, however, goes well beyond intentional disparate treatment to include unconscious disparities in the treatment of similarly situated persons, whether stemming from hostility, insensitivity, lack of empathy, or the use of stereotypes about a group. In our analysis of wrongful birth cases in chapter 5, for example, we question whether some courts' resistance to treating wrongful birth cases on a par with other cases of informed consent was influenced by cultural stereotypes of women as solely responsible for controlling sex, reproduction, and the raising of children and on an unwillingness to place responsibility upon physicians in this realm. Taking a page from statutory civil rights law, our conception of bias also encompasses facially neutral practices, doctrines, or policies that have a disproportionately harmful effect on women as a group and cannot be justified by reference to other competing interests or concerns.[45] We use this "disparate impact" meaning of bias, for example, in chapter 6 in discussing the effects of caps on noneconomic damages, where we marshal empirical research that documents the harshness of such caps on women, elderly plaintiffs, and children and counter arguments that such caps are necessary to curb excessive or runaway verdicts.

Finally, our conception of bias captures what is often referred to as cognitive bias, a process that affects the way we value activities, injuries, and other "things" that, strictly speaking, have no race or gender.[46] Thus, in several chapters, we discuss whether certain types of injuries (e.g., emotional harm) or certain types of damages (e.g., noneconomic damages) have been devalued in part because of their cognitive association with women and women's activities. This notion of devaluation also drives our view that gender-linked intentional harms, such as domestic violence and workplace harassment, have been marginalized and shunted off to other domains of law where full compensation is unlikely to be obtained. Further, in chapter 5, we connect three common cognitive biases identified by psychologists—the fundamental attribution error, the normality bias, and the omission bias—to race and gender bias in tort law by explaining how stereotypes and prototypes can affect the causal attribution process to the detriment of female and minority tort plaintiffs.

Our broad definition of bias and inclination to explore implicit gender and race bias in facially neutral standards tracks the approaches of feminist scholars from multiple schools of feminist thought that have made inroads in the law in the past thirty years. Like many contemporary critical scholars, we are not tied to a particular brand of feminism. Rather, our critical approach to tort law is influenced to a significant degree by liberal, cultural, radical, and intersectional feminism.[47]

Many of the insights and proposals in this book are compatible with liberal feminism. Although often derided as assimilationist and tied to male norms, liberal feminism has at times posed a formidable challenge to traditional legal doctrine by its emphasis on equal rights and its insistence on treating women as persons fully as capable as men to engage in all lines of work and activities outside the home. One major theme of this book is the desirability of incorporating liberal concepts from civil rights and equal protection into the mainstream of torts, including rights of protection against sexual harassment and hostile work environments and constitutional guarantees of reproductive choice. Our arguments in favor of mainstreaming domestic violence protection into intentional torts and insurance coverage also reflect the equal rights principle that violence against women in the home, perpetrated by spouses and other intimates, should be treated as seriously in the law as stranger violence. Likewise, the high priority liberal feminists have traditionally placed on gender integration in the workplace and on equal pay resonates with our objections to the methods used to calculate future income potential of female plaintiffs, which uncritically assume that historic patterns of lower pay and lower workforce participation for women as compared to men will persist into the future.

The broad themes of cultural feminism come out most clearly in our discussions of the devaluation of emotional distress and tort law's tepid response to women's reproductive and relational injuries. In particular, cultural feminists have sought greater support for maternal activities and have criticized the failure to recognize and attach a positive value to caring, nurturing, empathy, and intimate human connections. This failure can be seen most readily in tort law's reluctance to compensate pregnant women for losses stemming from miscarriages and stillbirths caused by physician negligence and for trauma experienced by mothers and other family members precipitated by the wrongful killing or injuring of children under their care. Especially in these contexts, we agree with cultural feminists that tort law reflects a masculinist viewpoint that values pecuniary interests over intimacy and family and seems oblivious or indifferent to the degree of suffering many women experience when these human connections are damaged or severed.

Radical feminist theory has left its imprint on our approach primarily in areas of tort law touching on sexual violence, exploitation, and legal notions of consent. From Catharine MacKinnon and other radical theorists, we take up the basic insight that widespread sexual abuse, exploitation, and objectification of women have been tolerated in the law and perpetuated by male-focused standards of consent and harm that suppress women's perspectives. From the refusal to provide meaningful compensation to domestic violence victims to the majority view that pervasive sexual harassment in the workplace does not constitute "outrageous" conduct actionable in tort, tort doctrine has generally been inhospitable to abuse victims and remains an area of law that has yet to adopt an egalitarian conception of consent in sexual relations. It is still often the case that sexually exploitative conduct accomplished through means other than the direct application of physical force—such as economic pressure, violation of trust, or deception—does not give rise to a tort claim.[48] In this book, we discuss the failure of both intentional tort and negligence doctrine to make the protection of sexual autonomy and integrity a high priority. We regard the centering of accidental harm (over intentionally caused injury) and the privileging of physical harm (over intangible injuries) as the chief structural means by which tort law has continued to submerge such sexualized injuries and rule them beyond the boundaries of tort law.

The contributions of intersectional feminism to this book are intertwined with and to a large extent indistinguishable from the impact that critical race theory has had on our approach to tort law. Perhaps the most important insight of intersectional feminism—sometimes also referred to as antiessentialist feminism—is that it is a mistake to treat one aspect of identity, such as gender, as primary or fundamental and to regard other dimensions of identity, such as race and ethnicity, simply as variations on a theme.[49] Instead, intersectional and critical race theorists have emphasized that systems of subordination intersect and interact in ways that often create distinctive experiences for subgroups, such as women of color, and that require close scrutiny of policies and legal doctrines for their differing effects on these specific groups. For this reason, in analyzing social phenomena, we can be misled if we conceptualize race bias plus sex bias as simply additive, serving only to intensify the same harm. Instead, the intersecting currents create a more complex picture and can at times give rise to a tension among interests of different subgroups of women. For example, in tracing out the development of nervous-shock cases at the turn of the 20th century, we show how the denial of recovery for what was perceived as emotional injury left many pregnant white women without redress for serious physical and relational harm, ignoring the pain and suffering they experienced from miscarriages and stillbirth. In the same era, however, some courts allowed recovery to white female plaintiffs for purported insults and emotional distress caused by encounters with black defendants whom they claimed did not treat them with sufficient deference and servility. Recovery for emotional harm thus had a dual character: it could serve to validate serious gender-linked harms for some women, whereas for others it bolstered white racial privilege and reinforced racial inequality.

From critical race theory, we borrow a broad conception of racial bias. In our view, racial bias certainly includes purposeful disparate treatment of whites and racial minorities, in violation of the constitutional and anti-discrimination principle of formal equality that requires that like cases be treated alike. This narrow conception of equality, however, does not exhaust the types of racial bias present in contemporary society. Thus, we agree with critical race scholars who regard racism as "endemic to American life,"[50] deeply woven into the national consciousness, with a profound impact on our institutions, culture, and discourse. In contrast to dominant mainstream views, critical race scholars emphatically reject the view that systemic race discrimination is a thing of the past and often use their scholarship to trace out the legacy of slavery and segregation in contemporary contexts. From this vantage point, race functions not simply to distort individual judgments but as an "ordering principle in a world of power, resources and privileges."[51]

Like feminists who seek out the gender implications of neutral rules and practices, critical race scholars are adept at asking the "race subordination question"[52] to ascertain the racial origins, racialized meanings, and race-linked effects of purportedly "colorblind" legal doctrines. Since Charles Lawrence first published his influential article on unconscious racism in 1987,[53] critical race scholars have employed a broad definition of racial bias that encompasses various forms of implicit bias, including unintentional disparate treatment, devaluation, negative racial imagery, and stereotypes. Another hallmark of much of the critical race literature is its critique of objectivity and its commitment to identifying and articulating legal harm from the perspectives of people of color.

In some areas of tort law, it is easy to appreciate the racial implications of neutrally phrased doctrines. In our discussion of workplace harassment cases in chapter 3, for example, we highlight a recent racial harassment case in which the coworkers of an African American woman engaged in a pattern of offensive behavior and name calling that traded on centuries-old negative images of blacks as animals, monkeys, and filthy creatures. The use of these offensive stereotypes, however, was not enough to qualify for tort liability under the "extreme and outrageous" conduct standard used by the court. In cases such as this, courts have placed little weight on the victim's perspective and have all but erased the significance of race as a factor in evaluating the seriousness of the defendant's conduct.

In other areas of tort law, the racial effects of "neutral" tort doctrines are harder to excavate and assess. A major theme in this book is that of racial devaluation, the process by which even unconscious value judgments can affect the way that the lives, injuries, and activities of people of color are measured. In agreement with critical race theory, we assert that one pernicious legacy of slavery and segregation has been the tendency to regard African American plaintiffs first and foremost as physical beings and to undervalue the emotional and intangible dimensions of their lives. Thus, in chapter 2, we recount a 1909 case of a black porter who was falsely accused of stealing from a passenger and falsely imprisoned. In an unusually explicit instance of racial devaluation, the court decided to slash the plaintiff's tort recovery because of its view that a black man would not suffer as much as a white man from such a humiliating experience. We detect similar patterns of devaluation in our study of wrongful death recoveries in Louisiana in a later era. Particularly because the tort system is committed to individualized determinations—with few checks for systemic bias—devaluation of this sort is largely invisible and unaddressed in contemporary law.[54]

Throughout our discussion of race and tort law, we follow the lead of critical race scholars in treating race as a social construction, rather than as a biological fact that tracks pertinent differences among human beings.[55] In tort litigation, what matters most is not the "fact" of a party's racial identity—indeed, as a doctrinal matter, a party's race is not a relevant fact—but the perception of such racial identity and the meanings that judges, juries, expert witnesses, and litigators attach to such identity. These racialized perceptions and meanings, however, are often difficult to glean from the cases. Like other areas of law, whiteness has long served as an unstated default in tort law, as evidenced by the tendency of courts to disclose the race of a party only when such party is identified as "black" or, in the language of older cases, as "colored" or "Negro."[56] Thus, a party's racial identity is often uncertain, and few cases delve into the complex racial and ethnic identities that characterize our increasingly multiracial and multiethnic society.

Given these practical difficulties, in this book we have looked closely at cases arising in contexts where race is prominent—such as negligent sterilization cases and cases involving injuries from lead paint poisoning—in which damage is concentrated in specific populations due to underlying social practices and economic conditions. Thus, negligent sterilization cases surfaced at a time when federal and state governments attempted to curb birth rates among low-income African Americans after welfare benefits were made available to black recipients. Lead paint litigation most often arises in low-income, predominantly minority communities, where there is a large stock of deteriorating older buildings that pose a lead paint hazard, especially to children.

These "racial-context" cases demonstrate the multiple ways in which race is constructed and racial meanings are produced in tort litigation. In negligent sterilization cases, for example, some courts have found it difficult to see injury or dignitary harm when a poor minority woman is pressured or coerced into being sterilized. In such cases, the harm is erased by tacit assumptions that minority women are purely physical beings who suffer no tangible harm through sterilization or that equate submission to the only medical treatment available with free choice. In the lead paint cases, race affects causal judgments about the role of genetics and family upbringing in producing cognitive disabilities when minority children are exposed to lead paint. In their attempts to avoid liability for failure to abate lead hazards, defendants have exploited the tendency to fix on race as a highly salient feature of the case, focus on the victim's personal characteristics, and deflect attention from situational factors, such as the condition of the premises. In these settings, the factor of race functions to overwhelm or override other causal factors and plays into the commonly held preference for simple, one-cause explanations in trying to understand complex phenomena. A similar process of "selective perception" can be seen in the overemphasis placed on race in calculating an accident victim's prospects for future income. The use of race-based tables to predict future earning capacity assumes that racial disparities in income will persist indefinitely into the future and discounts the degree to which increased job opportunities and other social changes can alter that pattern. In these racially charged contexts, race functions to activate negative stereotypes about the behavior and personal characteristics of minorities, eclipse other explanations for injuries, and reduce the chances for tort recovery. As a social construction capable of producing multiple meanings and effects, race operates subtly in tort cases to influence outcomes, even while the language of courts continues to treat race as an uncomplicated biological fact with a fixed meaning.

Critical Torts Scholarship

In addition to the more theoretically-oriented general literature from feminism, critical race theory, and related discourses, our approach builds on scholarship focused more specifically on gender, race, and tort law. Many of the themes we develop in this book have been foreshadowed in earlier writings that critically explored specific areas of tort law through a race and gender lens. This body of critical torts scholarship is still quite small in comparison to that generated from the schools of law and economics and corrective justice. And it is still the case that feminism and critical theory have not penetrated tort law and scholarship to the degree that they have other fields of law, such as antidiscrimination law and constitutional law. However, in the past twenty-five years, critical torts scholars have laid a foundation for works, such as ours, that attempt to theorize about race, gender, and tort law, more broadly, and to isolate recurring themes in a critical account of contemporary tort law. In the following paragraphs we select a few key writings, not explored elsewhere in the book, that form the intellectual backdrop for our approach.

In retrospect, we find the beginnings of critical torts scholarship in 1982, with the publication of Richard Delgado's article, *Words That Wound: A Tort Action for Racial Insults, Epithets and Name Calling.*[57] *Words That Wound* ignited a heated debate about legal responses to hate speech that eventually spilled over from torts to fuel controversies on college campuses and other settings. In the realm of tort law, however, Delgado was the first to take up a topic that would later arouse intense interest among feminist and critical race scholars, namely the degree to which common-law courts have offered or should offer relief to victims of race and sex discrimination in employment and other sectors of public life. In his article, Delgado criticized courts that had ruled that racial insults and harassment on the job were "mere insults" not actionable under the rubric of intentional infliction of emotional distress and proposed a new tort for racial insults. Aside from these specifics, Delgado's article was most notable for singling out torts as a site of inequality and as an area of law ripe for critical analysis. In this foundational piece, Delgado emphasized several themes that would subsequently become prominent in critical race theory: that racism and racial insults were endemic in the workplace; that racial harassment had an immediate devastating and often cumulative impact on its victims who faced similar bias in other situations; and that, in the long run, the negative racial stereotypes and imagery communicated by racial insults created a culture that reproduced racial injury in succeeding generations.

In their early writings, scholars such as Leslie Bender and Lucinda Finley likewise fixed on tort law as a site for feminist analysis.[58] In exploratory articles that widely canvassed the domain of tort law for potential male bias, these feminist scholars urged law professors to reexamine the substantive areas considered worthy of class time and the definitions of core concepts, such as reasonableness and injury, that permeate the field. Looking back, we find that Finley's list of ignored or marginalized sectors of tort law—encompassing liability for domestic violence and sexual harassment, relational and reproductive harms, and damages for emotional injury—was prescient in pinpointing those areas that had failed to compensate women for recurring injuries in their lives. Employing a cultural feminist perspective, Bender tried to envision what a more inclusive tort law might look like, imagining, for example, the replacement of the "reasonable man" standard with a more protective standard of care that required persons to act like responsible neighbors who had a stake in the well-being of others. Although these early writings were too preliminary to constitute a "revised treatise on tort law, which the subject really demands,"[59] they launched the kind of critical analysis of tort law we employ in this book.

Since the late 1980s, critical torts scholarship has mentioned and begun to develop many of the key themes that animate this book. Most prominently, scholars have noticed the distance between civil rights norms and ideals and the standards used to determine tort liability for discriminatory behavior.[60] In an early intersectional article, for example, Regina Austin focused on the inadequacies of the tort of intentional infliction of emotional distress to redress dignitary injuries of low-income workers. She argued for a transformation of the tort concept of "outrageous" conduct and identified multidimensional harassment based on race, ethnicity, gender, and "color of collar" as a major injustice that tort law should address.[61]

Our analysis of intentional torts and negligence claims also draws on the work of feminist scholars who have critiqued tort law's lack of recognition of gender-linked injuries, uncovered implicit male bias in neutral rules and practices, such as the reasonable person standard, and objected to male-focused definitions of consent that preclude redress for sexual exploitation.[62] Thus, in an important, controversial piece, Jane Larson relied on feminist conceptions of consent to make the case for expanding claims of intentional misrepresentation to include cases of sexual fraud.[63] Larson argued that the law's near-complete immunization of cases of sexual fraud, in contrast to its treatment of fraud in commercial settings, was a glaring omission that disproportionately harmed women. Larson's proposal called for tort liability in all cases involving "intentional, harmful misrepresentation made for the purpose of gaining another's consent to sexual relations." We sound a similar note in calling for more comprehensive tort coverage for harms of domestic violence, workplace harassment, and reproductive injury.

In this book, we have blended traditional doctrinal analysis and feminist and critical race theory with the goal of tracing, with some precision, the complicated paths through which gender and race bias infiltrate neutral rules in specific contexts. In this respect, we follow the example of Ellen Bublick's pathbreaking 1999 study of third-party rape cases, in which rape victims sue landlords or other institutional defendants for negligently failing to detect and remedy dangerous conditions.[64] Applying feminist principles to question methods of apportioning fault, Bublick argued that contemporary rules on comparative fault are built upon sexist assumptions that women have primary responsibility for preventing their own rapes and that tacitly accept and reinforce a discriminatory status quo in which rape and the fear of rape are pervasive features of women's lives. Bublick's skillful dissection of how various jurisdictions have dealt with victim "fault" in third-party rape cases after making the transition to a comparative fault system shows how gender hierarchy can be reproduced through new rules and procedures and does not always depend on retention of older doctrines.

The critical torts literature on racial devaluation, though less extensive than the gender-oriented research, has also managed to isolate some of the specific social and cultural practices that produce and reproduce racial disparities. With respect to the racial devaluation of claims brought by African Americans, torts scholars have zeroed in on litigation practices, particularly in the context of settlement, that drive down the amounts that minority plaintiffs are offered for their injuries. Frank McClellan, a law professor and torts litigator, details how race can enter into private negotiations among attorneys when they are called upon to predict how juries, experts, and judges will respond to their clients' stories of damage and loss.[65] The impact of race in these informal, everyday encounters is often hard to pinpoint and prove. McClellan recounts one case, for example, involving allegations of fraud against a computer company brought by three doctors. The defendant settled the claims of the two white doctors, but, in the case of the African American doctor, it decided without explanation to take its chances with an all-white jury, suggesting that it was race that tipped the balance in judging the potential value of the claims. Such low-level strategic decisions are closely tied to lawyers' perceptions about jury attitudes and the potential for implicit racial bias and unconscious race-based judgments of the sort we explore in chapters 5 and 6 in our discussion of causation and damages.

Finally, Regina Austin has recently argued that racial devaluation is not produced solely by biased decisions made by whites but is embedded in deep-seated cultural understandings, stereotypes, and assumptions, "shared by whites, blacks, and others," that establish the belief that "blacks are not deserving of the money they possess and furthermore do not know how to maximize its value."[66] To ground her theoretical discussion of the lesser "social and material value attached to black people's money," she highlights a recent Florida case involving an African American woman who was hurt in an automobile accident when she was hit by a truck that was changing lanes.[67] Jurors in that case drastically reduced the plaintiff's award by assigning her the lion's share of fault for the accident. Several jurors admitted that, during the deliberations, derogatory comments had been made about the plaintiff, who was then employed as a nurse's aide and receiving workers' compensation for a work-related injury. Characterizing her as a "fat, black woman on welfare who would simply blow the money on liquor, cigarettes, jai alai, bingo or the dog track," the jury was reluctant to award her any amount. Austin explains how, in this variation of racial devaluation, the jury presumably kept the award low, not necessarily because they trivialized plaintiff's injuries but because of racialized judgments about "who [plaintiff] was, where her money came from, and what she would do with any damage award." Austin's innovative take on devaluation, with its focus on the social value of money, looks beneath the disparities in economic and noneconomic damages that we discuss in chapters 2 and 6 and links jury bias to larger systems of segregation and cultural subordination.

It is important to note that the critical approach to tort law that we have assembled from these intellectual influences is not a unified theory of torts. Nor does the racial and gender lens through which we view tort law mean that we believe that gender and race equity should be the only goal of tort law or even the most important goal of tort law in every context. Instead, in this book we align ourselves with those "pluralist" scholars who regard the quest for a unified theory of torts as futile and undesirable and as invariably eclipsing the variegated richness and multiplicity of the field.[68] For pluralists, tort law can best be understood as "based on multiple rationales" and as furthering a variety of objectives, encompassing compensation, deterrence, and the promotion of social policies, including the particular goal of race and gender equity. Moreover, we share the conviction of Legal Realists and of so many scholars thereafter that, in understanding tort law and advocating reform, context is all important.[69] There is no substitute for a close examination of how various objectives complement or compete with one another in a particular class of cases. Thus, as the organization of this book suggests, we have constructed our approach to tort law in an "applied" fashion, after first investigating how gender and race operate to shape and affect doctrine in a variety of specific contexts.

Finally, this book operates on the premise that one of the virtues of tort law is that it is not a pristine field but is constantly changing to absorb concepts, principles and norms from other areas of law. Following the lead of historians of the field,[70] we regard as significant that tort law developed on an ad hoc basis, responding to new situations and developing particular rules to fit the context. G. Edward White concludes his intellectual history of tort law in America by noting that "from its origins the field of torts has been defined by its residual status."[71] More recently, Christopher Robinette has called torts the "catchall" of the common law, observing that it was "constantly intermingled with concepts from more 'pure' areas of law,"[72] such as criminal law, contracts, and property, and traversed legal boundaries with relative ease. In this book, we focus on a similar phenomenon in contemporary law and trace the migration of civil rights principles into torts. In several contexts, moreover, we argue for a more thorough integration of civil rights and equality norms into the mainstream of torts and criticize efforts to enforce a strict separation between torts and other domains of law. In our view, such a blurring of boundaries does not distort or damage tort law but rather recognizes its capacity to respond to and produce social change.

2

Historical Frames

It is not difficult to see the influence of gender and race on the recognition and valuation of injuries in judicial decisions of the past, particularly in cases decided before the Civil War. This enhanced visibility is partly a result of the fact that until the mid-19th century, recovery was linked to the legal and social status of the injured party. Race and gender determined who had a right to file a claim for injury in court and affected the nature and existence of substantive claims.

The institution of slavery, as well as the legal regime of coverture that denied independent legal rights to married women, prevented most African Americans and women of all races from suing for personal injuries in their own right. Because slaves were the property of their owners, personal injuries to slaves were treated as injuries to the slaveholder, rather than to the slave.[1] To be recognized in law, the personal injury to the slave had first to be translated into pecuniary loss to the slaveholder.

During the same period, married women also possessed no independent legal status. The doctrine of coverture operated to "merge" a woman's legal rights with those of her husband, essentially obliterating her individual legal existence. Thus, until the passage of the Married Women's Property Acts in the mid- to late 1800s,[2] husbands alone had the right to institute suits on behalf of their wives and possessed exclusive property rights in their wives' bodies and labor. Although married white women were not regarded as property itself, their subordinate status under coverture also resulted in a denial of recognition of substantive rights flowing from personal injury. Notably, for example, when a wife was tortiously injured, it was her husband who had a claim for the material value of her household and sexual services, known as the claim for "loss of consortium."[3] Comparable injury to the husband, however, gave no similar consortium rights in the wife for loss of her husband's services and society. Instead, her loss was regarded as intangible and not a proper subject for a legal claim. In short, there was no denying that race and gender held a central place in tort recovery, mirroring their overriding importance in larger society.

With the end of slavery and the formal abandonment of coverture in the latter part of the 19th century, tort doctrine began to look increasingly gender and race neutral. It is striking that throughout the period discussed in this book—from the turn of the 20th century to the present—judges have shown very little inclination to enunciate gender-specific or race-specific tort rules, even in times when gender-specific and race-specific thinking was the order of the day and regarded as unproblematic. This change in the law, however, was largely rhetorical. Gender and race may have vanished from the face of tort law, but considerations of gender and race remained relevant to the recognition and valuation of injury.

Long after married women were allowed to sue for personal injuries in their own name, tort claims brought by women were often marked by gender difference. Prevalent assumptions about gender—linked to an ideology of separate spheres—influenced how courts categorized certain tort claims associated with female plaintiffs and played a role in determining which types of claims would be legally compensable. Additionally, the legacy of slavery cast a long shadow over tort recovery. Although blacks could and did seek compensation in the courts for their injuries once slavery was abolished, the value placed on their lives and suffering was often lower than that for whites, reflecting and reinforcing blacks' lower status in America's racially stratified society. In marked contrast to this devaluation of claims brought by African Americans, however, courts often placed a positive value on white racial privilege and allowed white plaintiffs to seek recovery for racialized injuries stemming from social encounters with black people that they regarded as unacceptable and emotionally disturbing.

This chapter presents a portrait of two groups of tort cases that date from approximately the turn of the 20th century to the late 1930s to illustrate how gender and race ideology found their way into suits for personal injury, shaped evolving tort doctrine, and affected tort recoveries. The first group of cases is what was then known as "nervous-shock" cases, a precursor to the contemporary claim for negligent infliction of emotional distress.[4] Starting in the late 19th century, the "nervous-shock" cases were dominated by white female plaintiffs who claimed that they had suffered a miscarriage or stillbirth as a result of defendant's negligent behavior. Despite the physical aspects of these plaintiffs' injuries, many courts characterized these cases as mental disturbance cases and refused to grant recovery. The "nervous-shock" cases illustrate the importance of gender in an ostensibly gender-neutral area of the law and demonstrate how the dichotomy of mental versus physical harm becomes mapped onto debates over tort recovery for women plaintiffs.

The second group of cases consists of claims brought by African Americans. The focus in these cases is on race and the devaluation of injury, at a time and place when racial segregation was legally and culturally sanctioned. We closely examine one high-profile New York case decided in 1909 in which an African American Pullman porter had his damage award dramatically reduced expressly because the judge believed that an intangible injury suffered by a black man was worth less than a comparable injury suffered by a white man. We then trace similar patterns of devaluation in wrongful death awards for African American plaintiffs in a set of cases decided in Louisiana between 1900 and 1940. Although the devaluation in these cases was less explicit, the Louisiana courts were able to minimize losses suffered by black families by maintaining informal racially segregated methods for evaluating injury that tended to set a lower value on the lives and suffering of black victims. As a bridge between these two groups of cases, we examine a tort case from 1905 that was brought by a white woman who claimed that a frightening encounter with a black woman had caused her emotional distress and consequent injury.[5] Her success in that litigation serves as an example of how race privilege could bolster recovery in an ordinary personal injury suit and how racialized fear experienced by white plaintiffs was given value in an ostensibly race-neutral system of compensation.

We chose these cases because they are such good vehicles for seeing the influence of race and gender in tort law, even though the tort doctrines enunciated in the cases rarely explicitly advert to race or gender. It is our view that the application and development of tort doctrine in these cases is not truly neutral but is affected in important ways by the race and gender of the claimants. Race and gender emerge not only in the statements made by courts but in the particular language, the choice of analogies, and the tone of the cases, which betray cultural attitudes linked to race and gender. It is in these ways that race and gender are present in the two groups of cases, even if often somewhat under the surface.

Nervous Shock, Gender, and the Impact Rule

The legal doctrine governing nervous-shock cases demonstrates the complicated manner in which cultural conceptions of gender difference and gender hierarchy infiltrate legal categories.[6] Before the turn of the 20th century, it was the conventional wisdom that, standing alone, mental disturbance did not qualify as a legally cognizable harm. The case law constructed a legal dichotomy of interests—privileging physical harm over emotional harm—

that persists to this day. The early cases explained that the law was aimed chiefly at protecting material interests and physical harm, leaving emotions and relationships beyond the protection of tort law.[7] This basic demarcation line had important gender implications for compensation: losses typically suffered by men were often associated with the more highly-valued physical realm, while losses typically suffered by women were relegated to the lower-valued realm of the emotional or relational.

Even in the 19th century, however, the legal reluctance to compensate for emotional harm was not absolute. In fact, tort law routinely compensated for emotional disturbance, provided only that the defendant's conduct otherwise amounted to a legally recognizable tort. In the realm of intentional torts, damages for humiliation or other distress were generally recoverable, provided the plaintiff proved all the elements of the particular cause of action. For example, a plaintiff could recover for the humiliation of being spat upon by a defendant, once plaintiff proved the elements of a battery, that is, that he was touched without his consent in a rude or offensive matter.[8] Most important, as negligence law developed in the mid-19th century, it became settled law that damages for emotional injury, such as pain and suffering, were recoverable as "parasitic damages" if they accompanied a physical injury.[9]

By so specifying the elements of particular intentional tort claims and deciding the circumstances under which emotional distress could be "tacked onto" claims for physical injury, courts in effect selectively compensated for nonphysical harm. In some contexts, emotional harm was given value by the courts, but in others it was denied. Moreover, the courts managed to accomplish the selection without undoing the basic hierarchy that privileged the physical over the emotional. It was in this process of selective recognition of legal injury that the gender of the parties became highly relevant.

A dramatic example of the selective recognition of legal injury was the old claim for criminal conversation, the claim that a husband could assert against a man who had had sexual intercourse with his wife.[10] At common law, the husband's injury was legally cognizable, even though today we would regard the harm of adultery as an intangible injury likely to produce emotional distress in the "betrayed" spouse. To the 19th-century mind, however, the seduction of the wife by the defendant was regarded not simply as an event that caused emotional distress to the husband but as a loss of the husband's right of exclusive sexual access to his wife. Such an injury was viewed as analogous to a loss of property and was thought of as permanent in nature and as properly giving rise to a legal claim, regardless of the husband's subjective response. Accordingly, the claim for criminal conversation was classified as a discrete intentional tort that afforded the husband a right to recover all consequential damages, rather than a claim for emotional harm.[11]

It was also telling that the claim for criminal conversation was gender-specific; until the turn of the 20th century, it could not be brought by a wife against a defendant who had had sexual intercourse with her husband.[12] Courts reasoned that the wife lost nothing of permanent value when her husband committed adultery. Reflecting a sexual double standard, the prevailing norm was that a wife should ordinarily forgive her husband when he committed adultery and thereby repair the marital relationship. Because she had no right to her husband's sexual fidelity, any injury the wife suffered was relegated to the class of noncompensable hurt feelings and emotional disturbance, rather than analogized to a tangible property loss.[13] Crucially, when the plaintiff was a woman, the harm of adultery was conceptualized as an intangible harm; and, following the basic rule that denied recovery for mental disturbance alone, the law placed no value on the plaintiff's injury in such situations.

Rarely is the connection between gender and the recognition of injury as explicit and as straightforward as it was in the old tort of criminal conversation. As mentioned earlier, for quite some time, tort doctrine has been gender-neutral on its face—claims given to husbands are given to wives and vice versa. However, the example of the criminal conversation tort does highlight a prominent feature of the nervous-shock cases that arose at the turn of the 20th century. As in the criminal conversation tort, in the nervous-shock cases, the legal categorization of the claim as an "emotional distress" claim was affected by the gender of the plaintiff. The plaintiffs in each of the early classic cases that came to define the nervous-shock claim were women, and a connection between women and fright-based injury was forged from the beginning. Several of these women were pregnant at the time of the frightening occurrence and suffered miscarriages that they believed were caused by their fright. Many women seeking compensation for fright-based injury also alleged that they suffered from some form of hysterical disorder, a condition that was thought to be peculiar to women. Thus, it is not surprising that some courts viewed these claims as distinctive in nature and treated them less favorably than other negligence claims that also produced a combination of physical and emotional harms.

The most prominent early U.S. case arose in New York in 1896 when a plaintiff, Annie Mitchell, suffered nervous shock while waiting to board one of the defendant's horse-drawn railway cars.[14] The car came so close to hitting Mitchell that she actually "stood between the horses' heads when they were stopped." Corroborated by medical evidence, Mitchell claimed that her fright had caused her to lose consciousness and to suffer a miscarriage.

At the time the case was decided, the development of negligence law was still in its early stages. Particularly with the growth of railroad travel, courts were faced with the novel question of deciding how to categorize injury caused by nervous shock produced by the dramatic rise in the number of railway accidents and incidents.[15] Importantly, at the time, the conventional wisdom and the prevailing medical judgment held that trauma, and particularly nervous shock, could cause miscarriages, stillbirths, and hysterical illnesses and that transportation incidents posed these additional risks for female passengers.[16]

The physical/emotional dichotomy surfaced prominently in this context. Courts were called upon to choose whether to classify these cases as "physical harm" cases by focusing on the ultimate harm—including the miscarriages and stillbirths—suffered by the plaintiffs or to classify the cases as "mental disturbance" cases by focusing on the mechanism or cause of the injury, that is, the fright and shock produced by defendant's negligence. As with so many other legal disputes, the choice of classification was crucial: if the claim was for mental disturbance, there would be no recovery, but if it was classified as a claim for physical injury, the ordinary rules of negligence liability would apply, promising recovery upon proof of breach of duty and causation.

The categorization dilemma would play itself out in the courts in the doctrinal struggle over what became known as the "impact rule," a requirement that plaintiff first point to proof of some physical impact or contact upon her person before she could qualify for a damage award. *Mitchell* set the stage for acceptance of the impact rule by denying recovery and placing this fright-based miscarriage case squarely into the category of "mental disturbance." The highest court of the state declared that it was only "logical" to deny recovery for the physical consequences of fright—whether "nervous disease, blindness, insanity, or even a miscarriage"—because fright alone was not a legally cognizable injury. The court's reasoning, however, was soon assailed by critics. They argued that no logic required the New York court to regard Mitchell's physical harm as subordinate to her fright and that the legal question could just as readily be framed differently to ask why the law should treat physical injury produced by fright less favorably than physical injury produced by any other cause.[17]

Mitchell nevertheless spawned two very important decisions in the prestigious Massachusetts Supreme Judicial Court—*Spade v. Lynn & Boston Railroad*,[18] in 1897, and *Homans v. Boston Elevated Railway*,[19] in 1902—the latter case written by Justice Oliver Wendell Holmes. The Massachusetts decisions did so much to establish the impact rule that legal commentators shortly thereafter announced that the "general weight of authority in the American courts sustains the ruling that there can be no recovery for nervous shock, unaccompanied by physical injury."[20] This meant that a case would likely be classified as a mental disturbance case, regardless of the physical nature of plaintiff's ultimate injuries, if the plaintiff could not point to the all-important contemporaneous physical contact with her person.

Like *Mitchell*, *Spade* involved a female plaintiff who claimed that fright had caused her to experience severe physical consequences, in this case hysterical paralysis.[21] Margaret Spade was a passenger on the defendant's railway when the defendant's employees forcibly ejected two drunken passengers who were standing beside her. Even though plaintiff was actually grazed by one of the ejected passengers as he "lurched" off the car, she admitted that it was her fear that produced the subsequent paralysis and other ailments.

The *Spade* opinion was notable for its clarity and candor. The court articulated the impact rule in precise terms, stating that "[w]e remain satisfied with the rule that there can be no recovery for fright, terror, alarm, anxiety, or distress of mind, if these are unaccompanied by some physical injury; and if the rule is to stand, we think it should also be held that there can be no recovery for such physical injuries as may be caused solely by mental disturbance, where there is no injury to the person from without." For the Massachusetts court, if the source of the injury was external (i.e., from contact), there could be compensation. But if the source of the injury was internal (i.e., from fright), there would be no compensation, regardless of the physicality of the harm.

The text of the opinion in *Spade* also indicates a link between plaintiff's gender and the court's view that it was sensible and just to deny recovery in such nervous-shock cases. The *Spade* court focused directly on what it saw as the relevant qualities of the plaintiff and the defendant. It is significant to note that the court regarded the injury alleged by the plaintiff as real and as actually caused by her fright. But, notably, the court believed that only "a timid or sensitive person" would suffer a physical injury because of fright and that a normal person would not have had such a reaction. Echoing the language of an earlier influential case from Australia,[22] the court characterized plaintiff's injury as too "remote" to justify recovery and reached the normative conclusion that the law ought not to be structured to protect the interest of this group of unusually sensitive persons. For the Massachusetts court, a ruling for the plaintiff would jeopardize "[n]ot only the transportation of passengers and the running of trains, but the general conduct of business and the ordinary affairs of life." In its view, the "logical vindication" of the impact rule was that it would be unfair to hold "merely negligent" defendants to pay for the consequences of fright.

The image that emerges from *Spade* is one of a hypersensitive woman whose claims posed a threat to business-as-usual. The Massachusetts court characterized this case as a mental disturbance case—and solidified the impact rule—because it feared that application of ordinary negligence principles would impose a disproportionate liability on defendants. This sense of disproportion arose both from the court's view of plaintiff's injury as marginal and from its belief in the importance of defendant's activity. In the later *Homans* decision, Justice Oliver Wendell Holmes lent his imprimatur to the reasoning of *Spade* and the impact rule by stating that, although it was an "arbitrary exception" to negligence liability, it was nevertheless justified as a pragmatic accommodation of public policy interests.

In the line of cases that embraced the impact rule and denied recovery for even serious physical consequences of fright and shock, we can see the most punitive aspects of separate spheres ideology in play. The rhetoric of the opinions and the rationales for denying liability cast the plaintiffs as timid, sensitive, fragile, weak, and overly excitable. The portraits of plaintiffs, such as Annie Mitchell, that emerged from the opinions matched the prevailing stereotypes of white middle- and upper-class women at the turn of the century, often depicted as frail, dependent beings who were unfit for their assigned roles as childbearers and childraisers. The plaintiffs in the classic cases also responded in ways that were predictable and in line with a familiar narrative of how a lady traveler might well react in such a situation. In this respect, each performed a well-understood script of nervous shock and presented the courts with an opportunity to offer the protection implicitly promised by separate spheres ideology.

However, the ordinariness and the predictability of plaintiffs' responses did not impel these courts to regard their injuries as normal or predictable. Leading torts scholar William Prosser would later remark that "[i]t is not difficult to discover in the earlier opinions a distinctly masculine astonishment that any woman should ever be so silly as to allow herself to be frightened or shocked into a miscarriage."[23] Indeed, the "impact rule" precedents were more inclined to hold a woman to a "reasonable man" standard and to penalize women for responding to danger in stereotypical feminine ways. The judicial ascription of women's injuries as "remote" in this context can best be understood in the sense of injuries removed from the judges' experiences as men. Additionally, even the dispassionate endorsement of the impact rule on "public policy" grounds, which did not impugn the individual plaintiffs or feminine responses more generally, nevertheless seemed grounded on a balancing of interests that minimized women's physical, mental, and procreative injuries and that placed a much higher value on the financial interests of corporate defendants. This harsh side of separate spheres ideology limited protection to women outside the home and highlighted the danger of train and streetcar travel for them. Such a structuring of legal recovery also tended to reinforce the notion that women's proper sphere was domestic and that industry should not be compelled to accommodate women's interests, at least when they were pregnant.

By 1910, the harsh rule had been endorsed in the large industrial states—Pennsylvania, New York, Massachusetts, Illinois, Michigan, and Ohio[24]—and thus was in force in most of the major metropolitan areas of the country where transportation accidents and fright-based injuries were likely to take a toll. However, like so many common law doctrines, it did not find favor in all jurisdictions, and, from the beginning, a counterline of precedents emerged that refused to apply, or simply did not apply, the impact rule. In these jurisdictions, female plaintiffs received a more sympathetic response to their injuries, and their gender did not seem to hurt their claims in any way. Significantly, the courts in these cases also downplayed the mental disturbance aspects of the claims.

A good example of an early case that rejected the impact rule and applied ordinary negligence principles to a fright-based claim is *Purcell v. St. Paul City Ry. Co.*,[25] decided by the Minnesota Supreme Court in 1892. *Purcell* was a near-miss case that very much resembled the fact pattern in *Mitchell*. The plaintiff was a female passenger on a street car in St. Paul who became frightened when defendant's cable car rapidly approached her car and a collision seemed imminent. As the court described her injuries, the shock "threw her into violent convulsions," causing a miscarriage and subsequent illness. Ruling for the plaintiff, the court curtly dismissed the relevance of the axiom that the law provided no recovery for mental distress. For the Minnesota court, this clearly was a case of physical injury, "as serious, certainly, as would be the breaking of an arm or a leg." Once the court characterized the case as a physical harm case, the only issue left to be discussed before recovery could be authorized was that of proximate cause. In marked contrast to the court in *Mitchell*, the Minnesota court had no trouble finding proximate cause because it regarded plaintiff's response as predictable, especially given the confusion and alarm surrounding the incident. Most important, the court rejected defense counsel's argument that "plaintiff's pregnancy rendered her more susceptible to groundless alarm" and that she therefore should be held responsible for her own injuries. Instead, the court refused to embrace a view of pregnant women as supersensitive or abnormal or as posing an undue burden on carriers. It forthrightly declared that "[c]ertainly a woman in her condition has as good right to be carried as any one, and is entitled to at least as high a degree of care on the part of the carrier."

The liberal approach of the Minnesota court was followed in several jurisdictions in opinions that criticized the "impact rule" states for striking the wrong balance between the plaintiff's and the defendant's interests.[26] These courts did not disparage plaintiff's injuries by labeling them remote or abnormal but instead characterized them as "injuries of the most serious character," often highlighting damage to a plaintiff's reproductive interests. These courts also refused to categorize nervous-shock cases as mental disturbance cases, in one case noting that the debate was really "one of time only," because, under the impact rule, immediate physical consequences qualified for compensation, while consequences that surfaced later did not. This same court drove home the illogic of the impact rule by claiming that it might as well be said that "a death caused by poison is not to be attributed to the person who administered it, because the mortal effect is not produced contemporaneously with its administration." The court's choice of analogy, rhetorically linking plaintiff's injury to death, was a far cry from Holmes's sympathetic treatment of the transportation industry.

The liberal precedents that rejected the impact rule treated claims of miscarriages and other illnesses suffered by women as serious physical injuries and seemed to have little difficulty believing that negative consequences of all sorts could flow from fright. Cases such as *Purcell* complicate the story of nervous shock by showing that some courts of the time were capable of treating women's fear and response to danger as reasonable and deserving of legal protection. These liberal precedents were more in line with other pockets of negligence law involving transportation-related injuries in which turn-of-the-century courts acknowledged the distinctive situation of female plaintiffs, including the fact that women often wore cumbersome clothing that restricted their ability to move, and refused to punish them for complying with prevailing gender norms.[27] With respect to these cases, we are inclined to agree with Margo Schlanger's assessment that such courts treated women empathetically and did not presume either that women were incapable of acting reasonably or that they were unreasonable when they acted like women were expected to act.[28]

By 1925, the tide had turned against the impact rule, and a clear majority of states refused to apply the rule to cut off liability for the physical consequences of nervous shock.[29] But the rule nonetheless survived in many parts of the country for a long time thereafter. Several of the industrial states of its origin—notably New York[30] and Pennsylvania[31]—did not officially discard the rule until as late as the 1960s and 1970s. The rule also gained favor in some states that had not ruled on the issue before 1925,[32] and it is still in force in four jurisdictions to some degree today.[33] Although it may never have attained the majority-rule status that was sometimes attributed to it, it clearly had a significant impact on tort recoveries and is still considered the beginning point for contemporary discussions of the proper scope of recovery for negligent infliction of emotional distress.

In assessing the links among the impact rule, nervous-shock cases, and gender, one is drawn to ask how male plaintiffs were treated by courts and whether women plaintiffs received less favorable treatment than their male counterparts. Under a narrow formal equality framework, so familiar in constitutional and other areas of law, the key question in determining whether gender bias against women has occurred is to ask whether "similarly situated" males received better treatment.[34] However, what is striking about the early nervous-shock cases is that there were few male plaintiffs to use for such a comparison.

Historian Barbara Welke has speculated that the dearth of male plaintiffs, at least in the reported cases, was probably the result of several factors. She asserts that the nature of men's and women's claims tended to differ.[35] Of course, men did not suffer from the miscarriages and stillbirths that were a central element of many of the fright-based claims brought by women plaintiffs. Welke also notes that prevailing separate spheres behavioral norms may have prompted men and women to respond differently to similar incidents. For example, she compares cases involving trains that negligently failed to stop at a plaintiff's destination. When the train went past a man's appointed stop, he was likely to jump off and incur a physical injury. A woman, however, might well suffer a fright-based injury when she stayed on the train past her destination and was forced to walk back alone at night in a dangerous location. In line with gender norms, men were also encouraged to allege and emphasize direct physical injury when asserting legal claims and were discouraged from admitting in public that they had suffered damages from fright-based injuries.

Additionally, in the few cases in which male plaintiffs alleged injury traceable to fright, courts were not particularly receptive to their claims. For example, recovery was denied to a man who had lost his leg as a result of jumping from a fast-moving train.[36] He claimed that his fright had impelled him to jump because the conductor and other passengers had threatened to tie him up, take his money, and then throw him off the train. Overturning a jury verdict for the plaintiff, the Missouri Supreme Court found his story incredible, blamed him for jumping, and recited the axiom that mental anguish was not recoverable in tort law. Similarly, in an early Texas case, a man was denied compensation when he alleged injury based on fear for his personal safety, after a train let out a large burst of steam, frightened his team of horses, and caused his wagon to break.[37]

The influence of gender in the nervous-shock cases and the existence of gender bias thus cannot be shown simply by stacking women's claims for fright against identical claims brought by men and comparing the results. Instead, as in debates over the legal treatment of rape victims or other female-dominated areas of the law, any assessment of gender fairness requires resort to theories of equality that extend beyond requirements of formal equality that insist only that "likes" be treated alike. A deeper substantive equality inquiry[38] is necessary to analyze the treatment of nervous shock as a case study in how the law responds to recurring injuries women face, even if there are few similarly situated male tort victims whose treatment can be used as yardstick for fairness. This is a lesson that feminist legal theorists have stressed since the mid-1980s, when formal equality theories increasingly came under attack.[39] This broader approach to equality challenges male norms and pursues the question of whether predominantly-female groups have been treated equitably.

Looking at the nervous-shock cases in retrospect, we can see that, not surprisingly, the courts did not respond to the recurring claims of negligently caused miscarriages produced by nervous shock in a highly protective way, by, for example, recognizing a claim for negligent interference with women's procreative interests, comparable to men's interest in the exclusive sexual access to their wives afforded by the old tort of criminal conversation. Even today, such a "woman-friendly" response is hard to imagine, although some contemporary cases are more willing to allow recovery for emotional distress when the case arises in the "sensitive" context of reproduction. Rather, such a protective response seems unlikely even today, largely because of the courts' continuing refusal to value procreative and emotional interests as highly as interests in property and bodily integrity. In chapter 4, we discuss how, in negligence cases, the courts still have difficulty characterizing the distinctive relationship between a pregnant woman and her fetus and still do not yet regard a mother's response to a miscarriage or stillbirth as equivalent to a "physical" injury.

We regard the most significant and enduring legacy of the nervous-shock cases to lie in their struggle over the physical/emotional dichotomy in the law of torts. It is crucial that the debate over whether to allow recovery for fright-based harms was framed as a struggle over categorization and only indirectly as a struggle over gender. The defense strategy was to exploit the cognitive association between women and emotions and to link it to recurring injuries women sustained on trains and streetcars. Labeling the cases "mental disturbance" cases served to shift the focus from the admittedly physical aspects of the injuries and to minimize any relational harm that occurred as a result of miscarriages, stillbirths, and other consequences of nervous shock. Framing the issue as centering on the physical/emotional distinction in tort law also sounded a gender-neutral theme, even though gender seethed up from the facts of the cases.

As we explain in chapter 4, resort to the physical/emotional distinction to determine whether to provide legal compensation for a predominately-female group of injured plaintiffs would become a familiar move in tort law. After the impact rule was finally laid to rest in the 1960s and 1970s, courts were faced with another difficult issue—whether to allow mothers and other close family members to sue for trauma-based harm suffered as a result of witnessing the negligent killing or injuring of their children or other family members. In these so-called bystander cases, the prototypical plaintiff was a mother who often had suffered a combination of injuries—physical, emotional, and relational—and the issue was once again whether to treat such a case as a "mental disturbance" case and deny all recovery. The bystander cases represented round two in the legal treatment of fright-based harm and gave the courts another opportunity to confront gender and the boundary between emotional and physical harm.

Presently, as we detail in chapter 4, courts are struggling with the important question of the degree to which to allow recovery for "stand-alone" emotional distress when defendant's negligent conduct did not cause any ultimate physical symptoms or physical manifestations of injury. Many of these contemporary cases involve female plaintiffs who allege injury arising from sexual exploitation[40] or reproductive harm.[41] In the 21st century, the face of negligent infliction of emotional distress is still female, and the story of the impact rule, with its gender imprint, still resonates in contemporary clashes over the limits of tort recovery and the continuing relevance of gender to tort doctrine.

Racialized Fear and White Privilege

Because the story of nervous shock is largely about the legal treatment of white women's injuries, at first blush it may not appear to implicate race or racial ideology. Looking just a bit more closely at the cases, however, it is evident that race played into the separate spheres stereotypes that attached to many of the plaintiffs in the cases and influenced the rhetoric and reasoning of many courts. This happened because, at its base, the separate spheres trope was race-specific: only white women were regarded as fragile, delicate, timid, and in need of protection, in stark contrast to prevailing images of black women as stoic and impervious to pain. Although a few African American women were successful in fighting for the legal "right" to be treated as ladies (i.e., proper white women), traditional notions of femininity were inextricably linked to whiteness.

In addition to the racialized quality of separate spheres embedded in the nervous-shock cases, race was implicated in turn-of-the-century tort claims for emotional distress of another sort. These "emotional distress" cases typically involved allegations that defendant's conduct—or, more often, the conduct of employees or persons in the control of the defendant—was insulting or abusive in a specifically racial sense, giving rise to compensable claims for fear, humiliation, and mental anguish. In cases of this sort, white plaintiffs traded on the high cultural value placed on whiteness, that is, white privilege,[42] to convince courts that they had suffered a real injury, despite the absence of physical harm or other material damage. In marked contrast to the skepticism displayed by some courts in the nervous-shock cases, several courts in the racialized fear and insult cases credited white plaintiffs' allegations of injury.[43] For some courts at least, insult and abuse became more tangible when they also amounted to a challenge to white supremacy.

One of the most revealing cases of racialized fear and judicial recognition of white privilege is *Gulf, Colorado & Santa Fe Railway. Co. v. Luther*,[44] a 1905 decision from a Texas appellate court. The claim in that case arose from an incident in the "ladies waiting room" of a railway station. As part of the separate spheres notion that white women should be protected and shielded in public places, large cities in the segregated South at that time provided separate "ladies" waiting rooms for the use of white women, their children, and their white male escorts, typically their husbands. Black men and women were restricted to "colored" waiting rooms, while most white men used what was called the "white" waiting room. The only black women allowed in the "ladies" waiting room were black employees, not passengers.[45]

Mrs. Luther was traveling with her husband and her four small children when their train was delayed. The incident occurred when Mr. Luther left them in the "ladies" waiting room while he went into town on business. According to the testimony, one of the Luther children spilled water from a cup onto the floor. Shortly thereafter, Mrs. Luther and the female attendant in the waiting room, described repeatedly by the court as the "negro woman," had a heated exchange. Mrs. Luther apparently believed that the spill was an accident. But the attendant disputed this and allegedly told Mrs. Luther that "the child did know water was in the cup" and said that "[i]f you say the child did not know that water was in the cup you are a liar." In addition to disputing her account, Mrs. Luther claimed that the attendant's demeanor was frightening, saying that "she turned on me with an angry look." When Mrs. Luther told the attendant that she was not "accustomed to be[ing] treated that way by colored people," the attendant replied in kind, remarking, "I am used to your kind. I meet up with them every day." Mrs. Luther claimed that during this exchange, which lasted "about five minutes," the attendant stood right over her, shook her finger in Mrs. Luther's eye, and looked "vicious and angry." She sought compensation from the railroad for injuries stemming from the incident, which the court described as great fright, humiliation, worry, distress, nervous prostration, physical pain, and mental anguish.[46] Significantly, beyond the vague reference to physical pain, there was no allegation of physical injury or external physical contact and the court treated the suit as one for mental distress alone.

Because it was based on the intentional acts of the railroad employee, *Luther* presented a distinctive type of mental distress case that seemed more like an intentional tort claim for insult or abuse than a claim for negligence. Indeed, courts had developed what was known as the "common carrier" doctrine in response to such cases and had held that railroads and other common carriers owed a broad duty to protect their passengers from insulting or violent behavior by employees or even fellow passengers.[47] If the plaintiff could successfully lodge her case under the common carrier doctrine, she could recover without proof of physical injury, despite the fact that it could be argued that the claim against the railroad was not really based on any intentional conduct on the part of the railroad itself. However, an important element of such a claim, presaging the development of the contemporary claim for intentional infliction of mental distress, was plaintiff's proof that the employee's conduct was insulting or outrageous. Recovery thus hinged on a judgment about the quality of the employee's behavior and how it likely affected the plaintiff.

The jury in *Luther* rendered a verdict for plaintiff in the sum of $2,500, a sizeable recovery at the time.[48] In upholding the judgment, the Texas appellate judge wrote an opinion that emphasized the attendant's race and drew upon separate spheres stereotypes of white women to explain and underscore Mrs. Luther's suffering. Referring to her race no fewer than sixteen times, the court characterized the behavior of the attendant, whose name was never revealed, as "violent and outrageous" and had little trouble fitting this case into the line of common carrier cases that dispensed with the need to prove physical injury. In the court's view, the high jury verdict was reasonable, given the gender and racial identities of the parties. In the court's own words:

> [W]hat could be more humiliating to a frail, delicate, sensitive woman, with a babe at her breast and her other little ones around her, than to be pounced upon, vilified and traduced by a negro servant in a railway depot, where her relation as a passenger to its owner entitles her to be treated with respect and kindness? Is it any wonder to those who can contemplate the effect of such an outrage that the poor woman for months afterwards, as she testified, could not close her eyes without that angry, threatening negro arising before her and murdering sleep.

In our reading of the case, white privilege certainly worked to Mrs. Luther's advantage. It is far from clear that the attendant's conduct could fairly be characterized as outrageous or violent. The exchange between the women instead suggests that each had staked out a position on the facts and each had expressed some contempt for the other. Even if we concede that the attendant raised her voice and wagged her finger, her conduct can qualify as "outrageous" only if it is presumed that Mrs. Luther was entitled to be treated with some special deference, that is, to be accorded the respect owed to a white woman. In this view, the main problem with the attendant's behavior was that it was racially inappropriate or "uppity" and thus posed a challenge to Mrs. Luther's racial superiority. Apparently after Mrs. Luther reminded the attendant of her "place" by stating that she was not used to being treated that way by colored people, the "servant" was not supposed to get angry but was expected to remain courteous and obsequious.

The racial privilege that bolstered Mrs. Luther's case was also inseparable from her gender. In the court's view of the exchange between the women, it was critical that Mrs. Luther was white, female, and a mother and was thought to be acutely sensitive to emotional upset and pain. It is hard to believe that the court would have demonstrated quite as much sympathy for Mr. Luther if the incident had occurred while he was alone with his four children. Here, however, with Mr. Luther in town and away from his wife on unspecified business, it became the railroad's responsibility to protect her. As Barbara Welke has so eloquently documented in her history of railroad litigation, white racial supremacy in the South was fundamentally predicated on protecting white women and maintaining racialized gender norms.[49] In *Luther*, the race of the attendant and the race of the victim combined to make the harm acute. It was at this intersection of race and gender—in cases presenting claims of white female victims and black "aggressors"—that the privilege of whiteness emerged so prominently.

Luther also demonstrates how the power of race and racial threat affected the law's view of African American women. The fact that the attendant in the case was also a woman did not carry much weight in the case. In the extended passage quoted earlier, the court tellingly refers to her as a "negro servant" and a "threatening negro." This description both underscores her subordinate racial position and serves to masculinize her, emphasizing her supposedly aggressive behavior, including how she "pounced upon" the helpless Mrs. Luther. Again, it is hard to imagine that a black Mrs. Luther suing for a similar injury would have had as much success in court in comparable circumstances. Indeed, there could be no truly comparable case because an African American woman would not have had the services of a white (or any other) attendant in the "colored" waiting room. Most significant, because she lacked the race privilege of a white woman, a black Mrs. Luther would have had a much more difficult task convincing the jury that she was the kind of lady who could be devastated by rude behavior from a servant. In an earlier Kentucky case, for example, there was uncontradicted evidence that a black woman was accosted by a drunken white male passenger who had gone into the colored coach, offered her a drink, "perhaps laid his hand upon her," and made profane and indecent remarks to her. The jury nevertheless returned a verdict for the defendant railroad.[50]

Our reading of *Luther* indicates that mental distress and fear may arise from many sources and that an unavoidable exercise of normative judgment is required to determine whether the resulting harm should be recognized and compensated in law. The facts in *Luther* differed significantly from those in *Mitchell* and the nervous-shock cases discussed previously, where the defendants' negligence consisted of operating their horses and vehicles in a dangerous fashion and putting plaintiffs in fear for their lives. In contrast, in cases like *Luther*, the conduct deemed actionable was defendant's failure to prevent an encounter with a black person that the white plaintiff regarded as objectionable. Allowing recovery in *Luther* thus not only validated Mrs. Luther's claim of injury but also gave powerful incentives to defendants like railroads to protect whites from such contacts with blacks. It thus endorsed and reinforced a system of white supremacy. In so doing, it gave the intangible asset of white racial status a material value.

Race, Devaluation, and Wrongful Death

At the same time that courts in turn-of-the-century tort cases were according a positive value to white racial status, race surfaced in a negative way in suits brought by African Americans. In these cases, minority race status operated to devalue the lives and suffering of tort plaintiffs, resulting in lower awards for black plaintiffs than would likely have been awarded to white plaintiffs under similar circumstances. Although this form of bias seems straightforward, in the familiar sense of a failure to treat "like" cases alike, it is significant that, in the tort context, devaluation affected value judgments about the seriousness of an injury and operated to minimize the extent of the plaintiff's harm.[51] Thus, in some cases, the seriousness of an injury to an African American plaintiff could be so discounted that it actually appeared, to white decision makers, to be a type of harm different from that suffered by a white person. When this occurred, the cases did not look alike in the eyes of the judge or jury. Updated versions of this dynamic have reappeared in contemporary assessments of damage awards, as our discussion in chapter 6 of the use of race-based earning tables shows. Racial devaluation continues to be masked in a system that appears to give fair, individualized treatment to tort victims.

Perhaps the most celebrated instance of racial devaluation in early-20th-century tort litigation involved the 1909 decision in a case brought by George Griffin, an African American man who worked as a Pullman porter.[52] While publicized and contested at the time, the case has not made it into standard accounts of tort law. Griffin was accused of stealing property belonging to Daniel Brady, a prominent businessman and brother of the famous "Diamond Jim Brady," one of the best-known financiers of the gilded age. Brady's accusation of theft resulted in Griffin's arrest and jailing. It is not clear just how long Griffin remained in jail before he was cleared of all charges by a magistrate. The record indicates only that it was somewhere between two hours and an overnight detention.

After the incident, Griffin sued Brady for false imprisonment, seeking $10,000 in damages for maliciously causing his arrest and detention. As is the case today, false imprisonment in 1909 was a well-established intentional tort claim brought to redress injuries stemming from a detention or confinement.[53] Because its primary function has been to vindicate the plaintiff's interest in personal mobility and freedom, plaintiffs alleging false imprisonment have traditionally been allowed to seek damages for mental distress and humiliation as part of the legal recognition of this specific type of dignitary harm. As in other intentional torts, juries in false imprisonment suits are given considerable discretion to award a sum that reflects the community's judgment of the seriousness of the harm done to the plaintiff. In such cases, although the damage award is designed to compensate the plaintiff for actual damage suffered, calculation of such an award is inextricably linked to judgments about the nature of the defendant's behavior and the personal characteristics of the plaintiff.

In Griffin's false imprisonment suit, a jury in New York found Brady liable and awarded Griffin $2,500 in damages. As we noted earlier in discussing *Luther*, the 1905 race privilege case, this represented a sizeable sum for the time. Apparently, the Griffin case was so notable that the *New York Times* reported what transpired between the trial judge, Justice Phillip Henry Dugro, and the lawyers representing Griffin. Convinced that the damages were too high, Justice Dugro first told Griffin's lawyers that if they did not agree to a reduction of the damages to the dramatically smaller amount of $300, he would set aside the jury's verdict and order a new trial. When the lawyers refused, Justice Dugro went ahead and reduced the amount to $300 anyway. Griffin's subsequent appeals of the reduction order were all unsuccessful.[54]

That racial devaluation affected Justice Dugro's ruling was evident from his ruling, as he sought to justify his decision to reduce the award. According to the *Times* account, Justice Dugro fixed on Griffin's race and imagined how the harm Griffin sustained was less than what a white man would suffer if jailed on the basis of false information. Referring to plaintiff, Justice Dugro stated:

> [h]e was a porter, and while he is just as good as the President of the United States, and if he is imprisoned wrongfully he should be paid for it, it would be a bad argument to say that he is just as good in many senses. He would not be hurt just as much if put in prison as every man would be. That depends on a man's standing, what his circumstances are, and if he is a colored man, the fact that he is a colored man is to be considered. . . .[I]n one sense, a colored man is just as good as a white man, for the law says he is, but he has not the same amount of injury under all circumstances

that a white man would have. . . . In this sort of community I dare say the amount of evil that would flow to the colored man from a charge like this would not be as great as it probably would be to a white man.

For Justice Dugro, Griffin's race minimized his injury and meant that, even though plaintiff was entitled to a damage award, his injury had less value than if he had been white. At one point, he even noted that Griffin's employer had not lost faith in him as a result of the incident and that he was sure that Griffin would be happy to take $2,500 for being in jail two hours. In a headline reporting on the appeal in the case, the *Times* summed up the trial court's position, declaring: "Negro Not Equal to White: Suffers Less Humiliation in False Arrest, Court Holds."

The *Times* also published an editorial on the case that was critical of the trial judge's action.[55] Noting that the case had "made talk all over the country," the editorial recognized its potential significance beyond its individual facts and beyond New York. Perhaps in part because of the intangible nature of the injury, however, the *Times* appeared to believe that the fairness of the judge's assessment was open to debate. Referring to Justice Dugro's decision to reduce the award because of Griffin's race, the editorial went on to state that "[n]obody could deny that there was a sort of truth in it, and yet almost everybody had an instinctive realization that the thing was, or ought to be, wrong." In this respect, the editorial acknowledged a plausible connection between the race of the plaintiff and the degree of humiliation and suffering expected to flow from the tortious action. In the end, however, the *Times* editorial denounced Justice Dugro's action, in terms that echoed W. E. B. Du Bois's notion of a "talented tenth" of black Americans whose achievements and qualities deserved the respect of white Americans.[56] The editorial characterized Justice Dugro's approach as "the indictment and condemnation of a race, without regard to its better part or its exceptional members," and called the ruling "repugnant to the modern sense of equity."

The judicial treatment of George Griffin's case was also the subject of criticism in articles published shortly thereafter in newspapers and legal journals across the country.[57] One particularly trenchant attack first appeared in the *Virginia Law Register* and was later reprinted in a weekly law journal published in St. Louis.[58] Under the headline "A New York Court Draws the Color Line," the author sarcastically dubbed Justice Dugro's opinion "remarkable" and did not try to hide his glee that such a miscarriage of justice had occurred in New York. According to this critic, race should not have entered the case at all. He regarded the ruling as wholly unfounded, stating that the court would have had to go back to the 14th century to find support for its ruling. Apparently oblivious to similar devaluative judgments made in Southern courts, which we discuss later, the author proclaimed that:

> We are exceedingly glad that this decision came from a court of justice north of the Potomac. Had it occurred in a southern state we can imagine the agony of mind that it would have cost the New York Evening Post and a few other journals of that character. We do not believe that in our Court of Appeals the court would have listened for one moment to an argument based on the color of the suitor before it.

Today, such a heated debate about whether the degree of a person's mental suffering or humiliation depends on race seems unsupportable or even ludicrous. As we discuss in chapter 6, contemporary law recognizes and generally accepts that tort damages for lost earnings or other economic harm will often vary based on a person's income, a factor indirectly connected to race. However, it is equally widely accepted that nonpecuniary awards for pain and suffering, mental anguish, and dignitary harm are supposed to be purely individual and free of racial considerations. Certainly no contemporary court would follow Justice Dugro's lead and state that, simply because of his race, a black person could not have "the same amount of injury" as a white person when it comes to noneconomic harm.

In 1909, however, such a link between race and mental distress damages was not so unthinkable. As explained by interdisciplinary legal scholar Martha Minow, pain was often tied to race and ethnicity in 19th-century medical practice and medical literature.[59] Even the use of anesthesia was selective because it was thought that the need for painkillers varied, depending on the race, gender, ethnicity, and other personal characteristics of the patient.[60] Thus, when Justice Dugro assumed that George Griffin's suffering was less than that of a white man, he reflected a racist view with a long pedigree that built racial devaluation into purportedly individualized judgments about a person's case. In tort law, this kind of devaluation likely had its first appearance in early cases that assumed that the amount of injury depended on a person's class status or station in society. For example, a case report from 1302 quotes an English judge as expressing the view that "[A] buffet given to a knight or noble was as bad as a wound given to one of the rabble."[61] Translated into more modern terms, this statement is tantamount to saying that punching an upper-class gentleman causes as much harm as stabbing an ordinary man.

We conclude that Justice Dugro's ruling sparked a controversy not because it was based on a novel understanding of the connection between race and harm but because the racial devaluation in the ruling was so explicit. By the 20th century, it was exceedingly rare to find a reported decision that relied explicitly on race to justify lowering an award to a black litigant.[62] Griffin's case thus presented the issue of devaluation in a highly visible way and showcased its significant consequences. In that case, when the court reduced the award from $2,500 to $300, one might reasonably have concluded that the reduction represented the difference between a white and a black measure of harm. Put another way, race transformed a serious injury into a relatively minor one.

As is apparent by the jury's significantly higher verdict and the commentators' criticism of Justice Dugro's ruling, the proper role of race in tort law was contested even in 1909, rather like the contested nature of gender in the nervous-shock cases. Some writers of the day, like the caustic critic from the *Virginia Law Register*, recognized the circular and unpersuasive quality of the reasoning used to justify resort to race to discern the amount and quality of a plaintiff's suffering. In effect, Justice Dugro had relied on the inferior caste status of blacks to justify a lower, inferior award to Griffin, under the logic that because Griffin had low social standing to begin with, he did not have as far to fall as a white man who was falsely imprisoned. The author of the *Virginia Law Register* article shrewdly pointed out the problem with such an argument, noting that "[t]he injury to a man for false imprisonment might be far greater in the case of a humble man working for a daily wage than in the case of a millionaire. The fact that the former had once been in prison, although innocent, might cause him great trouble in securing a position such as a porter upon a Pullman car." He went on to conclude that "the injury, therefore, for false imprisonment to a porter on Pullman car, even though he was colored, might be greater than to a Vanderbilt or a Rockefeller." Thus, in the writer's view, even if the harm of false imprisonment had a reputational dimension beyond pure mental distress, racial devaluation of a black man's injury could still not be justified.

When we analyze Griffin from a contemporary critical perspective, we are also struck by how readily Justice Dugro moved from an individualized assessment of one person's suffering to hypothetical calculations about the measure of pain purportedly experienced by blacks as a group. Justice Dugro not only resorted to individual factors in the case to determine how much Griffin actually suffered (e.g., how long plaintiff had been confined and the specific circumstances surrounding his confinement); he also employed a group-based frame of reference that sought to measure how blacks could be expected to respond under such circumstances. He assessed the injury to "the colored man," rather than to the individual Mr. George Griffin. This black-only reference point clearly worked to Griffin's individual disadvantage: it linked him to others in his racial group and infused racial hierarchy directly into the tort award.

The racial devaluation so evident in the Griffin case was not an isolated phenomenon, even if it most often surfaced in more subtle guises. To understand how devaluation works in more ordinary cases, we examined a set of wrongful death cases decided by Louisiana appellate courts in the first four decades of the 20th century.[63] We chose wrongful death cases because they present a particularly good vehicle for ferreting out devaluation, given that each wrongful death case involves the same injury—the death of a family member—and thus provides some rough basis for comparison. In Louisiana at that time, the governing wrongful death statute allowed surviving relatives to bring two distinct types of related claims against a tortfeasor, although, confusingly, both claims are typically brought in one lawsuit and combined into a wrongful death case.[64] The principal claim was the technical claim for "wrongful death," which is designed to compensate the *survivors* for *their* losses as a result of the death. For these wrongful death claims, Louisiana's scope of recovery was quite generous: survivors were entitled to receive not only compensation for loss of financial support but also an amount to compensate for loss of emotional support and love and for the grief they had suffered as a result of the death. Additionally, in appropriate cases, the relatives of the victim could also assert a claim for damages that the victim could have brought on his own behalf had he survived, commonly referred to as a "survival claim." Survival claims are designed to compensate for the *victim's* losses; for example, if the victim was struck by a train and survived for hours or weeks before dying from his injuries, family members may assert a survival claim to recover for the victim's pain and suffering and for any lost income the victim sustained in the interval between injury and death.[65]

For our purposes, it is important to note that the structure of recovery for wrongful death in Louisiana permitted plaintiffs to recover for both intangible and tangible or pecuniary losses. First, recovery for emotional distress was available in wrongful death cases to compensate for the survivor's emotional distress. Second, recovery for emotional distress was available in survival actions to compensate for the decedent's emotional and physical suffering. Thus, courts were routinely called upon to place a dollar value on the intangible relational and emotional loss caused by the death of a loved one.

And, as happened in the Griffin case in New York, racial devaluation was apt to find its way into Louisiana wrongful death cases when courts measured these intangible losses.

Finally, one unusual feature of Louisiana law that deserves mention is that appellate courts were authorized to review the facts, as well as the law, in personal injury cases and could even conduct an independent review of the specific amount awarded to the plaintiff by the jury or trial court.[66] Thus, the reported cases in Louisiana cases frequently contain discussions of "quantum," that is, the specific amounts plaintiffs received, in contrast to cases in most other jurisdictions that do not have appellate review of facts.

During the period 1900–1940, both black and white plaintiffs filed and won many wrongful death and survival actions, obtaining recovery for relatives' deaths at the hands of railroads, gas companies, neighbors, and a variety of other defendants. As courts do today, Louisiana courts in the early 20th century struggled with the difficult task of how to quantify a loss so intimate and precious as the death of a child, spouse, or parent. The judicial treatment of wrongful death thus reveals how the law valued different people's lives, suffering, and connections to each other and how race in particular could influence that valuation.

Unlike an administrative system, such as workers' compensation, which groups types of injuries into predetermined categories in order to systematize compensation decisions,[67] the common law system of torts and common law courts are committed to the notion that every death and every injury is particular and different.[68] Within this system of individualized judgment, however, the principle of treating like cases alike comes into play when courts, particularly appellate courts, attempt to impose a rough consistency among the cases by adhering to precedents set in what they regard as "similar" cases. This adherence to precedents not only has the effect of limiting the discretion of courts and juries but also demonstrates what counts as "similar" or "different" for such courts and thus reveals their implicit frames of reference.

Strikingly, in some wrongful death cases, appellate courts in Louisiana determined the appropriate amount to award black families by comparing that amount only to amounts granted in other black-victim cases. This practice in essence relied on a segregated, black-only benchmark to determine quantum, similar to the black-only frame of reference Justice Dugro employed when he reduced the award for George Griffin. However, unlike the temporary notoriety of the Griffin case, the racial devaluation present in these Louisiana cases went unnoticed. It blended into the segregative patterns of the larger culture and apparently was subtle enough not to attract attention.

One clear example of the use of black-only precedents to determine damages is the 1939 case of *Young v. Broussard*.[69] The victim in that case was Pentard Young, a twenty-nine-year-old African American man, who was shot and killed by a night watchman at the sugar mill where he had worked for approximately one year before he was laid off. At the time, Pentard Young lived with his parents and contributed three or four dollars a week from his weekly wage of fourteen dollars. After he was shot, Pentard survived for two days, suffering considerable pain before he died.

A suit for wrongful death and survival damages was brought by his parents, his closest survivors, who sought to recover for lost support, for their grief and loss of love and affection, and for their son's pain and suffering prior to his death. Because the trial court had concluded that the defendants had not acted tortiously, the appellate court had the task of reviewing the case to determine both liability and the amount of the award.

After concluding that Pentard Young was entitled to recovery because he had not been at fault and because the sugar mill was legally responsible for the shooter's action, the court decided to set the damages at $3,500. In choosing this amount, the court mentioned three earlier cases decided by Louisiana appellate courts, each involving black adult victims, whom the court sometimes referred to as "boys." Two cases had been decided by the same court within the preceding two years.[70] Each of these cases involved the death of a young, unmarried black man; in one case the court had awarded $3,000, and in the other it had awarded $3,200. The third case had been decided more than thirteen years earlier by a different appellate court. It involved the malicious killing of a twenty-year-old black man and resulted in an award of $6,000.[71]

Without further explanation, the *Young* court stated that "[w]e have decided to fix the award in this case at $3,500, which amount we believe to be proper under the facts of the case." Although the court did not expressly so indicate, it is likely that the bulk of the award was meant to compensate for the mental suffering of the parents and the pain and suffering of the deceased, rather than for loss of financial support. This inference is warranted because the court made a point of stating that Pentard Young's financial contribution to his parents amounted to "little more than his own board" and that the family had "four other grown boys who help in the support of the family."

What is most significant about *Young* is that the court did not compare its $3,500 award in that case to an award of $8,780 in *Boykin v. Plauche*,[72] a potentially similar case involving a white victim that had been decided by the same court only three years earlier. As in *Young*, Charles Boykin died when he was a young man in his twenties, and, like Young, Boykin had never earned much money or contributed much to his surviving mother's support, with the exception of a few months' work at an oil company. Unlike Pentard Young, however, Charles Boykin did not suffer before his death: he was in a car accident and never regained consciousness after the impact. There were, of course, some other differences in the two young men's lives and deaths. Charles Boykin was in college at the time of his death, had ambitions to become a writer, and was described by the court as "exceptionally brilliant." He was also white.

When the appellate court in *Boykin* set the award for wrongful death at $8,780—an amount more than double the amount in *Young*—it was careful not to speculate as to how much the deceased son would have contributed to his mother's support. Perhaps because Charles Boykin was still in college and it was far from clear that he would have been a financial success as a writer, the court chose to duck that difficult issue and lumped all items of damage together in the final sum. Presumably, however, in addition to an undetermined sum for financial support, the award contained a sizeable recovery for the intangible losses suffered by Boykin's mother. We can assume the court did not grant any survival damages because Boykin never regained consciousness after the accident.

The *Boykin* court determined quantum in the case without citing any cases. Notably, and in contrast to *Young*, it did not reach back to cite the 1926 case involving an unmarried black man who also died in his twenties. Because it did not make that comparison, the court did not have to explain why the award in the 1926 case was only $6,000 or why the award in *Boykin* was considerably higher.

Putting *Young* and *Boykin* side by side reveals the potentially devaluative effect of using segregated precedents. The award of $3,500 in *Young* might appear reasonable and consistent when compared only to the other black-victim cases, particularly because the highest sum awarded in the black precedent cases was $6,000 and was awarded in a case of a malicious shooting. However, if the *Young* court had compared its award to the $8,780 award in *Boykin*, the award likely would have seemed too low. The court would have then have been forced to ask why the *Boykin* case was so different as to justify a significantly higher award.

It is possible, of course, that the disparity in the awards in *Young* and *Boykin* is entirely a result of the court's view that Charles Boykin would have contributed significantly more financially to his mother's support. Admittedly, because Boykin was in college, his prospects for financial success were likely greater than Pentard Young's. However, two considerations weigh against accepting this as a complete explanation for the disparity in the awards. First, Charles Boykin had not provided substantial support to his mother in the past, and the court refused to speculate about his earning potential. Second, even if it was reasonable to place a higher value on the "financial support" element of damages in *Boykin*, that should not account for the entire disparity, particularly given that only Young's family had the right to recover survival damages because only Young had suffered before his death.

Instead, a more likely explanation for the disparity in the awards, or at least some portion of it, is that the pain and suffering of Pentard Young and the grief and emotional loss of his parents were not given as high a value as the emotional harm suffered by the mother of Charles Boykin. In the invisible process of measuring grief and pain, it is likely that Louisiana courts in these cases were influenced by the race of the victims and shared Justice Dugro's views about the connection between race and mental distress.

When we switch from a comparison of individual cases to view the system of wrongful death recovery in Louisiana at the aggregate level, we can begin to get a rough sense of the potential impact that devaluation and other forces had in suppressing awards for black families during this period. Our survey of all published wrongful death and survival decisions decided in Louisiana from 1900 through 1940 indicates that the average recoveries for black families were less than half those for white families.[73] The same held true for median recoveries. During this period, the average award in lawsuits brought by blacks was $3,542 (median: $3,100); the average award in lawsuits brought by whites was $7,605 (median: $7,000). While this calculation cannot tell how much of the disparity was the result of racial devaluation or exactly how such devaluation occurred, it certainly suggests that race may have mattered as much in tort cases as it did in the larger culture.[74]

To frame the discussion of race and gender in contemporary tort law that follows, this chapter has identified and applied three important dynamics that have surfaced and resurfaced in this area of law for more than a century. The mapping of gender onto the debate over physical versus mental harm, the operation of white racial privilege, and the devaluation of claims brought by racial minorities are dynamics that have shaped the law of intentional torts, negligence, causation, and damages. When we see these dynamics in play in varying contexts over time, however, they do not always take the same form but tend to appear in updated versions that fit more comfortably within the cultural and legal struggles of the day. As legal historian Reva Siegel's theory of social and legal change describes it,[75] the dynamics reemerge encased in different rules and different rhetorics. As we seek to show in the remaining chapters, however, it is the underlying continuity of gender and racial hierarchy that often remains hidden in this process as it reproduces the same—yet different—tort law.

3

Intentional Torts

In the first few weeks of law school, beginning students discover that intentional torts are at the margins of contemporary tort law. Although most first-year torts courses still start with intentional torts, the professor generally moves quickly onto negligence liability and stays there for most of the semester, perhaps reserving some limited time at the end of the course to examine strict liability.[1] This pedagogical centering of negligence and downplaying of intentional torts mirrors an understanding of what is considered to be the intellectual and practical "core" of the field. At this core lie accidental injury and the rules governing recovery for physical harm caused by unintentional conduct. The rest of tort law—from cases involving a punch in the nose to those involving a deprivation of an intimate family relationship—are relegated to the periphery of the field and rarely count for much in the formulation of tort theory.

This vision of the basic structure of tort law was recently underscored in the drafting process of the most recent revision of the Restatement of Torts, the influential and ambitious undertaking of the American Law Institute that attempts to "restate" the rules and principles of tort law as gleaned from thousands of judicial decisions. For this Third Restatement of Torts, an initial decision was made to limit the revision project only to "basic" or "general" principles and to focus on the essentials. Starting from the premise that "the problem of accidental injury is what many see as the core problem facing modern tort law,"[2] the drafters initially chose not to update the sections devoted to the traditional intentional torts, such as battery, assault, and false imprisonment, and to treat cases of emotional harm as a special topic, reserving it for separate consideration at a later date.

The Third Restatement's concentration on negligence and physical harm is in line with the initial shaping of the field by such luminaries as Oliver Wendell Holmes and Roscoe Pound. For example, when Holmes, in 1897, searched for general principles that would define the then-new domain of tort law, he looked to railroad crossing and industrial accidents as raw material for his theories and set about to explain the duties modern enterprise owed to workers, customers, and the general public. Holmes did not pay much attention to intentional torts because for him they represented antiquated causes of action associated with "the old days of isolated, ungeneralized wrongs, assaults, slanders, and the like."[3] This alignment of intentional torts with preindustrial society was echoed by Roscoe Pound, who constructed a narrative of progress in which the law first dealt with and solved the problem of "intentional aggressions" in its path toward a "civilized society" and then went on to tackle more contemporary and challenging issues related to negligence and accidents.[4] Even a contemporary, left-leaning scholar such as Richard Abel accepts this basic account of the trajectory of tort law, noting that changes in "industrialization, urbanization, capitalism, and the state" tend to "reduce the salience of intentional torts [and] increase that of negligent injuries."[5]

A similar preoccupation with accidents and a neglect of intentional torts characterize the two major schools of scholarly thought that have dominated torts scholarship in the past four decades. For the most part, "law and economics" scholars have derived their accounts and critiques of tort law through an analysis of the efficiency of legal rules governing negligence and strict liability and, like their intellectual predecessors, have described their chief concern as determining the risk of loss from accidental injuries or destruction of property. At least since Guido Calabresi's famous 1970 book *The Costs of Accidents*,[6] the place held by intentional torts in economic analysis has been precarious and marginal, with some economics-minded scholars preferring to subsume intentional torts under the category of crimes, rather than within the realm of torts at all.[7] Even the "corrective justice" theorists, with their emphasis on the moral foundations of tort law and the importance of requiring defendants to pay for the harm they cause, also pay scant attention to intentional torts.[8] They are fascinated by the moral implications of the choice between negligence and strict liability in compensating for unintentional harms but tend not to consider whether tort law adequately responds to the most serious injuries caused by deliberate and immoral behavior.

One central problem with this de-emphasis of intentional torts is its tendency to render certain types of recurring harms largely invisible within the frame of tort law, even as they have gained prominence in the larger culture and in other areas of law. This focus on "accidents" to the neglect of intentional torts reinforces a tacit assumption that the intellectual and practical problems of intentionally-caused harm have already been addressed and presumably resolved. Pushing intentional torts from the center of the law school curriculum also means that new generations of lawyers are less likely to regard tort law as a proper vehicle for responding to widespread injuries caused by aggression and abuse of power that bear little resemblance to the prototypical automobile accident, products liability, or slip-and-fall case.

This chapter focuses on how tort law treats two such undertheorized intentional harms—domestic violence and workplace harassment—and what that means for victims, the evolution of tort doctrine, and tort theory. For each harm, the law has evolved from a point of near-total denial of tort liability to a softer regime of partial barriers that allows for recovery in a small number of cases. It is still the case, however, that domestic violence and workplace harassment are rarely thought of as intentional torts and have yet to appreciably affect the contours of tort law.

It is now widely appreciated that the injuries caused by domestic violence and workplace harassment are not evenly distributed in society but fall disproportionately on women and members of minority social groups. A comprehensive national study published in 2000 confirmed the conventional wisdom that women were far more likely than men to be victims of domestic violence and to sustain injury as a result of the violence.[9] Even though there is now greater awareness of domestic violence in same-sex households and of cases in which women attack or fight back against male partners, the harm has not lost its gendered character.[10]

The incidence of workplace harassment directed at women and minorities is harder to gauge because of the absence of comparable nationwide victimization studies and the fact that same-sex harassment, which disproportionately affects men, has received sustained attention only in the past decade. However, approximately 85 percent of formal complaints of sexual harassment received by the Equal Employment Opportunity Commission (the "EEOC") still involve complaints of men harassing women, and there is evidence that women of color and women in economically vulnerable positions are the most common targets of harassment.[11] Moreover, there is a significant number of racial harassment cases targeting minority men, most often brought as civil rights complaints.[12] Thus, despite the popularity of neutrally phrased descriptions, both domestic violence and workplace harassment are linked to larger structures of gender and race inequality and are commonly understood to be manifestations of continuing patterns of discrimination and subordination.[13] As such, they are good indicators of how tort law responds or fails to respond to injuries that are distinctively marked by the social group identity of its victims.

What is most striking about the categories of domestic violence and workplace harassment as they connect to tort law is that each fits rather comfortably within the familiar rubrics of intentional tort liability. As it is generally understood, domestic violence consists of a variety of abusive behaviors that occur over a course of time. Researchers and domestic violence advocates who study the dynamics of domestic violence stress that the touchstone of domestic violence is coercion and control, specifically the ability of the perpetrator to establish "control and fear in a relationship through the use of physical violence, intimidation, and other forms of abuse."[14] While the particular abuse in each case is different, it is now well known that domestic violence often involves physical battering, such as striking, beating, shoving, and slapping; sexual assault, including rape; restraint, including forcing the victim not to leave the house or to stay away from family and friends; and a pattern of psychological abuse, including insult, verbal humiliation, and belittling.

From a torts perspective, many of the behaviors associated with domestic violence are likely to fall under the classic intentional torts of battery, assault, and false imprisonment. For example, much of the physical abuse in domestic violence constitutes a battery, defined in tort as an intentional harmful or offensive bodily contact with the plaintiff against her will or wishes.[15] Marital rape falls within this category and is actionable as a battery, particularly now that most jurisdictions have abolished criminal law immunity for such violations.[16] Likewise, when there is no physical harm, intimidating behavior may nevertheless amount to an assault, in instances in which the defendant's threatening action puts the victim in fear of an imminent battery.[17] And, finally, a false imprisonment may take place in cases in which the abuser restrains the victim's freedom of movement by means of force or threat of force.[18]

When the domestic abuse consists solely of a pattern of verbal abuse, it is somewhat more difficult to characterize as tortious behavior. The best candidate for liability in such a case is the relatively new tort of intentional infliction of emotional distress.[19] This cause of action provides recovery for severe emotional distress, even when not accompanied by physical harm, in cases in which the defendant engages in "extreme and outrageous" behavior. Although there is no clear definition of "extreme and outrageous" conduct, the concept is used to articulate a standard that marks off behavior that is "intolerable in a civilized community."[20] As the intentional infliction tort has evolved in the past half-century, courts have been most willing to declare conduct "outrageous" in those cases in which a defendant exploits an existing power disparity between the parties, particularly when the defendant knowingly takes advantage of a vulnerable or powerless plaintiff. On its face, this flexible tort seems especially well suited to address those frequent cases of domestic violence in which an abusive spouse or partner uses his physical and economic advantage to heighten the disparity of power between the parties and to intensify feelings of helplessness on the part of the victim.

Similarly, tort law is an appropriate location for suits alleging workplace harassment. In such suits, plaintiffs typically complain of being the target of repeated abusive behavior by supervisors and coworkers and allege a variety of harms, from severe emotional distress to consequent physical and economic injury. Because such a large number of harassment cases involve plaintiffs who have been singled out because of their sex, race, or other "outsider" status in the workplace, they are now commonly thought of as civil rights claims and are most often brought under statutes that bar employment discrimination, most notably Title VII of the Civil Rights Act of 1964. Starting in the mid-1970s, the hostile environment cause of action emerged in Title VII litigation that allowed targets of workplace harassment, under the definition first adopted by the EEOC, to recover if they proved that they suffered "severe or pervasive" harassment that had "the purpose or effect of unreasonably interfering with [their] work performance or creating an intimidating, hostile or offensive working environment."[21]

Like suits for domestic violence, tort claims for workplace harassment fall readily under the available intentional tort categories. The reason for this is that, in addition to generating claims of battery or assault in cases of physical harassment, the typical hostile environment case is tailor-made for the intentional infliction tort. Abuse of the kind of economic power wielded by employers and supervisors is a marker of what many courts regard as "outrageous" behavior. Additionally, much harassing behavior is of a repeated nature and has the capacity to create a cumulative harm that is "worse than the sum of its parts." These features map closely onto the intentional infliction tort, which was designed to capture not only discrete tortious acts but a wrongful course of conduct that occurs over a period of time.

Rather than being a principal site for litigation alleging domestic violence and workplace harassment, however, tort law has played only a marginal role in protecting against these intentionally caused injuries. Suits alleging tort claims for domestic violence are still exceedingly rare. Thus, a study published in 1992 detected only fifty-seven reported cases seeking tort recovery for domestic violence in the decade 1981–1990.[22] Similarly, a review of reported cases for the year 2003 turned up only thirty-four cases.[23] When these tiny numbers are compared to the high rate of injury suffered by women from domestic violence—somewhere on the order of nearly 2 million injuries per year[24]—it is clear that tort liability barely enters the picture of legal responses to domestic violence, even if we assume that the number of settled tort claims is far greater than the number of reported cases.

The situation with respect to workplace harassment cases brought as tort actions is not so stark, although here too tort law plays only a supplemental role in providing legal relief, taking a clear back seat to claims brought under civil rights statutes. In a recent study of successful sexual harassment cases from 1982 to 2004 in which plaintiffs won damages, Catherine Sharkey found that fewer than half the cases (98 out of 232) contained a state tort claim.[25] Even when tort claims are asserted, moreover, they are often treated as secondary by courts and litigators, as evidenced by the term "collateral tort," commonly used to refer to intentional infliction claims alleged in the employment context. Beyond cases of sexual harassment, there are no similar data available for racial or other types of workplace harassment claims.[26] However, there is little reason to suspect that tort liability is relatively more important for these types of claims, except perhaps for the class of cases alleging conduct not currently covered by most employment discrimination statutes, such as harassment based on sexual orientation or language.

Over time, the barriers to asserting tort claims for domestic violence and workplace harassment have shifted, tracking changing attitudes about the nature and seriousness of the two harms. Before the era of civil rights and the battered-women's movement, harms caused by domestic violence and workplace harassment were largely denied, justified, or forced underground.[27] Powerful doctrinal barriers to tort claims made liability nearly impossible, and there was little protection for victims beyond tort in either the criminal or civil side of the law. In the aftermath of the civil rights and feminist movements, the law regulating these potential tort claims has become more complex. Barriers to tort liability now take diverse doctrinal, institutional, and ideological forms that tend to avoid explicitly characterizing the harms as trivial or offering justifications of the actions of abusers. Instead, the small number of tort claims today sends the more palatable message that these harms are taken care of elsewhere in the law and are best kept out of tort law.

Tort Claims for Domestic Violence

With respect to tort claims for domestic violence, the insuperable barrier to liability was once the doctrine of interspousal immunity, which prohibited one spouse from suing the other for injuries inflicted during the marriage.[28] When Holmes and Pound centered the field of torts on accidents and declared the problem of intentional injury solved, domestic violence was legal and interspousal immunity was the law of the land. The immunity was originally supported by the fiction of "marital unity" or "coverture," by which the identity of a married woman was said to merge into that of her husband's, giving him the sole legal right to institute suit on her behalf. In line with this fiction, it was said that neither spouse could bring suit against the other because to do so implied the logical impossibility of suing oneself. States clung to interspousal immunity even long after passage of Married Women's Property Acts and Earnings Acts that recognized women's separate legal identities and their right to sue third parties for their own injuries. The disability imposed by the marital unity doctrine lived on, however, as courts interpreted the progressive legislation narrowly and refused to allow married women to assert their independence by filing suit against their husbands.[29] For all practical purposes, interspousal immunity perpetuated the law's historical tolerance for domestic violence that had once openly declared that a husband had a right to exact obedience from his wife and to "chastise" her insubordination through the use of physical force.[30]

In the 20th century, the justifications for interspousal immunity shifted to more functional ground: rather than expressing the unitary nature of the marriage, courts embraced interspousal immunity in the name of promoting "marital harmony," protecting "marital privacy," and preventing fraud. The common rationales offered in support of immunity were that denying a tort claim prevented spouses from using the courts to air petty grievances or to seek revenge. It was also said to prevent spouses from colluding to secure tort recovery.[31] Further, immunity presumably served the courts' interest by shielding judges from having to scrutinize and pass judgment on family relationships, with all their class, race, and cultural differences, at a time when it was feared that the reputation of the family could be tarnished simply because it was the subject of a public lawsuit.

The support for interspousal immunity was gradually undercut by a general consensus that fraud could be prevented by means other than a ban on liability and by the growing realization that interspousal immunity did not promote marital harmony but often served to protect the self-interest of abusive husbands, who could rely on the doctrine to avoid legal consequences for their abuse. Before interspousal immunity was eventually abolished in the 1980s and 1990s, it had the effect of steering potential claims of domestic violence into family law, where the subject might or might not emerge as one of several issues raised during divorce proceedings. Under the old fault-based system of divorce in force prior to the 1970s, allegations of abuse might surface to support a woman's right to dissolve the marriage and her right to secure alimony or a favorable division of assets from a husband judged to be at fault.[32] However, divorce proceedings were not designed to compensate one spouse for injury done by the other. Instead, family courts were preoccupied with determining whether the marriage was salvageable or irredeemably broken, which spouse had been at fault, who should be awarded custody of children, and how to divide the couple's assets. Although an "innocent" wife might receive alimony and a greater share of the assets, this monetary award was not the same as "damages" in a tort action.

With the advent of no-fault divorce, in the 1970s, even the relevance of allegations of domestic violence could be questioned. Under a no-fault regime, regardless of personal fault—including the commission of violence—a spouse has the right to obtain dissolution of the marriage and to ask the court to distribute the assets of the marriage equitably. There is thus little room for considering the effect of domestic violence on the injured spouse or her need for compensation. Accordingly, divorce proceedings rarely provide a venue for thoughtful assessment of domestic violence.

Once interspousal immunity was lifted by the 1990s, one might have expected that domestic violence cases would become a staple of tort law. By that time, the feminist movement had raised awareness of the pervasiveness of domestic violence, and each state had enacted statutes that allowed domestic violence victims to obtain civil "protection orders" to compel abusers to stay away from their victims and refrain from further abuse.[33] For a variety of reasons, however, very few instances of domestic violence ended up as tort cases, despite the good fit between intentional tort doctrines and domestic violence.

Interestingly, the marginal status of domestic violence as a tort derives in part from its classification as an intentional tort claim. In two important practical respects relating to insurance and statutes of limitations, intentional torts are treated less favorably under current law than are claims for negligence. Given the widespread view that intentional torts constitute more serious invasions of personal rights than negligently inflicted harms, this prioritizing is anomalous and explainable largely by the fact that little attention has been paid to intentional torts generally.

The most important barrier to tort claims for domestic violence is the absence of liability insurance as a fund that victims can tap into to secure compensation. Unlike other recurring types of injuries, such as automobile accidents, injuries from domestic violence are not currently covered by insurance. Although homeowners' insurance policies provide broad coverage for torts committed anywhere in the world by the homeowners, they typically exclude coverage for "intentional acts." They may also contain a "family member exclusion" that denies coverage whenever one member of the family sues another.[34] Together, these exclusions are quite effective in keeping cases of domestic violence out of civil courts and in denying a secure basis for monetary relief for victims.

The lack of liability insurance coverage for domestic violence torts means that victims may have a very difficult time finding a lawyer to take their case. Personal injury lawyers generally rely on contingency fee agreements, which provide that the lawyer will advance the plaintiff the costs of litigation, taking a set percentage (often 33 percent) from the total recovery if the litigation is a success. In virtually every context, the presence (or absence) of liability insurance plays so crucial a role in determining the volume of litigation that it can be said that "insurance drives litigation," rather than vice versa.[35] Tom Baker has observed that plaintiffs' lawyers far prefer to sue a defendant who has insurance over suing a wealthy defendant with no insurance.[36] Not surprisingly, the vast majority of tort judgments and settlements are not paid from defendants' own pocketbooks but come from liability insurance policies paid for in advance by defendants. Without insurance, there is typically no reliable pool of assets from which to satisfy judgments: retirement assets are shielded from tort judgments by federal law, and jointly owned residences are often not available for tort compensation. Additionally, unlike victims of other gender-linked harms, such as rape and sexual harassment, domestic violence victims are not able to look to third-party defendants, such as landlords or employers, for compensation based on a failure to prevent the injury from occurring.[37] Thus, the exclusion of domestic violence from liability insurance, largely because of its classification as an intentional tort, effectively takes this class of injuries out of the mainstream of personal injuries.

When the exclusions from liability coverage are closely examined, however, it is not easy to justify this unfavorable treatment of intentional torts, particularly with domestic violence uppermost in mind. The "family member exclusion" in homeowners' liability policies was added by insurance companies shortly after courts began dissolving interspousal immunity. As applied to domestic violence claims, the exclusion is largely a recapitulation of interspousal tort immunity and thus is vulnerable to the same attacks levied against that immunity. Particularly in cases involving an allegation of domestic violence, it is not fair to assume that spouses will collude to defraud insurers or will engage in other fraudulent conduct that cannot be detected by insurers. Notably, in the context of automobile insurance, some courts have struck down similar family member exclusions as arbitrary and irrational.

The exclusion for "intentional acts" is considerably more debatable, if only because it may intuitively seem wrong to permit a person guilty of domestic violence to escape personal liability by insuring against his own aggression. This intuition is sometimes couched in "moral hazard" terms, that is, the concern that if persons are able to insure against a particular harm, they will take fewer measures to avoid the harm and may even suffer it on purpose or exaggerate their losses once the harm occurs.[38] A classic example is that of an automobile owner who may be less careful to lock her car door if she has insured her car radio. In the domestic violence context, the critical question becomes whether providing liability insurance will have the perverse effect of increasing the level of violence once abusers realize that an insurance company may end up paying for the consequences of their actions.

If the idea of providing liability insurance to cover domestic violence were to become the subject of serious debate, however, the flaws in such a moral hazard objection would quickly surface. At bottom, the objection rests on the insupportable assumption that the current institutional framework—with no insurance coverage and very few tort suits—represents an appropriate mix of deterrence and compensation. The unstated premise seems to be that potential abusers are currently deterred from committing acts of violence because they are uninsured and theoretically subject to tort liability. However, the high incidence of domestic violence and high levels of uncompensated injury point to a very different baseline and a very different reality, one in which domestic violence is largely left immunized in tort and, if addressed at all, is the subject only of civil protection orders and the criminal law. As with many other areas of tort law, from auto accidents to products liability, the goals of deterrence and compensation are not likely to be achieved unless there is a real threat of tort liability. And, since litigation does indeed follow insurance, the threat of liability for domestic violence will not be credible unless and until the harm is insured.

Despite its familiarity and intuitive appeal, the "intentional acts" exclusion prohibiting coverage for domestic violence injuries is neither inevitable nor obviously justified. Insurance can now be purchased to cover "social" problems that once seemed intractable, such as injuries caused by uninsured motorists and even harm inflicted by terrorists.[39] According to insurance scholar Kenneth Abraham, the insurance business is "remarkably creative" at covering risks that at first seemed uninsurable.[40] If and when a societal consensus emerges that victims of domestic violence urgently need and deserve compensation, insurance companies are capable of creatively adapting their products to fill the need. Looked at from this perspective, the most formidable barrier to tort recovery for domestic violence victims lies not simply in the legal classification of domestic violence as an intentional harm but in the law's failure to require or encourage insurers to provide adequate protection for victims of intentional harms. The effect is to make both the injuries and the potential claims invisible.

The other respect in which tort claims for domestic violence are impeded by their categorization as intentional torts relates to the applicable statutes of limitations. In the United States, statutes of limitations for intentional torts are typically shorter than those for negligence.[41] Statutes of limitations for the older torts of battery, assault, and false imprisonment are typically between one and two years. They range from one to ten years for intentional infliction of emotional distress but are most commonly set at two or three years. In contrast, the statutes of limitations for negligence are typically longer, ranging from two to six years. This seemingly small difference, however, has been repeatedly cited as posing a significant obstacle for domestic violence victims because the pattern of coercion and control that characterizes domestic violence can make consideration of filing a tort claim near the time of the injury inconceivable for many victims. Consideration of a tort claim generally comes, if at all, only after the injured spouse has left the relationship and has established an independent existence for herself and her children, not infrequently years after serious incidents of battering have occurred. For this reason, domestic violence advocates have long argued for extending the statute of limitations in this context, proposing, for example, that domestic violence be treated as a "continuing tort" and that the statute of limitations be "tolled" until the abusive relationship has ended.[42]

Although the shorter statutes of limitations are applied neutrally to all intentional torts, their application is particularly harsh in the domestic violence context, given the enormous pressures upon abuse victims not to give up on their marriages or partnerships and to keep their families together. As apparently neutral rules, moreover, short statutes of limitations do not strike most observers as gender biased, unless their effect on survivors of domestic violence is noted. If they were the subject of serious scrutiny, however, it is likely that the disparities in tort limitations periods would be abolished or a longer limitations period set for intentional torts than for negligence, based on the relative moral culpability of offenders. There is nothing to commend the shorter statutes of limitations save tradition. That tradition derives from an Act of Parliament in 1623, the rationale behind passage having long since been lost to obscurity. Most important, the usual justifications for limitations statutes—to bar "stale" claims, avoid the problem of fading witness memories, and foster predictability so that potential defendants can cease worrying about getting sued—apply with equal force to claims based on intent and negligence. In the United Kingdom, where numerous official bodies have systematically reviewed statutes of limitation and made recommendations for revisions, the limitations periods are now longer for intentional torts than for negligence.[43]

In addition to the insurance and statute-of-limitations restrictions applicable to intentional torts generally, tort claims for domestic violence are also hampered by doctrines and arguments that focus specifically on the purportedly distinctive nature of domestic violence. There is still a tendency to steer domestic violence cases into family court. For example, recent cases have confronted the issue of whether a tort claim for domestic violence must be brought at the time of divorce or be precluded under the legal doctrines of res judicata or collateral estoppel, which require that claims arising from the "same transaction or series of transactions" be brought simultaneously. Admittedly, this joinder rule does not prevent a victim of domestic violence from raising a separate tort claim along with her matrimonial claims and in this respect differs from a regime of tort immunity. The practical effect of this new procedural barrier, however, is to discourage tort suits and to reproduce the old regime.

Clare Dalton, a specialist in domestic violence, has argued that, for many abuse victims, escaping a violent marriage is their first priority and that pursuing a tort claim is "simply too dangerous, until such time as her separation from her abuser has been successfully accomplished, and a structure has been put in place that sets limits to his interactions with her and her children."[44] Confronted with the prospect that asserting a tort claim at this early stage might prolong and complicate the divorce proceedings, many abuse victims will simply forgo the tort claim. Some courts have taken notice of the "extreme hardship and injustice" that victims of domestic violence face because of delays in securing divorce and custody decrees and have refused to require joinder. In 2005, for example, New York's highest court reversed its joinder rule and permitted an abused wife to sue her husband for damages relating to an incident of domestic violence, even though the claim could have been brought earlier as part of the divorce proceedings.[45] A minority of states, however, continue to require joinder, thus erecting a powerful, if partial, obstacle to tort recovery.

The idea that domestic violence is a "family matter" and that family law ought to be accorded primacy in handling domestic violence cases also finds expression in some courts' unwillingness to apply the tort of intentional infliction of emotional distress in the marital context. Early on, New York refused to allow recognition of the infliction tort between spouses, and at least one other jurisdiction followed suit.[46] Although this position has been expressly rejected in a few states, the issue has yet to be addressed in a significant number of jurisdictions and thus is still on the table. The principal concern of those who would deny protection of the infliction tort in the marital context is the fear that spouses will routinely assert intentional infliction claims in divorce proceedings and that the usual screen of requiring plaintiffs to prove that the defendant's conduct is "extreme and outrageous" will not suffice to stem the tide of cases. Echoing earlier rationales for interspousal immunity, this objection also stresses the uniqueness of the marriage relationship, which purportedly makes it inappropriate for courts to judge the parties' behavior as if they were strangers and counsels against a rule that would allow a "pervasive inspection of spouses' private lives."[47]

Beneath the narrow issue of the applicability of the intentional infliction tort in the divorce context is a more fundamental debate over how to conceptualize and handle cases of domestic violence. The tension is over whether to treat domestic abuse as a species of marital discord inseparable from other disagreements that typically surface during a breakup or to treat it as coercive, controlling behavior that invades important individual rights of the abused party. Taking the first view, Ira Ellman, the major author of the American Law Institute's *Principles of the Law of Family Dissolution*, has argued, with coauthor Stephen Sugarman, that the intentional infliction tort should be available in the context of a divorce only where physical abuse amounting to a violation of the criminal law has taken place.[48] In contrast, the Third Restatement of Torts refuses to so limit the ambit of the intentional infliction tort, mentioning only that liability may not be imposed simply because a spouse chooses to exercise his or her right to file for divorce. Without staking a position on the nature of domestic abuse and its connection to outrageous behavior, the Third Restatement anticipates that courts will apply the intentional infliction tort in the marital context on a case-by-case basis, judging the particular behavior against the standard of outrageousness that courts have fashioned in that state.[49]

The larger significance of both the joinder rule and the argument against applying the intentional infliction tort in the domestic context is that they each would steer domestic violence cases back into the family law realm, without closing the door to tort law completely. They each set up significant barriers to enforcement of tort law against domestic violence but are couched in gender-neutral terms, making them less recognizable as gender bias. The end result is that the trickle of cases that make it into the torts domain are far too few to "mainstream" the injury and affect prevailing prototypes of intentional torts.

Tort Claims for Workplace Harassment

With respect to claims for workplace harassment, the principal barrier to tort liability is a cluster of legal doctrines that attempts to mark out torts as a distinct legal domain, wholly separate and apart from the growing body of workplace antidiscrimination law. Unlike domestic violence victims, targets of workplace harassment often have a cause of action for damages under federal and state civil rights statutes, such as Title VII of the Civil Rights Act of 1964, which prohibit discrimination based on race, sex, and other forms of discrimination in employment.[50] These statutory antidiscrimination claims are so prominently linked to harassment that it is often assumed that the statutory remedies are sufficient and that victims need not bother with other avenues of redress.

From a practical perspective, however, plaintiffs often gain a considerable advantage by bringing a tort claim for workplace harassment. First, tort offers the prospect of greater damages, in contrast to recoveries under civil rights statutes, which are typically capped at very low amounts. In federal civil rights suits, for example, Title VII sets a total cap on a plaintiff's combined compensatory and punitive damages at $50,000 to $300,000, depending on the size of the employer. Because most states have set no caps or have set higher caps on tort damages, a harassment plaintiff stands a better chance of securing an adequate recovery in tort. Indeed, a recent empirical study of sexual harassment cases conducted by Catherine Sharkey found that including a tort claim in such cases had the effect of increasing an award on average by $137,176, after controlling for independent variables that might affect the level of damages.[51]

Aside from the possibilities of upping a damage award, tort law is attractive to some harassment claimants because of its universal character and the looser formulation of required elements of proof, compared to the technicalities of civil rights laws. As mentioned earlier, for quite some time, the best candidate for situating a tort claim for harassing behavior has been the tort of intentional infliction of emotional distress. The elements of the intentional infliction claim are quite straightforward and intuitive, requiring the plaintiff to prove (1) intent or recklessness, (2) extreme and outrageous conduct, (3) causation, and (4) severe emotional distress. The intentional infliction tort invites a functional inquiry into fault and harm, placing an emphasis on the egregious nature of defendant's behavior and the seriousness of plaintiff's injury. It is also framed in universal terms, protecting all persons against abusive and egregious behavior.

In contrast, the threshold inquiry under statutory civil rights laws is more formal in character and screens out many claims at the outset: an employee asserting a statutory civil rights claim must first demonstrate that his or her mistreatment falls under one of the specified bases of discrimination. Under Title VII, for example, a plaintiff must prove that he or she suffered discrimination because of race, color, sex, religion, or national origin. A claim that asserts "language" discrimination, rather than discrimination based on "national origin," or a claim that amounts to discrimination based on "sexual orientation," rather than "sex," is subject to dismissal, even if the harassment is egregious and the harm severe.

As a result, many contemporary forms of bias are likely to fall through the cracks of the preset categories of statutory civil rights laws. There is little space, for example, for claims of same-sex harassment,[52] multidimensional discrimination (with overtones of both race and class bias),[53] or discrimination against subgroups.[54] Additionally, because of the status-based character of civil rights statutes, it is often difficult to reach bias directed at persons because of how they perform their identity (e.g., the "effeminate" man)[55] or against persons who refuse to cover their identity and resist assimilation (e.g., the African American woman who wears her hair in braids or corn rows).[56] Given these limitations, it is not surprising that some harassment victims have turned to tort law, with its universal character, where plaintiffs are not required to pinpoint the discriminatory motivation behind their harassment or abuse in order to recover.

Beyond these immediate practical impacts, whether courts allow a tort claim for conduct that also amounts to a statutory civil rights violation is a significant cultural index, signaling whether new understandings of discriminatory behavior such as "sexual harassment" and "hostile environment" have made it into the mainstream and have altered traditional thinking about the proper domain of tort law. The central issue is whether discriminatory conduct, as first articulated in statutory civil rights cases, should also qualify as "extreme and outrageous" conduct in tort. The degree to which courts permit civil rights principles to migrate into tort law and to influence basic tort concepts is a good gauge of the responsiveness of the common law to distinctive types of injuries that disproportionately affect minority social groups.

Given the widespread agreement regarding the elements of proof for the claim for intentional infliction of emotional distress, one might expect to see uniformity in the treatment of workplace harassment claims brought under this tort. At present, however, the doctrine governing tort claims for such workplace harassment is technically complex and varies greatly from state to state. The divide in the courts mirrors the strong opposing social forces surrounding issues of equality in the larger culture. The results range from a hefty migration of civil rights principles into tort law in some states to a complete cutoff of such tort claims in others.

Through the complex welter of cases, however, one can discern two basic approaches to using the intentional infliction claim to redress workplace harassment: the majority of courts treat the claim of intentional infliction as a mere "gap filler," an extraordinary remedy that should be allowed only infrequently or when no other remedy is available. This means, of course, that when a plaintiff has a viable claim for harassment under Title VII or some other statute, a tort claim is generally not allowed. A minority of states, in contrast, treat the intentional infliction claim as an independent cause of action that may be brought regardless of the availability of other claims. These states believe that the intentional infliction claim serves the important function of reinforcing the state's public policy of promoting civil rights and equal employment opportunity. They see no need to restrict plaintiff to relief under the statutory claims. We refer to these two approaches as the "gap filler" and the "mutual reinforcement" approaches.

At the outset, it is important to note that, in most jurisdictions, proof of discriminatory workplace harassment—the kind of discrimination that looks most like a tort—is not sufficient to guarantee tort recovery. For the most part, courts do not equate every act of discrimination with outrageous conduct. With the notable exception of California,[57] courts have refused to classify workplace sex or race discrimination as per se outrageous conduct. Many courts have even hesitated to declare the "severe or pervasive" harassment required to prove a hostile environment claim under civil rights statutes as sufficient to meet the threshold tort requirement of "extreme and outrageous" conduct.

Some states set the bar of proof of "outrageousness" so high that they allow recovery only in extremely aggravated—some might say bizarre—cases that do not resemble the typical hostile working environment case. In these states, something more is needed to establish outrageousness in the employment context, although most courts have been unable to articulate precisely what constitutes that extra element. For example, the Pennsylvania Supreme Court is willing to impose tort liability only for "the most clearly desperate and ultra extreme conduct," taking an extremely narrow view of the intentional infliction tort. The court has disavowed any precise formula for determining such extreme conduct, however, clinging to a holistic approach and judging each case on its particular facts. [58] Not surprisingly, decisions in this area often lack analysis: courts tend to recite the facts of an instant case, indicate that recovery was denied in other cases of equally bad conduct, and rule that the conduct in the instant case does not meet the demanding standard for outrageousness.

A racial harassment case decided in 2000 exemplifies the incredibly high standard of proof some courts require before allowing a jury to decide whether the defendant has engaged in outrageous conduct. In *Walker v. Thompson*,[59] a federal appeals court affirmed a summary judgment in favor of a manufacturer whose supervisors had harassed an African American woman who worked as a clerk. Starting a month after she began employment, plaintiff was subjected to a series of demeaning comments and disparate treatment by the general manager of the facility and by plaintiff's immediate supervisor, the office manager. The comments directed at plaintiff and two other African American women working in the office were not oblique but followed familiar scripts that linked black people to animals, accentuated and caricatured their color and physical appearance, and underscored their inferior position in the company. Plaintiff was compared to slaves and to monkeys; her hair was mocked as "nappy" and as resembling that of a cat or a dog; she was told that people at a work-related anniversary party "would think that she was there to rob them"; and the word "nigger" was used in conversations in her presence. At one point, the office manager proudly displayed a greeting card with the picture of a monkey on it in a window facing the desks of the African American employees and repeatedly made jokes about the "little black monkey."

The general manager, who was assigned to investigate plaintiff's complaints of discrimination, was himself guilty of blatantly racist remarks: he told plaintiff that she "did not look like she swung from trees" and asked her if she were "picking fleas" from another black woman's hair one day when the plaintiff was removing a piece of lint from her coworker's braid. In addition to the frequent derisive comments made over the course of three years, the plaintiff was also subjected to heightened surveillance and scrutiny of her behavior. The office manager told the three African American women employees that they could not talk to one another, physically separated them from one another, and instructed the receptionist to listen in on their phone conversations. Eventually, all three women resigned, citing pervasive racial discrimination as the reason for their resignations. They brought suit alleging both a Title VII race discrimination claim and a tort claim for intentional infliction of emotional distress.

The appellate court had little difficulty concluding that the incidents could add up to a hostile environment and that a jury should decide whether to hold defendant liable under Title VII. When it came to plaintiff's tort claim for intentional infliction of emotional distress, however, the court upheld the summary judgment for the employer and prevented the claim from being tried by a jury. With little discussion, the court stated that "condemnable conduct [does not] necessarily translate into conduct that rises to the level of extreme and outrageous" and noted that the Texas courts had found that only "few incidents" qualified under this demanding standard. Apparently, neither the repeated nature of the verbal abuse, nor the fact that more than one black employee was subjected to abuse, nor the persistent unequal working conditions the workers endured were enough to classify the case as something other than mere "insults, indignities, threats, annoyances or petty oppressions," insulated from tort liability. Like many other courts, the *Walker* court employed a standard of "outrage" that failed to capture severe, pervasive harassment that looked like the typical—if still quite egregious—hostile environment case, leaving the matter to be decided exclusively under federal civil rights laws.

Other states are even more explicit about keeping the domains of tort and civil rights separate: they preempt tort claims altogether, based on the existence of another civil remedy. Interestingly, because Title VII, the federal civil rights law, contains an express "anti-preemption" provision that indicates that it was not designed to preempt state law claims, courts have had to be creative to bar tort claims. States that have taken the preemption route either have relied on their own state's civil rights acts or have ruled that tort claims are barred by the exclusivity provision of the state's workers' compensation statute. Only a few states have decided that their states' antidiscrimination acts were intended to occupy the field and have preempted tort claims on that basis.[60] The more powerful barrier to asserting tort claims has proven to be the willingness of some courts to interpret their workers' compensation laws very broadly to cover workplace harassment.[61] In this genre of preemption challenges, the "proper domain" issue comes up indirectly as courts grapple with whether the legislature intended to channel claims for harassment and discrimination into workers' compensation, which was designed principally to respond to industrial accidents and occupational disease. Because workers' compensation is also well known for its ungenerous awards, it is generally regarded by victims and their lawyers as no substitute for tort recovery. Harassment claimants are thus likely to rely exclusively on their statutory civil rights claims if their only other option is workers' compensation.

Whether courts employ the doctrine of preemption or give a restrictive legal interpretation to "outrageousness" in the context of workplace harassment, the result is the same, namely to push harassment claims back into the statutory civil rights law, screening social equality issues out of intentional torts. In these "gap filler" states, harassment is seen not as an intentional tort with a civil rights dimension but only as a public law violation.

In marked contrast, a minority of jurisdictions have refused to so limit the domain of torts and have used tort law to reinforce the state's public policy against workplace harassment. A 1970 case from the California Supreme Court was the first to allow a black male truck driver to sue for intentional infliction when his supervisor hurled racial epithets at him before firing him without just cause.[62] The court regarded the infliction tort as particularly appropriate for application in the workplace context and stated that it was entirely reasonable to expect "Negroes to suffer severe emotional distress from discriminatory conduct." [63] Similarly, a leading decision from the Supreme Court of Florida in 1989 took a broad view of that state's commitment to eradicating sexual harassment, insisting that "[p]ublic policy now requires that employers be held accountable in tort for the sexually harassing environments they permit, whether the claim is premised on a remedial statute or on the common law."[64] Comparable sentiments about the importance of allowing "cumulative remedies" for harassment victims to reinforce the "strong public policy" against sexual harassment were more recently echoed by the Supreme Court of Colorado in a 2001 same-sex harassment case alleging intentional infliction and other tort claims against an employer.[65] For these states, preservation of a tort remedy serves to vindicate the "intangible injury to personal rights" caused by harassment that "robs the person of dignity and self esteem."[66]

Beneath discussion of the technical issues that dominate the case law in this area lie more fundamental judgments about the respective domains of torts and civil rights and the proper location(s) for claims of workplace harassment. Whether judges permit an intentional infliction claim to proceed depends on whether they believe it "fits" within torts or should be handled exclusively under the theories and remedies provided by civil rights statutes. The choice between the "gap filler" and the "mutual reinforcement" approaches thus tends to hinge on this categorization.

Because workplace harassment is a new cause of action first brought to life by the women's movement in the early 1970s, it is not surprising that it initially did not fit particularly well under either torts or Title VII. In some respects, it is an interloper in both domains. The lack of a perfect fit for claims of workplace harassment reflects the multidimensional quality of this harm, which defies categorization under traditional headings. One reason courts have so much trouble positioning claims of harassment is that such claims articulate a type of injury—disproportionately experienced by members of subordinated groups—that cannot be pinned down as psychological, economic, or physical in nature or as clearly individual- or group-based.

Scholarship on the distinctive harms produced by workplace harassment, using both antisubordination and antistereotyping theories, has revealed the social dimension of harassment: it can effectively devalue its target and reinforce that person's inferior status in the workplace.[67] Through harassment, women workers are sexually objectified and reminded of their subordinate status in the family and in the private sphere of sexual relationships; male harassment victims are punished for not conforming to gender norms or for being gay or perceived to be gay or effeminate; and racial minorities are subjected to bullying behavior that trades on symbols of slavery and segregation. The ubiquity and the everyday nature of sexual, racial, and other forms of workplace harassment may make it particularly hard for individuals to define and contest their treatment, the more it is naturalized and seems indistinguishable from just the way things are.[68]

Notably, when claims for sexual harassment were first introduced in Title VII litigation, they were initially resisted by some courts in part because they did not look like prototypical civil rights violations, such as a discriminatory firing, demotion, or refusal to promote, which resulted in direct economic harm. Many courts continued to embrace traditional notions about the harmless and inevitable nature of sexual propositioning, teasing, hazing, and other forms of sexualized conduct. They categorized such interactions as personal in nature and as stemming from sexual attraction or some other individualized motivation, rather than from sex-based bias.[69] Although the hostile environment claim for both racial and sexual harassment was eventually recognized by federal courts, it is still treated as somewhat suspect and as qualitatively different from core violations of civil rights law.

With respect to tort law, the marginalization of claims alleging workplace harassment stems from these claims' failure to resemble the classic personal injury. As we discuss at greater length in chapter 4, when a cause of action is characterized as an emotional distress claim, the ordinary rules of liability tend not to apply. Instead, similar to other "stand-alone" claims for emotional distress, tort claims for harassment sit precariously at the margins of recovery, with considerable variation among the states in the specific rules applied and in the prospects for success.

The current reluctance to use the intentional infliction tort as a vehicle for civil rights is partly rooted in tradition. Although there has been a long history of protecting some dignitary interests against tortious intentional invasion, those dignitary interests were exceedingly narrow in scope and have incorporated traditional views about the proper behavior of the sexes. Thus, the tort of assault was fashioned to afford recovery only for physically threatening conduct and was originally designed to reduce the incentive for retaliation and escalation of physical violence. In the words of Dean Prosser, the older torts, such as assault, provided a remedy for "the kind of conduct likely to lead to a breach of the peace by provoking immediate retaliation."[70] To warrant recovery, the physical harm threatened had to be imminent, and it was sometimes said that "words alone do not constitute assault." These limitations have meant that a claim for assault was generally unavailable in contexts where it was perceived that targets would not fight back and would respond more passively by internalizing the pain. Most notably, a "mere" solicitation to have sex was not generally regarded as actionable, no matter how insulting or offensive to the target.[71] One leading commentator of the day famously remarked that in the realm of torts, "there is no harm in asking."[72]

Similarly, the tort of slander has so far proved incapable of responding to the harms of sexual harassment. Traditionally, slander actions were designed to provide redress for damage to reputation, including sexual reputation, and often centered on a female plaintiff's reputation for chastity. In the 19th and early 20th centuries, women plaintiffs often prevailed in defamation suits when they alleged that defendants had made false statements impugning their reputation for sexual propriety. Many courts even adopted the view that such claims amounted to slander per se and dispensed with the need to prove special damages.[73] However, when the locus of slander suits changed from the private sphere to the more public sphere of work, women had far less success convincing courts that the kind of sexual slurs and taunts that characterize a hostile working environment amounted to actionable defamation. According to Lisa Pruitt's extensive history of defamation cases, contemporary courts are now apt to deny recovery and to regard the offending statements as utterly lacking in content and incapable of being judged as either true or false.[74]

Because the older, particularized torts have not been reshaped to capture either racial or sexual harassment, the migration of civil rights and equality principles into tort law now largely depends on the scope given to the intentional infliction tort and on the courts' willingness to expand the tort beyond its marginal "gap filler" function. The critical question is whether the intentional infliction tort will be opened up to allow juries to decide whether discriminatory actions violate contemporary norms of just and decent behavior.

The intentional infliction tort is unlikely to be very useful in promoting social equality unless courts are willing to make the transition from an honor-based standard of outrageous conduct to a dignity-based standard of outrageous conduct informed by civil rights law. Before the era of civil rights, the intentional infliction tort tended to protect older conceptions of male honor and female chastity. As Israeli scholar Orit Kamir describes it, an "honor culture" is a system highly dependent on one's relative standing in society in which "reputation is all."[75] Kamir explains that, in such cultures, a person's honor can "easily be lost through the slightest social error, or stolen by another" and requires "specific, daily (sometimes ritualistic) behavior" to police the boundary between the honorable and the disreputable. Under such a system, the severity of sexualized conduct directed at women is generally judged by its capacity to sully the reputation of a "respectable" woman. Not surprisingly, the early intentional infliction cases reflected such an honor-based culture and displayed little concern for protecting an individual woman's sexual autonomy or her right to self-determination. Courts were not then inclined to plumb the facts of a case to see whether a woman "welcomed" a particular sexual advance or whether particular attentions were "unwanted," to borrow from the vocabulary of contemporary sexual harassment law.

In contrast, under a dignity-based system informed by civil rights, the inquiry shifts to whether a defendant's conduct, as a whole, has the effect of seriously harming the plaintiff by targeting her as a second-class citizen who does not deserve to be treated with equal respect and consideration. Under this approach, the discriminatory aspect of the behavior is part of what qualifies it as outrageous conduct and sets it apart from less virulent forms of incivility, rudeness, and disrespect. Under a dignity-based approach, courts would no longer search for some unusual or bizarre feature of a harassment case that sets it apart from the recurring hostile environment cases. Instead, they would consider whether a defendant's conduct should be classified as outrageous in part because it conforms to a pattern common to civil rights violations, creating the potential for cumulative harm for targeted victims and the continuation of persistent social inequalities. This concept applies with equal force to both sex- and race-based harassment and discrimination.

The kind of transition from honor to dignity that we envision in the interpretation of the tort concept of "outrageous" conduct is similar to the approach of Canadian law, which has successfully woven equality principles into its fundamental notion of dignity. Canadian courts tend to regard equal treatment as an essential component of human dignity. This contrasts sharply with the dominant approach in the United States, which tends to separate the two concepts, assigning to civil rights the task of protecting equality, while tort law is assigned the task of protecting dignitary interests. Thus, the Canadian Supreme Court defines human dignity along civil rights lines, declaring that "[h]uman dignity means that an individual or group feels self-respect and self worth . . . and is harmed by unfair treatment premised upon personal traits or circumstances that do not relate to individual needs, capacities, or merits." Seeing a social equality dimension to dignity, Canadian courts find an injury to human dignity "when individuals and groups are marginalized, ignored or devalued."[76] Under the Canadian vision of human dignity, it is far easier to characterize persistent racial, sexual, or other group-based forms of harassment as serious harms that warrant protection under both statutory and common law.

In those states that have been more willing to permit tort claims for workplace harassment in the United States, courts have yet to explain or theorize about how the migration of civil rights concepts might affect tort law more generally. In line with the case-by-case approach to the intentional infliction tort, courts have not yet articulated a theory regulating the intersection of torts and civil rights, beyond noting the important public policies underlying civil rights laws. In large part as a result of the development of the hostile environment claim under Title VII, however, tort law now has something to borrow to give meaning to outrageous conduct in intentional infliction cases and to allow the tort to move toward a dignity-based standard informed by civil rights.

In some respects, the development of Title VII sexual harassment law over the past thirty years has been remarkable, contributing to a transformation in the way sexualized conduct in the workplace is understood and evaluated, at least in some quarters. Simply put, the emergence of sexual harassment law has challenged the belief that there is no harm in asking. The entire body of sexual harassment law is premised on the view that solicitations for sex and other sexualized conduct in the workplace can produce harm, most notably in instances when they are backed by economic coercion or pressure, and can reinforce the subordinate status of a group of workers. In marked contrast to an earlier era which presumed that women were always free to accept or refuse sexual solicitations, Title VII law now recognizes how disparities in power and status can produce offers that cannot be refused and can construct unequal working conditions for targeted workers. This deprivatization of the harm of sexual harassment and separation of sexual harassment from the category of consensual sex was the pivotal move toward legal recognition of the claim under Title VII. The change in vocabulary from "solicitation" to "harassment" effectively conveys the distance traveled, from harmless offer to form of abuse.

At the doctrinal level, the feature of the "hostile environment" harassment claim that potentially could have the greatest impact on determinations of "outrageousness" in tort claims for intentional infliction is the incorporation of "multiple perspectives" to guide judgments about the harmful quality of harassing behavior. The multiple perspectives approach acknowledges that the meaning of an action may differ, depending on the perspective from which the action is viewed. In statutory civil rights cases, many courts have begun to consider events from the perspective of the target of the harassing conduct, as well as from the perspective of the harasser or that of a disinterested third party.[77] This attempt to look at a case from the viewpoint of the "reasonable person in plaintiff's condition" often highlights salient individual characteristics of the plaintiff, such as race or gender, and focuses attention on the impact of situational factors, such as the plaintiff's token status in the workplace or the inferior position of her social group within a particular organization. In addition to attending to the "totality of the circumstances" in a particular case, the multiple perspectives approach gives factfinders room to consider the background social identities of the actors and the power dynamics at the workplace before they decide whether harm has occurred.

A similar approach could readily be incorporated into intentional infliction cases. In intentional infliction cases, courts have often noted that "taking advantage of a plaintiff known to be vulnerable" enhances the likelihood that the actions will be deemed outrageous. Civil rights law adds the important insight that race, gender, and other markers of outsider status can operate as vulnerabilities in the context of the workplace, especially as experienced from the perspective of the targeted group.

Domains and Devaluation

Tort law's treatment of domestic violence and workplace harassment as intentional torts is marked by ambivalence and mixed messages. Although there is no longer a categorical denial that these behaviors qualify as intentional torts, the intricate doctrines that impede tort recovery for these injuries send the clear signal that torts is the wrong domain to handle such cases and that such harms are not to be regarded as "core" personal injuries. With respect to domestic violence, victims are largely left without a civil damages remedy, and their concerns, if addressed at all, are handled by criminal courts, through protection orders or by family law. There is little real chance for compensation because the law provides no sustainable claim against third-party defendants and victims are unable to tap into liability insurance coverage. Despite public campaigns decrying the high incidence of domestic violence and its huge societal costs, tort law has not stepped in to provide an additional measure of deterrence or a source of compensation for victims.

Victims of workplace gender or race harassment fare somewhat better. Statutory civil rights laws provide a measure of compensation, and suits may be brought against employers that have failed to prevent or correct hostile environments. However, for the most part, harassment victims have been steered away from torts, resulting in lower awards and leaving some classes of plaintiffs without a remedy. The continued separation of torts and civil rights, moreover, threatens to stunt the development of general tort principles. Leaving harassment and discrimination out of tort law runs the risk of artificially shrinking the concept of "outrageous" conduct and minimizing the importance of civil rights to individuals and to society as a whole. Compared to stark doctrines of the past, the contemporary practice of cordoning off domestic violence and workplace harassment from the domain of torts may be a more palatable way of handling these intentional tort claims because it avoids a declaration that the claims are not worthy of compensation. However, the underlying message and the practical effect of the containment are not so very different from the outcomes of older doctrines that viewed domestic violence as a private, family matter, treated sexual harassment as simply the inevitable byproduct of mixing the sexes at work, and ignored racial harassment altogether. Both the old and the new strategies serve to devalue the harms by suggesting that they do not quite merit full incorporation into the premier system designed to protect against civil wrongs, namely tort law. Their omission from the main body of tort law has contributed to the relative lack of importance of intentional torts and has left the misimpression that tort law is, or should be, all about accidents.

4

Negligence

It is well recognized that negligence is the preeminent theory of liability in U.S. tort law. Generations of law students have dutifully memorized the five elements of a plaintiff's prima facie case of negligence: duty, breach, cause-in-fact, proximate cause, and damages. In common parlance, the first two elements—duty and breach—are often lumped together and referred to as the negligence inquiry. Strictly speaking, however, the two elements are separate: there can be no requirement to act reasonably (i.e., nonnegligently) unless there is an antecedent duty imposed on the defendant to take care to safeguard plaintiff's interests. Absent a duty, there can be no breach.

In the discussions leading to the Third Restatement of Torts, a lively debate broke out among academics as to whether the concept of duty should be considered obsolete.[1] The issue arose because the existence of a duty to exercise reasonable care is often presupposed in contemporary tort law, except for truly exceptional situations in which public policy clearly dictates relieving defendants of responsibility.[2] Although the debate was not finally settled, there is general agreement that the duty to act reasonably now operates as the default standard and that deviation from that standard requires explanation and justification. To a large degree, negligence plus causation is synonymous with tort liability.

What is not always acknowledged or understood, however, is that this general duty of care due extends only to cases of physical injury and property damage.[3] Significantly, there is no general duty to protect against emotional harm or relational loss.[4] This huge exception from the duty-to-act-reasonably requirement encompasses a wide spectrum of harm. Under the heading of emotional harm fall mental disturbances of all sorts, from fear, shock, and trauma to grief, anxiety, humiliation, and shame. Although also intangible, relational injury is distinct from emotional injury; it is centered on the damage or destruction done to important human relationships.[5] For example, relational claims for wrongful death and loss of consortium compensate for the severing of ties between spouses or for the severe impairment of the parent/child relationship. It is interesting that, outside the realm of law, the state of a person's emotional and relational life is regarded as central to that person's well-being. Tort law, however, continues to regard these interests with a high degree of skepticism. In this respect, the preoccupation of tort law with physical harm seems outdated and out of touch with social reality.

The standard story told about the rationale for limiting claims for emotional harm has shifted over time.[6] Early cases tended to doubt the genuineness of emotional distress claims. There were fears that plaintiffs could easily fake injuries and that it would be impossible to trace the invisible causal chain from the accident to the plaintiff's injury. Additionally, early courts also often faulted plaintiffs for not being "tougher," suggesting that emotional distress was more a function of the idiosyncrasies of the victim than the dangerous quality of the defendant's action.

This skepticism toward plaintiffs in emotional disturbance suits still surfaces today. The new Restatement of Torts, for example, attempts to explain the "caution" that courts have historically displayed in granting recovery for emotional distress by noting that "emotional distress is less objectively verifiable than physical harm and therefore easier for an individual to feign, to exaggerate or to engage in self deception about the existence or extent of the harm."[7] Comments to the Restatement also echo a distaste for compensating timid, supersensitive plaintiffs, reciting the familiar view that "some minor or modest emotional harm is endemic in living in society and individuals must learn to accept and cope with such harm."

As courts and commentators have long noted, however, these twin concerns about genuineness and seriousness of emotional injuries are incapable of justifying a total ban on recovery for this type of harm.[8] Over time, plaintiffs have had considerable success convincing courts that fraudulent claims can be weeded out if courts and juries rely on their own good judgment and on the wealth of medical knowledge describing and documenting various types of emotional disturbances.[9] In this respect, many emotional injuries are not qualitatively different from physical injuries, which can sometimes be difficult to prove and verify. Additionally, it is now well accepted there is no need to deny recovery for all emotional injuries in order to screen out cases of trivial or insubstantial harm. Taking a page from the development of the tort of intentional infliction of emotional distress, most courts seem to understand that claims for negligent infliction of emotional distress can be expressly limited to cases of severe emotional harm, as defined by each particular jurisdiction.

Given the weakness of these traditional rationales for denying recovery, it is not surprising that, in more recent cases, the hesitation to award damages for emotional distress is often couched in terms of pragmatic concerns about imposing disproportionate liability of defendants and providing a clear stopping point for liability.[10] In other words, the rhetorical ground has shifted from concerns about the worthiness of plaintiffs and their claims to worries about the effect of liability on defendants and the courts. In a negligent infliction claim decided in 1994 by the U.S. Supreme Court under the Federal Employers' Liability Act, for example, Justice Clarence Thomas stressed that, unlike physical harm caused through impact, injuries produced through the mechanism of fear or other distress can occur far from the time and place of the original accident.[11] This particular feature of emotional injury means that many more people can be subjected to a risk of harm and that damages can mount if multiple victims pursue their claims. Even proponents of liberalization of tort recovery for negligence acknowledge that these pragmatic concerns are not groundless. There is thus a recognized need for line-drawing in emotional distress cases and for the development of fair rules that limit the scope of liability. As the new Restatement puts it, some courts have been "more sympathetic to liability when the circumstances are such that any reasonable person would suffer serious emotional disturbance, when the severity of the harm or effect limits the victim's ordinary activities, and when the scope of liability is sufficiently limited."[12] While these pragmatic limitations on recovery for emotional distress are still "considerably more" than those imposed for physical harm, they do represent an opening in the law and greater comfort on the part of at least some courts with allowing recovery for intangible harm.

The shift in rationale for limiting claims of emotional distress highlights that concerns of judicial administration are central to this fast-developing area of law. In our view, the crucial question regarding compensation for emotional distress is no longer *whether* compensation for negligently inflicted emotional distress should ever be allowed. Some legal protection already exists and has existed for quite some time. Rather, the crucial policy choices have to do with *when* to provide compensation, that is, with identifying those contexts in which the genuine emotional distress suffered by victims is so compelling that it deserves recognition in law. In this chapter we identify three contexts—cases involving sexual exploitation, cases involving reproductive injury, and cases involving harm to close family members—that we argue deserve special scrutiny, in part because of their close connection to women's interests and to gender equality.

One of the main points we stress is that, despite the trend toward liberalizing recovery, treating emotional harm and relational losses differently from physical harm and property loss remains an important structural feature of tort law.[13] The dichotomy between physical and emotional harm (or between damage to property and damage to relationships) does not simply set up a system of contrasting legal interests; it constructs an implicit hierarchy of value, as well. Although the standard texts do not always state so explicitly, there is little question that a higher value is placed on physical injury and property loss than on emotional and relational harm. This well-entrenched hierarchy is reinforced in the Third Restatement, which has a separate section on emotional harm and no treatment at all of relational harms.[14] For these less favored types of harms, tort law still imposes a welter of special rules and limitations on recovery.

The special doctrinal rules governing emotional and relational harms are stated in gender-neutral terms and initially do not seem to be tied to any gender or other social group. As they operate in social contexts, however, the implicit hierarchy of value privileging physical injury and property loss has an important gender impact. It tends to place women at a disadvantage because important and recurring injuries in women's lives are more often classified as lower-ranked emotional or relational harm.[15] This gender effect cuts across racial lines, affecting subgroups of women in differing ways.

As mentioned previously, the lower ranking of emotional and relational injuries in contemporary law does not always cut off relief altogether. Courts no longer flatly declare that mental disturbance does not qualify for legal protection or refuse to recognize any relational injuries. Rather, through stringent requirements placed on recovery for emotional and relational harm, the law makes it harder to sue for gendered injuries such as sexual exploitation; damage connected to pregnancy, fertility, and childbirth; and suffering arising from injury to children and other family members. Under the guise of setting boundaries for recovery of intangible harm, courts routinely confront gender-inflected issues of sex, reproduction, and parent/child relationships. Mired in the intricacies of doctrine, however, they rarely see the larger picture and only rarely advert to gender in such cases. Instead, they tend to lump these claims together under the general rubric of "emotional distress" claims, masking the gender dimension underlying such lawsuits and often trivializing the harm. To be clear, the gender dynamic in these cases is not that of favoring individual male plaintiffs over individual female plaintiffs. Rather, gender disadvantage flows from disfavoring the type of claim that women plaintiffs are likely to bring, thus placing them—and any male plaintiffs who bring similar claims—at a structural disadvantage.

When emotional distress cases are analyzed through a critical lens, two features emerge as especially problematic. The first consists of judicial handling of contests involving consent to sexual encounters and the evaluation of harm caused by coerced or forced sex. Many cases involve plaintiffs who claim they were pressured or deceived into having sex with the defendant or otherwise exploited sexually. A key question in these cases is whether courts will embrace a feminist conception of consent that takes into consideration the power and social situation of the parties and understands that harm can flow from being forced or pressured to acquiesce in sexual conduct, even absent the application of physical force or threat of physical force.[16] The second feature present in many emotional distress cases involves the recognition and valuation of intimate relationships, particularly the mother/child relationship. Plaintiffs in these cases often ask courts to award damages for conduct that disrupts, damages, or severs such intimate relationships. A crucial issue in these cases is whether tort law will respond to the criticism posed most vigorously by cultural feminists who maintain that the law has not treated intimacy on a par with property rights and that essential cultural activities associated with women, such as childbearing and childrearing, have been undervalued.[17]

In this chapter, we discuss the evolving rules on recovery for negligent infliction of emotional distress, a particularly volatile area of the law that is often crowded out of the torts curriculum and marginalized in torts scholarship. This chapter builds upon the discussion in chapter 2 that treated "nervous-shock" cases. In chapter 2, we described how the distinction between physical and emotional harm was deployed in negligence law well into the 20th century to deny recovery for any injury—even physical injuries such as miscarriages or stillbirths—caused by fright or trauma, unless there was proof of physical contact with the person of the plaintiff. This "impact rule" is now rejected in virtually all states.[18] Recognizing the shift, the Third Restatement makes it clear that recovery for physical harm produced by any means is governed by ordinary negligence principles, including the imposition of a duty of reasonable care.[19] However, as we show, milder versions of the physical/emotional distinction are still very much alive and scattered throughout this area of law.

It is conventional to break down cases of emotional harm into two groups: (1) direct victim, and (2) secondary victim or bystander cases. In the latter group of cases, the injury to the plaintiff is caused through witnessing or otherwise experiencing harm to another, most often a family member. In our view, these bystander cases, while conventionally categorized as emotional-harm cases, are better understood as claims for relational injury. The "direct victim" category is the large residual category that encompasses all other claims for emotional harms.

Direct Victims and Gender

The most chaotic pocket of the law is that governing recovery in direct victim cases. This is in part due to the fact that cases in this category range over such disparate territory. Perhaps the most familiar negligent infliction of emotional distress claims are those for emotional distress arising from fear of physical harm that never materializes (the "near-miss" cases) or from fear of contracting a disease or physical illness in the future (e.g., fear of AIDS or cancerphobia cases).[20] In this genre of cases, there is no clear gender dimension or disparate gender impact. Over the years, we have witnessed a liberalization of rules governing recovery in this strand of cases. Thus, the Third Restatement now endorses recovery for "stand-alone" emotional distress in cases in which the plaintiff is placed in "immediate danger of bodily harm," an approach commonly known as the "danger zone" rule.[21] As one commentator notes, the danger zone rule is really a physical risk rule, a subsidiary of the physical/emotional distinction that limits recovery to those plaintiffs regarded as most at risk for physical injury, even if it never materializes.[22] Despite liberalization of the rules for emotional harm, it appears that courts are still most comfortable permitting recovery in cases that conceptually can be linked in some way to physical harm, even though the ultimate harm is purely emotional.

In contrast, the type of direct victim litigation that very often has a gender dimension consists of suits between parties in either a professional or a significant personal relationship. These suits often implicate not only a plaintiff's interest in emotional tranquility—the quaint term used by the Restatement to describe the interest at stake—but also a plaintiff's interest in sexual integrity and autonomy and in reproductive health and choice. Such cases typically are saturated with gender: the plaintiffs are disproportionately women, and their claims of emotional distress implicate cultural norms relating to gender roles, sexual relationships, and personal identity.

The courts are most in conflict when it comes to rules governing this second strand of negligent infliction of emotional distress cases. Many states continue to refuse to allow recovery in such cases unless the plaintiff can point to a "physical manifestation" arising from the emotionally distressing conduct of the defendant.[23] This stepchild of the impact rule insists on proof of physicality of the injury, even when it is clear that the emotional distress is severe and the plaintiff's response is not unreasonable under the circumstances. Other states have been more willing to impose liability in such cases, often by stretching the definition of "physical manifestation" beyond recognition.[24]

Surveying this disarray, the Third Restatement has wisely chosen to reject any attempt to broaden the definition of physical harm and to support recovery for "stand-alone" emotional distress unaccompanied by physical manifestations in certain contexts. Under the Restatement's more sensible approach, recovery for negligent infliction of emotional distress is allowed in cases in which the harm occurs in "the course of specified categories of activities, undertakings or relationships in which the negligent conduct is especially likely to cause emotional disturbance."[25]

The Restatement's emphasis on the relational context in which the tort is committed and its move away from basing recovery solely on the categorization of the injury marks an important development, especially if it influences the development of future case law. Significantly, however, the Restatement does not express an opinion as to which specific activities, undertakings, or relationships would give rise to liability. Whether there will be greater protection against gendered injuries thus depends on how courts interpret this proposed new synthesis of the rule.

In the past, some courts have limited recovery solely to cases in which plaintiff and defendant are in a contractual relationship.[26] Courts have envisioned this genre of emotional distress case as the modern version of an old line of cases that permitted recovery against a telegraph company that negligently failed to deliver a telegram announcing the death of a family member or against a funeral parlor or burial service that negligently mishandled a corpse.[27] These courts essentially treat this strand of negligent infliction of emotional distress as an appendage to contract law, providing recovery for emotional distress only in that special subset of contracts in which emotional distress is highly predictable given the delicate nature of the undertaking. In such cases, it is sometimes stated that the contract supplies the "independent duty" toward the plaintiff that justifies protection against emotional distress. Like the search for a physical manifestation, the search for an independent duty highlights the degree to which courts are uncomfortable finding a duty to protect against emotional harm and are still scrambling to discover another doctrinal peg on which to hang recovery.

The preexisting contract limitation does capture many cases—particularly those involving interference with reproduction—that occur in the context of the doctor/patient relationship.[28] It also potentially permits employees who claim that their employers have negligently failed to protect them from sexual harassment and exploitation to sue for negligent infliction of emotional distress. However, envisioning the tort as an expansion of contract rights suggests that the primary interest at stake is bolstering and enforcing the parties' voluntary agreement, that is, the general interest in private ordering protected by contract. By foregrounding contract, the exclusive source of the duty becomes private undertakings, rather than social norms or public policy. This conceptualization of the tort also misses a key relational dimension of the cases, beyond simply the fact that there is often (but not always) an underlying contract between the parties.

In our view, a critical feature of this strand of negligent infliction of emotional distress cases is that the defendant's conduct often damages a plaintiff's well-being in noncommercial contexts central to her identity as an individual, mother, or family member. Today, the negligent infliction of emotional distress tort is often the repository for claims involving harm to plaintiff's interest in sexual integrity and autonomy and in reproductive health and choice. Notably, these interests are not invariably linked to voluntary contractual arrangements between the parties and possess a relational as well as an individualistic quality. Women's control over their sexuality and their decisions about bearing and nurturing children are often at stake.

The Restatement and some courts do recognize that this strand of negligent infliction of emotional distress involves sensitive and personal activities that, if handled negligently, "are especially likely to cause emotional disturbance." The commentary to the Restatement also indicates that, like claims for intentional infliction of emotional distress, claims for negligent infliction of emotional distress often occur in situations in which "one person is in a position of power or authority over the other and therefore has greater potential to inflict emotional harm."[29] However, it is still far from clear whether courts will insist on the existence of a contract between the parties before they permit recovery or how they will evaluate the sensitive nature of the activity or the presence of exploitation or abuse of power, absent a contract.

The important step that the Restatement and even more liberal courts have failed to take is explicitly to prioritize the interests in sexual integrity and reproduction as fundamental interests, worthy of heightened protection against privately inflicted damage in tort law. Neither makes the analogy to the heightened protection these fundamental interests receive against government-based interference in constitutional law. Thus, the U.S. Constitution prohibits state action that interferes with an individual's choice of a sexual partner or with an important decision relating to childbearing and childrearing, absent proof that such interference is necessary to further a compelling state interest.[30] In constitutional doctrine, it is the fundamental personal interests at stake that trigger the court's "strict scrutiny" in such cases. As yet, there is no similar strict scrutiny or similar condemnation of private activities that pose equally potent threats to these personal interests.

Sexual Exploitation Cases

Two cases from the highest courts of Texas and Illinois illustrate the courts' ambivalence toward plaintiffs in negligent infliction of emotional distress cases involving allegations of sexual exploitation. The Texas decision was a rare instance in which gender bubbled up from the surface and became a key factor in the case.[31] *Boyles v. Kerr* was a 1993 Texas case involving a nineteen-year-old woman whose boyfriend, with the aid of his friends, cooked up a scheme secretly to videotape the couple having sex. Before the surreptitious taping, the friends set the stage for the video by taping themselves making crude comments and jokes about the event that was about to take place. After the taping, the boyfriend took possession of the video and showed it to ten other people, purportedly even charging money for one viewing. The video eventually was widely circulated and gossiped about at the college campuses the plaintiff and her now ex-boyfriend attended. The plaintiff found out about the tape two months after the event, when she discovered that she was becoming known as the "porno queen" among her classmates.

The woman sued her ex-boyfriend and the others involved in the scheme, asserting a variety of legal theories. The trial focused, however, primarily on the claim for negligent infliction of emotional distress, the theory that most readily reached the behavior of all of the defendants and would presumably allow plaintiff to tap into the homeowners' insurance policies of defendants' parents that covered negligence but not intentional injury.[32] The plaintiff alleged that the events significantly interfered with her ability to study and caused her severe emotional suffering and humiliation, culminating in a diagnosis of posttraumatic stress disorder. Apparently the jury agreed: it ruled for the plaintiff, bringing in a verdict of $1 million for both compensatory and punitive damages, which the appellate court affirmed.

By the time the case reached the Texas Supreme Court, it had garnered considerable attention from women's organizations, which submitted amicus briefs to the court supporting the verdict and imploring the court to recognize the claim for negligent infliction of emotional distress in the context of sexual abuse and exploitation cases. Amici stressed that denying recovery in a case such as *Boyles* would send a message to sexual abuse victims that they were "second-class citizens" and that it "defies logic to have a system of justice that will compensate the victim of a car wreck but that will refuse to compensate the recipients of the most devastating of emotional injuries."[33]

The impassioned arguments, however, did not persuade the majority of the court, which overturned the jury verdict and declared that, absent a finding of an "independent duty," there could be no recovery for negligent infliction of emotional distress in Texas. Tellingly, the court did not consider the special relationship between intimate sexual partners sufficient to create a duty. Justice Alberto Gonzalez, in a concurring opinion, flatly declared that "[t]his case has nothing to do with gender-based discrimination or an assault on women's rights."[34] The majority denied that it was leaving sex abuse victims wholly without a remedy, however, and remanded the case for retrial on an intentional tort theory.

The strong dissents in *Boyles* regarded the outcome in the case as an injustice to "the women of Texas" and chided the majority for treating what had happened to the plaintiff as if it were "a mere trifle or any other distress associated with daily existence." In response to the majority's claim that the case should be litigated solely as an intentional tort, Justice Spector—the lone female justice on the Texas Supreme Court—noted that in many cases, severe emotional distress may be caused by an actor who does not desire to inflict severe emotional distress and who may be oblivious to the fact that such distress is substantially certain to result from his actions. In this case, for example, Justice Spector speculated that Dan Boyles may have videotaped the sexual intercourse with Susan Kerr, "not for the purpose of injuring her, but rather for the purpose of amusing himself and his friends." She was of the view that "[b]rutish behavior that causes severe injury, even though unintentionally, should not be trivialized."[35]

Justice Spector's dissent was notable for her take on the gender dimension of the negligent infliction tort. She emphasized that the claim of negligent infliction of emotional distress was of special significance to women because "the overwhelming majority of emotional distress claims have arisen from harmful conduct by men, rather than women." While recognizing that both men and women could have an interest in recovery for emotional distress, she expressed concern that historically "men have had a disproportionate interest in downplaying such claims." For the dissent, the court's rejection of the negligent infliction claim represented a "step backward" in the law's response to the sexual mistreatment of women and was "especially troubling" given the high incidence of sexual harassment and domestic violence throughout the country.

Boyles is a striking example of how tort law can miss the mark when it lumps together all negligent infliction cases, without regard to context. Rather than battle over the abstract issue of whether there exists an independent duty upon which to base tort liability, cases such as *Boyles* should be resolved more concretely by focusing on whether the defendant's conduct could be expected to jeopardize plaintiff's interest in sexual integrity and autonomy. Because it was clear in *Boyles* that secretly videotaping and distributing the sex tape would reasonably be expected to and did seriously erode plaintiff's control over her own sexuality, a duty of due care should have been triggered. Interestingly, all the members of the Texas Supreme Court seemed to regard the case as one of unacceptable sexual exploitation, yet disagreed as to whether there was a duty of due care. Focusing more directly on the interest at stake in this case would have had the advantage of delimiting the scope of negligent infliction claims without downplaying the seriousness of the injury. Perhaps most important, it is not enough to say that plaintiff might have succeeded if only she had pursued a claim for intentional infliction of emotional distress or intentional invasion of privacy. In addition to the issue of availability of insurance, it is far from clear that the conduct of all the defendants in *Boyles* would be classified as outrageous, particularly under the high threshold of proof Texas courts have applied in intentional infliction cases.[36] Placing a high priority on the interest in sexual integrity and autonomy, moreover, means that the interest is regarded as so important that it should be protected against negligent as well as intentional interference.

Not all courts have been as reluctant to provide protection to sexual exploitation victims through the negligent infliction tort. In contrast to Texas, the Supreme Court of Illinois in 1991 allowed a negligent infliction claim based on sexual exploitation to proceed to trial in *Corgan v. Mueling*,[37] a case involving an unregistered psychologist who had had sex with a patient under the guise of therapy. After she ended the professional relationship, the former patient sued the therapist, alleging both intentional and negligent infliction of emotional distress. She claimed that the sexual encounters were shameful and humiliating to her and forced her to undergo more extensive counseling and psychotherapeutic care. Perhaps because it was easier to think about this case as an instance of professional malpractice, the allegations in Corgan's complaint focused on the particular ways in which the therapist had failed to take due care, mentioning his negligence in treating female patients when "he was incapable of maintaining appropriate professional objectivity," allowing the relationship with the plaintiff "to become a vehicle for the resolution of his own psychosexual infirmities," and failing to consult with other psychologists when "he realized that his relationship with plaintiff was adverse to her psychological well-being." [38]

In ruling for the plaintiff, the majority of the Illinois court dispensed with the need to demonstrate a "physical manifestation" of injury and held that the therapist/patient relationship gave rise to a duty to exercise due care. The majority opinion highlighted the risks and harms of sexual exploitation, citing recent legislation in the state that addressed the problem and an article in a feminist law journal that analyzed the exploitation of women patients.[39] In sharp contrast to the Texas court, the Illinois court was not concerned that the case might also have been framed and litigated as an intentional tort case. For the Illinois court, the extra measure of protection to an abuse victim afforded by a negligence claim was regarded as an appropriate legal response, given the gravity of the injury and the relationship of the parties.

It is important to note that the *Corgan* decision was not unanimous and drew a stinging dissent from a member of the court who had a very different idea of what constituted sexual exploitation and what should be the proper legal response in such cases. The dissent would have disallowed the claim, characterizing the case as one of "mutually agreeable sexual intercourse" and concluding that the moment the sexual relationship began, the treatment by definition ended.[40] Because the plaintiff was not "a minor, mentally retarded or under some other legal disability," the dissenting justice refused to regard her submission to sexual intercourse as sexual exploitation or sexual abuse. In the mind of the dissenting justice, negligence liability should be inexorably tied to physical injury. He opined that this was not a proper negligence case because "[t]here was no allegation that the parties fell off a bed or injured any part of plaintiff's anatomy." The justice's hostility to the majority's ruling was so intense that he ended his opinion by declaring that "to hold the defendant legally liable under such conditions is to countenance a legal form of extortion or blackmail" and complained that the plaintiff was using "the legal system as tool for a shakedown."

On display in both *Boyles* and *Corgan* are two very different stances toward allegations of sexual exploitation in tort cases. The majority in *Corgan*, as well as the dissenters in *Boyles*, were greatly affected by the context of the case and used it to justify liberalizing rules for recovery of damages under the negligent infliction tort. They seemed to start from an assumption that sexual exploitation was a serious societal problem and that tort law should respond to such a public policy concern. Although they stopped short of declaring that plaintiffs should receive heighted protection in sexual exploitation cases, they were aware of the importance of their decisions to women's rights and sexual equality. In their opinions, one can discern traces of the influence of radical feminist theorists such as Catharine MacKinnon, who have long argued for a transformation of legal notions of consent and an appreciation of the severity of the harm caused by sexual exploitation.[41]

In contrast, the majority in *Boyles* and the dissenter in *Corgan* thought it unnecessary and undesirable to expand the legal protection against sexual exploitation, particularly if it meant exposing insurers to claims in such cases. Significantly, the dissenter in *Corgan* also clearly blamed the victim for her own suffering. Although the justices in the Texas majority did not condone Dan Boyles's behavior, they were also careful to downplay the significance of the parties' relationship and noted that the plaintiff and defendant were "not dating steadily" but "had shared several previous sexual encounters," suggesting perhaps that Susan Kerr was foolish to trust a sex partner under such circumstances. These judges saw no connection between recovery for emotional distress and the larger cultural issues of gender equality and preservation of women's sexual integrity.

Aside from differing judicial attitudes toward sexual exploitation, of course, *Corgan* can be distinguished from *Boyles* because it entailed a contract for psychological treatment and an allegation of abuse of the therapeutic relationship. Noting those admittedly salient differences, however, only highlights what we believe to be a critical question posed by such cases: whether the protection of tort law from sexual exploitation in seemingly "consensual" sex settings should arise only when a contract exists. In our view, it is more relevant to focus on the fact that the women in both cases were unjustifiably misled and used. From a feminist perspective, the plaintiff in *Boyles* had as much right to expect that her boyfriend would not tape their sex for the amusement of others as did the patient in *Corgan* to trust that her therapist would not exploit her vulnerability to his sexual advantage. Of fundamental importance is that these expectations arise from normative standards of ethical behavior and decent treatment, not from contract. Admittedly, like most cultural norms, the norm against sexual exploitation is not universally accepted but remains contested. Like the dissenting justice in *Corgan*, many people still hold to the belief that, unless sexual intercourse is extracted through means of physical force or the threat of physical force, it is socially acceptable and ought not to be legally punished. And there is no escaping the sometimes difficult question of whether a defendant's conduct can fairly be characterized as sexual exploitation or abuse. However, this is the cultural terrain over which such contests should be waged, rather than deciding negligent infliction cases on less central features, such as whether a contract exists between the parties or whether the injury manifested itself physically.

Perhaps the most difficult question courts must address if and when the scope of protection against sexual exploitation is enlarged to encompass negligence claims is whether third parties who did not personally sexually exploit the plaintiff may be held liable for failing to prevent the exploitation or otherwise facilitating or enabling the conduct. This question comes up most frequently in the context of employment, when sexually harassed employees attempt to hold their employers liable for the damage caused by the harassing conduct of supervisors or co-employees. Particularly if the jurisdiction does not impose vicarious liability on employers for intentionally harassing conduct, negligent infliction claims frequently surface as another strategy to hold the employer accountable.[42]

In many respects, the tension points in the doctrine governing the intentional infliction tort in harassment cases are recapitulated in cases alleging negligent infliction of emotional distress. As mentioned in chapter 3, many jurisdictions now cut off intentional tort claims altogether, on preemption grounds or by defining "outrageous" conduct narrowly, without ever reaching the question of whether the employer should be held vicariously liable for supervisory harassment. Likewise, when a claim for negligent infliction is asserted against an employer, the claim might fail at the outset for failure to allege physical injury or physical manifestations before getting to the question of employer liability. When the issue is the employer's negligence, however, it should be noted that an employer might well defeat the charge by showing that it has instituted and regularly enforced antiharassment policies in its workplace and thus has exercised due care to prevent such conduct.[43] This "no-breach" defense is sufficiently protective of employer interests in such cases. There is no need to cut suits off at the outset by declaring that there is no duty to act reasonably.

Cases Involving Reproduction

Negligent infliction claims in the reproductive context have also caused courts enormous difficulties. Frequently brought against hospitals, physicians, and other health professionals, there is typically an underlying contract in the background of the case, although, in addition to the actual patient, a spouse or partner of the patient may join as a plaintiff. Thus, there have been negligent infliction claims brought by women who suffer emotional distress resulting from stillbirths and miscarriages caused by physician negligence and by couples who have sued fertility clinics for losing the sperm of a man about to undergo chemotherapy.[44] Women who have lost their capacity to reproduce through sterilization have also sued under lack of informed consent and other theories. Claims can also arise after a child is born. Parents have sued when their newborn was abducted from the hospital and when babies were switched at birth as result of hospital negligence. In this category also belong claims of "wrongful birth," discussed in chapter 5, typically brought against doctors who negligently fail to advise their patients about the risks of giving birth to a child with serious disabilities.

As a doctrinal matter, courts have often struggled with whether to impose a "physical injury" or "physical manifestation" requirement in negligent infliction cases in the reproductive context. This inquiry is itself related to gender because such cases often require courts to characterize the relationship between a pregnant woman and her fetus. Many courts have had a particularly difficult time seeing and categorizing the physical and emotional connection between a mother and fetus. The intertwined physical and emotional nature of the response of a woman who experiences a miscarriage or stillbirth does not seem to fit neatly into the standard repertoire of injuries suffered by torts plaintiffs.

Only in 2004 did the New York Court of Appeals finally decide to allow a claim by a woman who had suffered emotional distress after the stillbirth of her twins.[45] In that case, the woman's obstetrician had failed to diagnose and treat her for a condition (known as incompetent cervix) that put her pregnancy at risk. Before this case, the New York courts had clung to the "physical injury" rule and had insisted that a female plaintiff demonstrate a physical injury to herself, "distinct from that suffered by the fetus and not a normal incident of childbirth." Despite the existence of a doctor/patient relationship—which presumably carries an expectation that the doctor will exercise reasonable care to protect both the expectant mother and her unborn child—the New York courts had looked for something more before recognizing a duty and allowing recovery for the mother's clearly foreseeable emotional distress. Importantly, New York also disallows wrongful death suits in such cases, leaving the parents without a remedy in cases of negligently caused stillbirths and miscarriages.

New York's formalistic approach requiring that there be a separate physical injury to the mother that was not a normal incident of childbirth fails to comprehend a woman's distinctive interest in reproduction that encompasses a period during her pregnancy in which she and the fetus are linked physically. To try to isolate a wholly separate injury to the mother—and to deny recovery when it is lacking—is a dramatic example of refusing to recognize an injury unless an identical harm can be suffered by a man. Plaintiffs have argued that it is enough that no one disputes that the medical treatment of a woman during pregnancy is the kind of activity that, if handled negligently, is highly likely to give rise to serious emotional injuries thereafter. In the 2004 case, the New York Court of Appeals finally agreed. Reversing a long line of cases, the court acknowledged that, "[b]ecause the health of the mother and fetus are linked, we will not force them into legalistic pigeonholes."

Some courts that have historically been reluctant to allow claims for "stand-alone" emotional harm, however, have been impelled by the reproductive context of the claim to make an exception to the denial of recovery. A 1990 decision by the Iowa Supreme Court is a good example of judicial extension of the negligent infliction claim to protect plaintiff's reproductive interests, without stating so in precise terms. In *Oswald v. LeGrand*,[46] a woman who was five months pregnant was horribly mistreated by nurses and doctors at the emergency room of Mercy Hospital in Dubuque. Despite the woman's extensive bleeding and cramping, the nurses chided her for coming into the hospital, one even telling her that if she miscarried, it would not be a baby but rather "a big blob of blood." One of the doctors charged with treating the plaintiff was so eager to go on vacation that he left plaintiff in the hospital corridor, "hysterical and insisting she was about to deliver," minutes before she actually began delivering the baby in the hallway. After the delivery, the nurses and a doctor declared that the baby was stillborn and left the infant on an instrument tray for nearly one-half hour. Remarkably, it was the baby's father who discovered that the infant was still alive, when the infant returned his grasp to her finger. After twelve hours in intensive care, however, the infant subsequently died.

The negligent infliction claim was crucial to this case because the couple could not prove that the hospital's mistreatment of the mother and infant had somehow caused the infant's death or that the infant could have survived longer if the medical care had been otherwise. The court thus had to confront the question of whether an emotional distress claim could lie, even absent a claim of physical injury to the mother or the infant. Relying on old cases involving false death telegraphs and mishandling of corpses, the court permitted recovery. It observed that the "life-and-death" context of childbirth was comparable to the old cases presumably because both involved the "negligent performance of contractual services that carry with them deeply emotional responses in the event of a breach." Under the circumstances, the court believed that liability for emotional distress should also attach to the delivery of medical services. The court's decision was thus quite sensitive to context, even if it stopped short of declaring that plaintiff's interest in reproduction was a fundamental interest deserving of heightened protection.

One reason that courts in torts cases alleging reproductive harm may not be quick to draw an analogy to constitutional rights cases asserting deprivation of procreative rights may be that the latter generally involve the assertion of "negative" rights against government interference, while tort claims most often involve the assertion of "positive" rights against private defendants who have failed to protect plaintiffs' interests.[47] This dilemma over duty is at the heart of a larger cultural controversy about the scope of civil rights, with progressives arguing for more expansive protection against harms inflicted by private interests while conservatives generally aim to limit protection narrowly to abuses of official governmental power. In the real world, of course, there is often no strict separation between governmental power and private power, particularly for low-income persons who are forced to rely on the government for essential services such as medical care.

One prominent context in which constitutional claims for deprivation of reproductive rights have merged with tort-like allegations of lack of informed consent involves suits over the sterilization of poor women who qualify for Medicaid. Several high-profile suits were brought in the early and mid-1970s,[48] often alleging violations of 42 U.S.C. §1983, the Reconstruction-era statute that authorizes damage claims for civil rights violations committed under color of state law. The plaintiffs in these cases were typically minority women who claimed that they had been pressured to undergo sterilization procedures by doctors who believed that they were they were irresponsible "welfare" mothers who already had too many children and were a burden on the public fisc. In some respects, these cases were similar to the miscarriage and stillbirth cases discussed earlier, in that both alleged serious, if intangible, damage to the plaintiffs' reproductive interests at the hands of negligent and often callous medical professionals. The sterilization cases, however, differed from the typical miscarriage case in that the plaintiffs in the sterilization cases also asserted that the doctors or hospitals had followed a discriminatory policy toward plaintiffs tied to their race, gender, and class. Moreover, such claims were brought and classified as statutory civil rights claims and were frequently pursued by civil rights organizations or poverty law centers that had little strategic interest in linking their efforts to tort suits for negligent infliction of emotional distress, despite their obvious similarities.[49]

Legal scholar Dorothy Roberts has chronicled the sterilization suits and their significance for the reproductive rights of minority women.[50] Her history details that, prior to the late 1970s, the practice of performing unnecessary hysterectomies and tubal ligations on poor women without their knowledge or consent was widespread in the North, as well as in the Deep South. At the time, hospitals and doctors used a variety of tactics to coerce consent from poor pregnant women, from offering tubal ligations to women while they were in labor to refusing to treat indigent patients unless they agreed to be sterilized.

The extent of the sterilization abuses in some states has only recently been uncovered. Due to research by historian Johanna Schoen[51] and investigative reporting by journalists at the *Winston-Salem Journal*,[52] new details about the cases and procedures of the North Carolina Eugenics Board have surfaced. In its forty-year history—which lasted until 1974—the Board authorized the sterilization of more than 7,600 persons. By the late 1960s, more than 60 percent of those sterilized were black women, compared to North Carolina's population that was only approximately 25 percent black.[53] Social workers in the state adopted a policy of targeting young, unmarried black women who had given birth to a child. They threatened drastic actions, such as sending the teenage women to an orphanage or cutting off welfare funds to their entire families, including siblings and parents, if they did not submit to sterilization.[54] The revelation of the contents of the formerly sealed records of the Eugenics Board prompted the North Carolina House of Representative, in 2007, to vote to establish a commission to determine how to identify and give reparations to the victims, although no such program has yet been implemented or funded.[55]

Two notable civil rights cases from the 1970s exemplify the radically different positions courts took toward plaintiffs' claims of deprivation of reproductive rights and assertions of injury from coerced sterilizations. One case gained considerable notoriety, probably because the doctor involved was so explicit about his policy of pressuring poor black women to undergo sterilization. In *Walker v. Pierce*,[56] Dr. Clovis Pierce, the attending obstetrician at a county hospital in South Carolina, admitted that he had a policy of refusing to treat any woman who was on Medicaid or who was otherwise unable to pay her bills if she was having a third or subsequent child and did not agree to be sterilized. As recounted by the dissenting judge, Dr. Pierce told one patient that it was his "tax money paying for this baby" and that he was "tired of paying for illegitimate children." He bluntly said to the patient that if she didn't want to be sterilized, she could "find another doctor." Pierce was apparently unashamed of his practice and refused to sign an affidavit stating that he would not discriminate against Medicaid patients.

The two African American women who brought the suit in *Walker* testified that Pierce had used coercive tactics to enforce his policy: he had threatened to have one woman's state assistance terminated if she did not cooperate and ordered the immediate discharge from the hospital of another woman just after she gave birth, when she refused to submit to a tubal ligation. As could be expected, many women eventually gave in to the pressure, signed the requisite forms, and submitted to the sterilization procedure. The evidence indicated that the policy had an overwhelming negative impact on black women. Of the eighteen welfare mothers sterilized, sixteen were black.

From a torts perspective, *Walker* looks like a clear case of coerced consent, in the important sense that these women did not desire to lose their capacity to have children and there was no claim that the sterilization would somehow benefit their health. Nevertheless, the majority found no civil rights violation. The court first characterized the doctor/patient relationship as "one of free choice for both parties," even though it was clear that indigent pregnant women, such as the plaintiffs, rarely had alternatives to medical care besides the county hospital. The court then disputed both the racial character and the public nature of the doctor's policy, characterizing it as a "personal economic philosophy," despite the fact that most local welfare children were black and that Medicaid had paid Pierce more than $60,000 during the period in question. For the majority of the court, the civil rights statutes posed no obstacle to the doctor's decision to "establish and pursue the policy he had publicly and freely announced" and indicated that the doctor had every right to maintain his "professional attitude toward the increase in offspring" and then to set on a course of action to see his views "prevail." Apparently, the majority considered it reasonable for a doctor to place only subordinated women (who were poor, disproportionately minority, and receiving public assistance) to the Hobson's choice of sterilization if they desired medically necessary health care.

The lawsuit that had the biggest impact on public policy, however, was a class action brought by Minnie Lee Relf and Mary Alice Relf, two African American sisters from Montgomery, Alabama, who claimed that they had been involuntarily sterilized at a federally funded clinic when they were only fourteen and twelve years old. Initiated by the Southern Poverty Law Center and the National Welfare Rights Organization, this class action represented more than 125,000 class members consisting of poor persons, including minors and disabled persons, who had been involuntarily sterilized under federally funded programs, such as Medicaid and Aid to Families with Dependent Children. *Relf v. Weinberger*[57] was brought as a challenge to regulations promulgated by the Department of Health, Education, and Welfare (HEW) that had been drafted in response to the nationwide attention given to the experience of the Relf sisters and the consequent exposure of the widespread abuses in sterilization procedures.

In an usually strong opinion, Judge Gesell of the Washington, D.C., federal district court found that an estimated 100,000 to 150,000 low-income persons had been sterilized annually under the federal programs and that "an indefinite number of poor people have been improperly coerced into accepting a sterilization operation under the threat that various federally supported welfare benefits would be withdrawn unless they submitted to irreversible sterilization." He ruled that funding such coercive practices and tactics violated HEW's authority because it was Congress's intent that "federally assisted family planning sterilizations are permissible only with the voluntary, knowing and uncoerced consent of individuals competent to give such consent." As one of the remedies for the illegal action, Gesell ordered that federally funded providers of medical care change their consent procedures to ensure that patients would not be subjected to pressure from doctors or others and that they would, among other steps, receive special oral and written assurances that federal funds could not be withdrawn because of their unwillingness to accept sterilization.

Judge Gesell's order and other public-policy initiatives to end sterilization abuse had a significant impact. In 1978, HEW issued new rules that restricted sterilizations performed under programs receiving federal funds. The rules strengthened the requirements of informed consent, providing for consent in the preferred language of the patient and a thirty-day waiting period between the signing of the consent form and the sterilization procedure.[58] For our purposes, what is striking about these regulatory reforms is how closely they implicate issues that are at the heart of tort claims for negligent infliction of emotional distress in the reproductive context. The heightened protection against abuse afforded by the HEW regulations is predicated on the importance of the interest at stake, which justifies regulating the doctor/patient relationship. Moreover, the regulations implicitly disavow the *Walker* court's narrow view of informed consent by acknowledging that physician pressure and economic coercion can make a woman's "choice" to accept sterilization less than free and voluntary. While the ruling in *Relf* has no direct application to tort claims, its civil rights principles could easily be absorbed to guide courts in tort cases alleging malpractice and claims for negligent infliction of emotional distress. From our perspective, the take-home message of *Relf* is that medical personnel owe patients a heightened duty of care when advising and treating them on matters of reproductive choice and health and that they should guard against conduct that undermines or injures such patients' interests, whether it results in emotional or physical harm.

In her history of race and reproductive rights, Dorothy Roberts cautions that the federal regulations have not stopped sterilization abuse, citing the continued exceptionally high sterilization rates of black women.[59] However, today's cases are more likely to arise in individual, rather than class-wide, settings, and in what otherwise appear to be ordinary malpractice and informed consent suits. It is unlikely that physicians today would openly acknowledge that they had unilaterally decided to sterilize a patient because she was receiving Medicaid and had too many children. Traces of the old paternalistic and racist attitudes, however, can still be found in the medical treatment of pregnant minority women and in judicial responses to their injuries.

One troubling recent case is *Robinson v. Cutchin*,[60] a lack of informed consent case from Maryland decided in 2001 involving a pregnant African American woman. In that case, Glenda Robinson was treated by Dr. Cutchin in connection with the birth of her sixth child. The controversy centered on whether Robinson had given her consent to a tubal ligation in the event that she had to undergo a cesarean section. Dr. Cutchin alleged that she had given such consent, while Robinson denied it and asserted that she and her husband were planning on having a seventh child.

As it turned out, it was necessary to perform an emergency C-section for the delivery of Robinson's baby. Cutchin then went ahead and performed the tubal ligation. According to Robinson, she did not even discover that the sterilization had been performed until nearly two years after the birth of her child, when she learned she was incapable of conceiving. Robinson's suit against Dr. Cutchin alleged a variety of tort claims, including lack of informed consent, battery, and intentional infliction of emotional distress. Because the negligence claim of lack of informed consent resulted in a settlement, the only published opinion in the case involved the intentional tort claims for battery and intentional infliction of emotional distress.

The opinion of the district court dismissing the intentional tort claims displays skepticism toward claims of reproductive injury and casts doubt on the seriousness of plaintiff's alleged injury. Reminiscent of *Walker*'s disapproval of black women who choose to bear multiple children, the district court thought it relevant to point out that, before she was married, Robinson had "three prior children born out of wedlock" and that Robinson also had three children with her current husband. Assuming for the sake of argument that the tubal ligation had been performed without Robinson's consent, the court nevertheless concluded that it did not amount to a battery, defined as a harmful or offensive touching. To the court, the forced sterilization was not harmful "because it did not cause any additional physical pain, injury, or illness other than that occasioned by the C-Section procedure." In the court's view, the sterilization was also not offensive because it purportedly "did not offend Mrs. Robinson's reasonable sense of personal dignity." Remarkably, the court concluded that the injury to plaintiff's reproductive capacity had no connection to dignitary harm or harm to personal identity: the court bluntly stated that "the fact that she was not able to have a seventh child after previously giving birth to six children is hardly something which would offend a reasonable sense of dignity." Not surprisingly, given this assessment of the situation, the court also dismissed the intentional infliction claim, concluding that there was no evidence that the doctor had acted outrageously.

Although Robinson's negligence claim survived—and, with it, the prospect of recovering damages for emotional distress traceable to the sterilization procedure—the district court's opinion revealed a disconcerting tendency to devalue plaintiff's procreative interests and to minimize her suffering. The opinion seems oblivious to the constitutional principle that it is an individual woman's right to decide whether to bear children and to determine the size of her family. Particularly given that African American women have historically been denied the right of self-determination in these matters, the court in *Robinson* should not have been so quick to dismiss plaintiff's distress as "unreasonable" and to treat her lack of consent as having nothing to do with her sense of personal dignity.

In our view, the heightened protection for reproductive interests in negligent infliction cases should not be limited to cases of sterilization, stillbirth, and miscarriage. Even after a child is born, the connection between mother and infant should be recognized and valued. Rather than deny the special ties parents have to newborns or focus exclusively on an infant's separate injuries, courts should impose a duty of care upon medical professionals to protect parents against emotional distress in the important period during and immediately following childbirth. Thus, there should have been little difficulty finding liability in a recent case in which an employee of a hospital brought a one-day-old baby to a mother for breastfeeding, neglected to see that the mother was heavily sedated, and left them alone.[61] The infant was then smothered to death when the mother fell asleep on top of him. Rather than struggle with whether the mother was a bystander to her child's injury, was in the "danger zone," or satisfied some other artificial limitation imposed in negligent infliction cases, it should be easy to find tort protection simply on the defendant's failure to safeguard plaintiff's reproductive interests. Similarly, the emotional injury done to a parent when a hospital negligently loses a newborn [62] or switches a baby at birth[63] should be readily compensable. The absence of legal protection against negligence in such cases creates a legal anomaly whereby a person may recover tort damages for the value of damaged physical property but not for the far more serious emotional injury stemming from the hospital's failure to protect her newborn baby. This treatment supports the criticism of cultural feminist writers who have argued that women's contribution to society as childbearers and caretakers has been misunderstood and undervalued.[64] In real world terms, the period of reproduction stretches from conception until the parents take the baby home from the hospital. The parents' special interest at stake during this period deserves heightened protection and warrants finding a duty to protect against the negligent infliction of emotional distress.

Admittedly, not all cases involving negligent infliction in the reproductive context are easy cases. A good example of a difficult case is *Harnicher v. University of Utah Medical Center*, a 1998 case decided by the Utah Supreme Court.[65] This claim of negligent infliction of emotional distress arose from a terrible mixup at a fertility clinic. At the recommendation of their doctor, a couple agreed to an in vitro procedure in which the husband's sperm was to be mixed with that of a donor selected by the couple. Under the procedure, the couple could not be sure whether the sperm that actually fertilized the ovum was from the husband. They chose a donor with physical characteristics similar to those of the husband and authorized the use of only that donor sperm. The wife gave birth to triplets. One of the infants had red hair, unlike the husband, who had curly dark hair and brown eyes. When one of the children got sick, the couple had blood tests conducted that revealed that two of the children could not have been the child of either the husband or the selected donor. A DNA test on one of the infants established that his biological father was actually another donor.

Both parents sued for negligent infliction of emotional distress and claimed injuries as a result of the clinic's negligence. The wife's symptoms were more severe than her husband's. He alleged depression and anxiety. She was diagnosed with "major depressive disorder." One major issue in the case was whether mental illness, as experienced by the wife, should qualify as physical harm. This seemingly paradoxical inquiry was necessitated by precedents that arguably refused to allow recovery for stand-alone emotional distress.

Ultimately, a badly split Utah Supreme Court (2-1-1) denied recovery. The plurality dodged the issue of whether mental illness, without accompanying physical injury or manifestations, was compensable. Instead, the plurality ruled that plaintiffs could not prevail because they had not shown that "a reasonable person, normally constituted, would be unable to cope with the mental stress engendered by the circumstances of the case." The plurality was influenced by the fact that the children were "normal, healthy children" and that their physiological characteristics could not have been "reliably predicted" even absent the mixup. The plurality seemed to be saying that the couple's response—perhaps especially the wife's—was extreme, and it refused to allow recovery for such "eggshell plaintiffs." The dissent, however, would have allowed recovery based on clear negligence on the part of the clinic and the fact that emotional distress to the parents was entirely predictable.

Our approach to negligent infliction cases does not point to a clear result in *Harnicher*. Because plaintiffs' interests in reproduction were clearly at stake, we would find a duty to exercise reasonable care. However, a persuasive argument can be made in this case to deny recovery on other grounds. The wife's reaction to the revelation was extreme, flowing solely from the fact that the children turned out not to be biologically linked to her husband, a possibility of which the couple had been aware from the outset. Mixup cases, such as *Harnicher,* sometimes also involve reactions to race, when, for example, a child from an unintended donor turns out to be of a different race than the mother or siblings.[66] To award a couple damages for emotional distress in such a case might well reinforce racial prejudice or racial antipathy and might be understood as making a statement that it is reasonable for a person to reject a child for the sole reason that his skin color or physical attributes are different from the plaintiffs'. In such highly unusual cases, it is justifiable to use the doctrine of proximate cause to cut off liability, with full recognition of the policy-laden nature of that inquiry. In any event, it is preferable that courts decide whether permitting tort recovery in such cases would undermine important public policies, such as promoting racial equality or furthering the best interests of the child. Shifting the focus away from "duty" to "proximate cause" will not make the decision any easier, but at least it does not eclipse the central issue. As in other reproduction cases, nothing can be gained from having recovery turn on whether the plaintiff suffered physical as opposed to emotional harm.

Bystander Cases and Family Relationships

The final strand of negligent infliction cases is infelicitously known as bystander cases, signaling that the plaintiff in such cases is not the primary accident victim but a mere bystander who happens to witness an accident to another. In line with the highly individualistic character of the common law, courts have historically denied all recovery in such cases where the emotional distress is produced by fear for another.[67] It has been said that the negligent defendant owed no duty to the plaintiff or that harm to such a plaintiff was unforeseeable. In reality, however, the vast majority of plaintiffs who have sued in such cases were not mere bystanders, in the everyday sense of the word. Instead, the prototypical plaintiffs in such cases were mothers who saw their children die or suffer severe injury before their eyes.[68] In such cases, it strained credulity to argue that the presence of a mother or caregiver was unexpected and that her shock and distress were unforeseeable. Importantly, bystander plaintiffs in such cases were not basing their claims in any strict sense on their child's injury but instead sought recovery for their own pain, emotional distress, and often accompanying physical injuries. There was, however, an important relational element to the bystander claim that flowed from the fact that it was often the injured party's family member who was on hand to witness the injury and suffer distress as a result. To this degree, bystanders' claims looked very much like mothers' claims or caregivers' claims seeking recovery for the extra shock and pain that come from experiencing the suffering of a loved one in the plaintiff's care.

Over the years, tort law has steadily liberalized to allow compensation in some bystander cases. Replacing the rule of no recovery, courts gradually allowed bystander plaintiffs to prevail if they could prove that they were in the zone of physical danger and might well have been physically injured along with the direct victim, if circumstances had been slightly altered. This liberalization allowed recovery in cases in which mothers or other caregivers of children narrowly escaped physical injury but nevertheless suffered emotional harm primarily because they feared for their child's safety. Because the "danger zone" rule was based on a risk of physical harm, however, it did not represent a tremendously significant departure from prior law with its insistence on linking physical harm to the plaintiff.

The landmark case of *Dillon v. Legg*, decided by the California Supreme Court in 1968, broke from this tradition, furthered liberalized recovery, and, we suggest, may have altered the basic trajectory of bystander cases.[69] That case involved a mother who suffered nervous shock when she witnessed her child run down by a negligent driver. At the time, the mother was in a position of safety outside the physical danger zone. The California Supreme Court nevertheless allowed the claim and crafted guidelines for courts to follow in such cases. The *Dillon* factors, as they became known, permitted recovery when (1) plaintiff was located near the scene of the accident, (2) the shock to plaintiff resulted from a direct emotional impact upon plaintiff from sensory and contemporaneous observance of the accident, and (3) plaintiff and the accident victim were closely related.

In retrospect, the most innovative aspect of *Dillon* was its blending of individualistic and relational harm. Unlike traditional recovery for emotional distress in direct victim cases, *Dillon* did not provide a rule of universal recovery but limited claims to close family members. This "family members" limitation resembles the restriction typically placed on tort claims for wrongful death and loss of consortium, which compensate directly for damage to important personal relationships.[70] Thus, in relational harm cases, damages are predicated directly on the adverse change—in both pecuniary and nonpecuniary terms—that defendant's negligence caused in plaintiff's life because of the absence or injury of the loved one. There is no need for such relational claimants to witness the accident or the injury. In contrast, in the *Dillon*-type bystander claim, only a first-hand witness to the accident is given a claim. This requirement not only limits the number of claimants but also is said to restrict compensation to those who suffer the "extra trauma" of such a first-hand experience. This aspect of the negligent infliction of emotional distress claim fits more comfortably with other negligent infliction claims with their focus on damage to the individual; from this perspective, the bystander claim is still basically a nonrelational claim in which severe distress just happens to flow from the perception of suffering by another. Under this view, the family member requirement serves mainly to guarantee the genuineness of the distress and to limit the number of potential claimants.

Dillon's reception in other jurisdictions has been uneven. The Restatement reports that fourteen states have rejected it outright and have clung to the danger zone rule; four jurisdictions have even continued to insist on proof of physical impact.[71] However, some variation of *Dillon* is now in force in twenty-nine states, allowing the Restatement to adopt a rule authorizing recovery when the plaintiff "perceives the event contemporaneously and is a close family member of the person suffering the bodily injury."[72]

To some degree, this liberalization of the bystander rule recognizes the special harm that mothers and other close family members suffer in such situations. However, the courts' experience with applying *Dillon* has brought its own difficulties, particularly because of the artificial line drawing created by the requirement that a plaintiff witness or contemporaneously perceive the traumatic event. Thus, recovery has been denied to parents who see the bloodied body of their child moments after the accident occurs or shortly thereafter at the hospital.[73] Although no one would deny that their suffering is genuine and serious, it is not clear that they have suffered the "extra trauma" required by *Dillon*, particularly in jurisdictions that treat the *Dillon* factors as requirements and not merely guidelines.[74]

In the forty years since *Dillon* was decided, however, one point is clear: all courts embracing *Dillon* agree that recovery should be limited to close family members.[75] Accordingly, the Third Restatement has called this limitation "a specific and independent requirement" and not merely "a factor to be balanced against other factors."[76] This consensus underscores the relational dimension of the claim. Indeed, the most lively and important dispute in *Dillon*-type jurisdictions today centers on the meaning to be given to the term "close family members," and in particular whether same-sex partners, fiancées, and extended family members may qualify as "family."[77]

The dominant approach adopts a "bright-line" standard that limits family members to legally recognized relationships of blood, marriage, and adoption and excludes all but nuclear family members. Not surprisingly, this exclusion of nontraditional families can have a negative effect on minority families, which often do not mirror the white middle-class ideal. Thus, in one recent case from California, *Guzman v. Kirchhoefel*,[78] the court refused to allow plaintiff's claim when she witnessed the death of her second cousin in an accident caused by a negligent driver. Plaintiff described how she had lived with her cousin in the same household most of her life and was living with her at the time of the accident. She explained that the families resided together "out of economic necessity" and that their living arrangements arose because "there was nowhere else to go." The California court, however, declined to regard plaintiff's relationship as a close family relationship, concluding that the cousins did not qualify as members of the "immediate family unit." The court also characterized their living arrangement as mere "happenstance." Notably, the court's strict interpretation did not permit an inquiry into the social reality of whether plaintiff in fact had close everyday emotional ties with her cousin and left no room for a definition of "family" that encompassed extended families brought together in part because of economic exigencies.

Some courts, however, have adopted a more functional approach to the meaning of "family" in bystander cases. The leading case from New Jersey, *Dunphy v. Gregor*,[79] allowed a fiancée to recover when she witnessed her partner struck by an oncoming car. The couple had been living together for more than two years, and the court believed that a jury might well conclude that their relationship was an "intimate familial relationship," characterized by mutual dependence and shared experiences. Given the growing social acceptance of unmarried persons living together, the court concluded that sound public policy favored protecting such relationships when they were "substantial, stable, and enduring." This move to a more functional analysis, of course, paves the way for same-sex couples and persons in nontraditional families to argue that their ties deserve the same measure of respect. This position recently received a boost from the Third Restatement, which indicated its approval of the *Dunphy* approach and declared that "when defining what constitutes a close family relationship, courts should take into account changing practices and social norms and employ a functional approach to determine what constitutes a family."[80] Additionally, the functional approach was recently embraced and extended beyond the bystander context to cover purely relational claims of loss of consortium. In *Lozoya v. Sanchez*,[81] the New Mexico Supreme Court permitted the claim of a woman whose long-term male partner was injured in an automobile accident. The couple had "been together" for more than thirty years and had three children. Citing feminist scholarship,[82] the court decided that the ease of administration of "bright-line" rules did not justify excluding the claims of "persons whose loss of a significant relational interest may be just as devastating as the loss of legal spouse."

These recent developments indicate that the legitimacy of the bystander claim is grounded in large part on damage to an intimate relationship. In this important respect, the bystander claim shares a kinship with "direct victim" negligent infliction claims centering on abusive sexual relationships or relationships to newborns or fetuses. Looked at in this way, the bystander claim is primarily a way to vindicate damage to a relationship and has as much to do with recognizing the value of intimacy and family ties—most prominently, maternal ties to children—than with compensating for nervous shock and trauma.

Reconceptualizing bystander claims as relational injury claims could finish what *Dillon* started. The arbitrary distinctions of the bystander rule could give way to a simpler regime in which all close family members—whether at the scene of the accident or not—are afforded a claim for their relational loss.[83] The difficulty states experience in drawing the line for recovery could be eased by making proximity to the scene of the accident relevant to damages, not to a finding of duty. Reframing bystander claims as relational injury claims would allow states to harmonize recovery for negligent infliction of emotional distress with claims for wrongful death and loss of consortium.[84] Most important for our purposes, it would elevate the status of injury to relationships in the law of torts and help soften the hierarchy of claims that has long plagued recovery for negligent infliction of emotional distress.

5

Causation

A central proposition in tort law is that, without proof of causation, there can be no liability, regardless of the wrongfulness of the defendant's behavior. It is causation that ties the defendant's act to the plaintiff's harm and justifies singling out the defendant as the party who should provide compensation for the plaintiff's loss. On the surface, there may seem to be no obvious link between causation on the one hand and gender and race on the other. In this respect, causation initially seems different from tort concepts such as "outrageous conduct" or "negligence," discussed earlier, which require the court or jury to make normative judgments about the parties' conduct and thus may more readily be seen as implicating cultural attitudes toward different social groups.

This chapter, however, challenges that conventional wisdom and seeks to show how gender and race issues can also be important to legal determinations of causation, at least in certain factual contexts. For this purpose, we focus on two substantive areas—one that highlights gender and reproduction and one that highlights issues of race, gender, and social class. We examine the treatment of causation issues in what are known as "wrongful birth" cases, a relatively new cause of action in which pregnant plaintiffs sue their physicians for malpractice, alleging that their doctors' negligence prevented them from making an informed choice about whether to undergo an abortion or to proceed with the pregnancy and give birth.[1] We next analyze how courts have treated tort claims made on behalf of children claiming injury from exposure to lead paint,[2] a group of plaintiffs that is disproportionately minority and predominately from low-income families. In these lead paint cases, courts have had to grapple with difficult causation issues, as they determine whether a child's cognitive impairment is caused by exposure to lead paint or is traceable to preexisting factors, such as inherited family traits.

In some respects, our approach to causation in these two types of cases is quite traditional. Our analysis applies fundamental causation principles as articulated in the Third Restatement of Torts and looks at the wrongful birth and lead paint cases from this traditional vantage point. Additionally, however, we draw upon insights from the fields of social and cognitive psychology to explain how considerations of race and gender may affect causal judgments in tort law, even when the legal standards for causation are cast in objective, neutral terms. Our notion that causation is sometimes saturated with social policy is, of course, nothing new; starting in the 1930s, the Legal Realists argued that it was a mistake to believe that causation was a quasi-scientific concept that could be divorced from public policy.[3] Recent research in cognitive and social psychology does, however, offer us a new vocabulary and a new way of understanding how gender and race stereotypes, race- and gender-based schemas, and other common cognitive "shortcuts" influence causal judgments in subtle ways.[4] These habitual—and sometimes biased—ways of thinking create expectations in the minds of judges and jurors about what is possible and what is ordinary and likely, expectations that in turn affect decisions and doctrine. The upshot is that "simple" judgments as to cause and effect may mask more complex, and arguably more controversial, judgments about blame and responsibility.

As background for the discussion of the wrongful birth and lead paint cases, we first describe some traditional causation principles most pertinent to these two types of cases, introducing the crucial concept of "factual causation" and discussing how plaintiffs shoulder their burden of proof on this element in a typical tort case. In this background section, we also discuss key psychological concepts that arguably come into play when judges and jurors are called upon to make causal judgments. Employing the language of cognitive and social psychology, we explain how a legal determination of factual causation may be recast as a process of "causal attribution," one that is highly dependent on expectations and judgments of normality.

Factual Causation and Causal Attribution

It is axiomatic that a plaintiff in a tort case must prove that the defendant's act or omission "caused" the injury. As with other fundamental elements in a tort claim, the plaintiff is generally assigned the burden of proving causation by the traditional standard of proof in civil cases, namely, proof by a preponderance of the evidence. That much is simple and uncontested in virtually every tort case. Over the years, however, confusion has set in because the term "cause" has been used to describe more than one concept in the law. The main challenge for beginning law students is to learn to recognize the difference between "factual causation" (or cause-in-fact) and what is variously known as "proximate causation," "legal causation," or what the Third Restatement calls "scope of liability."[5] For the practicing attorney, the distinction between factual cause and proximate cause does not loom so large, particularly because the plaintiff is always required to prove both elements. In this chapter, we focus principally on issues relating to factual causation as most important for our analysis of gender and race issues in wrongful birth and lead paint cases, with only brief mention of proximate cause and scope of liability.

The Third Restatement endorses the venerable "but-for" test for determining factual causation.[6] Accordingly, it provides that "conduct is a factual cause when the harm would not have occurred absent the conduct." The test is not demanding: the Restatement makes it clear that "[t]ortious conduct need only be one of the factual causes of harm."[7] Under this formulation, factual causation is not designed to do much work in fixing responsibility for harm. The test envisions that there will often be multiple causes for single harms and serves to rule out only conduct that played no role at all in plaintiff's injury. Under the "but-for" test, the plaintiff need only identify the defendant's conduct as a "necessary condition" leading to an injurious outcome. In fact, early on, courts developed a policy-oriented rule—known as the eggshell plaintiff rule—that fits well with the modest role of "but-for" causation in multiple-cause cases.[8] Under the eggshell plaintiff rule, a defendant "takes the plaintiff as he finds him," meaning that a defendant is held responsible for the plaintiff's entire injuries, even if they are greater than expected and result in part from the plaintiff's preexisting condition. Under the doctrine, a defendant cannot escape liability for aggravating a preexisting condition of the plaintiff, provided only that the defendant's conduct played some role in hastening or worsening the condition.

At its base, the process for determining factual causation is a "counterfactual" process.[9] It requires the factfinder to engage in a hypothetical inquiry in order to answer the question of "what would have occurred if the actor had not engaged in the tortious conduct." In some cases, applying the "but-for" test is simple. A classic example involves a plaintiff who sues for the physical injuries she sustained in a car accident when the defendant driver struck her car immediately after running a red light. In such a case, the plaintiff need only convince the court and jury that if the defendant had not been negligent and had stopped for the red light, the plaintiff would not have been injured.

In many other cases, however, the counterfactual "proof" needed to prove causation is more complex and debatable. For example, in a claim for failure to diagnose and detect breast cancer, a plaintiff may argue that "but for" the defendant's negligent failure to read the plaintiff's mammogram correctly, her cancer would have been stopped by surgery. In such a case, however, the defendant can often be expected to respond that even if the mammogram had been read correctly, the cancer was so far advanced that the result would have been the same. Put in other words, that the defendant's mistake did not "cause" plaintiff's injuries. Particularly in medical malpractice cases, in which defendant's negligence consists of a failure to act, the counterfactual process may require the factfinder to speculate on various medical outcomes and probabilities in an attempt to reconstruct what might have been. Most recently, in toxic tort cases, such as asbestos and lead paint litigation, the courts have delineated several steps necessary to resolving the factual causation inquiry, including ascertaining whether the plaintiff was exposed to the substance in question, whether the substance was capable of causing the disease from which the plaintiff suffers (known as general causation), and whether the substance caused the individual plaintiff's disease (known as specific causation).[10]

The comments to the Third Restatement acknowledge that "courts have kept the bar for proving causation at only a modest height."[11] As David Robertson writes in an influential article, *The Common Sense of Cause in Fact*, "courts often emphasize that it is a mistake to insist on too much certainty when applying the but-for test."[12] This leniency is driven partly by recognition of the limitations of the counterfactual process and partly by an appreciation that, in litigation, judgments about causation are inevitably intertwined with judgments about negligence and harm. According to Robertson, "[T]he central idea is that when a defendant has engaged in conduct that we consider to be wrongful in major part because such conduct often leads to the kind of harm that the plaintiff has suffered, we are rightfully impatient with the defendant's claim that plaintiff cannot prove that the conduct caused harm on this occasion."[13] Thus, in the classic case of a stout woman who fell down unlighted stairs leading from a railroad's platform to its tracks, the court dismissed the railroad's contention that she might well have fallen even if adequate lighting had been provided.[14] Because the conduct of the defendant in failing to light the stairway "greatly multiplie[d] the chances of the accident" and was of a "character naturally leading to its occurrence," proof of causation was held to be satisfied, even though we know that many people suffer injuries from falling down adequately lighted stairs.

It is important also to note that there is a crucial distinction between proof of causation in tort law and proof of causation in the scientific context. Because the endeavors of medicine and science, as compared to law, are so different, it is not surprising that each field has developed its own standard for causation. A chief purpose of science and medicine is to identify and cure illness and disease, while the law is principally designed to resolve individual disputes. Given the therapeutic objective of medicine and science, the nature of medical and scientific proof is thus continually evolving, while legal proof calls for a more timely and final resolution. The Restatement warns that, even in cases involving complex factual causation questions in the medical context, the law should not rely too heavily on science.[15] In tort law, the crucial task in resolving a contest about factual causation is often to discern the line between "permissible inference" and "prohibited speculation." For such purposes, the Restatement cautions that "scientific standards for the sufficiency of evidence to establish a proposition may be inappropriate for the law, which itself must decide the minimum amount of evidence permitting a reasonable (and therefore permissible) inference as opposed to speculation which is not permitted."[16] Particularly when it comes to assessing liability for toxic torts, the comments to the new Restatement criticize courts that in the past have "over[relied] on scientific thresholds" to formulate "bright-line legal rules" for factual causation or to take the issue of causation away from the jury.

Behind the Restatement's cautionary message is a realist acknowledgment of the policy dimensions of both legal and medical judgments about causation. The Restatement comments admit that "scientists are subject to their own value judgments and preexisting biases that may affect their view of a body of evidence" and that judgments about causation in both domains can be affected by differing professional assessments of "the comparative costs of errors."[17] Overall, the comments suggest that courts cannot seek refuge in the "objective" realm of science and medicine to escape the need for making difficult causal judgments in light of the specific aims and policies of the law.

The Restatement's stance on factual causation is a sign that there is now widespread agreement with the sentiments expressed by legal realist scholar Wex S. Malone in his classic 1956 article, *Ruminations on Cause-in-Fact*.[18] At that time, Malone challenged the orthodoxy that factual causation was wholly different in character from proximate cause, a troublesome legal concept that had already been unmasked as bound up in policy. Instead, Malone claimed that even conclusions about cause-in-fact were in part driven by intuitions, preconceptions, and the "mysterious relationship between fact and policy," as the courts struggled with the ultimate legal objective of attempting "to offer an approximate expression of an accepted popular attitude toward responsibility." As the Restatement describes Malone's insight, "the rigor with which courts hold plaintiffs to their burden of proof [on factual causation] . . .

depends on the importance of the claim being enforced and the connection between the harm and the interest that the claim seeks to protect."[19]

More recently, Malone's former student, David Robertson, has untangled the strands of the "but-for" test, with the aim of showing how the counterfactual process works in practice.[20] His deconstruction emphasizes the centrality of "framing" in this conceptual process and provides a bridge between the legal discourse on factual causation employed by Malone and the Restatement and the discourse of cognitive and social psychologists. In Robertson's view, the but-for/counterfactual inquiry actually involves five interrelated steps: (1) identifying the injuries in the suit; (2) identifying the wrongful conduct; (3) mentally correcting the wrongful conduct to the extent necessary to make it lawful, leaving everything else the same; (4) asking whether the injuries would still have occurred had the defendant been acting correctly in that sense; and (5) answering the question. Robertson regards the first four steps as setting the legal frame for the causation question so that it poses a manageable question for tort litigation. However, as Robertson acknowledges, these four framing steps also amount to a "significantly complex mental operation,"[21] and one, we believe, that calls out for a fuller explanation than the traditional legal account of factual causation provides.

Recent research in cognitive and social psychology is particularly helpful in understanding the counterfactual reasoning process central to the "but-for" test for factual causation. The research proceeds from the proposition that the process by which people draw conclusions about cause and effect is not one of passive discovery of objective fact but consists of an active process of social construction. Thus, rather than speaking of cause-in-fact, psychologists analyze "causal attribution," the process by which human beings determine that a causal relationship exists, and the common mistakes humans make when they reach such determinations.[22] Not surprisingly, like other human reasoning processes, scholars have noted that "people's perceptions and descriptions of cause-and-effect relationships vary according to their time, place, culture and interest."[23] We can thus expect causal attributions —and, correspondingly, determinations of legal responsibility—for the same type of injury to change as "new" causal relationships are validated by changing perceptions of the nature of the accident, the accident victim, or the defendant's connection to the harm.

For our purposes, three key concepts from cognitive psychology are particularly relevant: what psychologists call (1) the fundamental attribution error; (2) the bias toward normality; and (3) the bias toward omission. Each of these concepts sheds light on how judges and juries tend to judge and misjudge causal relationships and how social factors like race and gender subtly come into play when they reason about events that might have been but never actually occurred.

As psychologists see it, the causal attribution process is crucial to our understanding of how people explain negative events, particularly whether people attribute negative events to factors beyond the victim's control or believe that such events were caused by and are the responsibility of the victim. Legal scholars conversant in cognitive and social psychology have explained the potential importance of this dichotomy for the trial of actual cases, despite contemporary legal doctrines that recognize the existence of multiple causes and endorse apportioning fault comparatively among plaintiffs and defendants in a tort action. Neil Feigenson, for example, tells us that people prefer simple explanations for events and behavior to complex ones and that they tend to be "content to rely on what first strikes them as a plausible sufficient cause for an event."[24]

This preference for a simple, one-cause explanation means that, in making causal judgments,[25] people are likely to interpret an event or behavior in one of two ways. They may interpret the event or behavior as being caused by something having to do with the character or personality traits of the actor herself. This interpretation is called "dispositional" because it is grounded in the internal disposition (broadly defined) of the actor. Or, alternatively, they may attribute the result to forces outside the actor. This interpretation is called "situational" because the causal explanation centers on external circumstances and fixes on the influence of the specific situation, rather than on the character or traits of the actor.

The fundamental attribution error occurs when people choose between such dispositional and situational explanations. Empirical evidence demonstrates that when it comes to selecting "dispositional" or "situational" explanations for events and behavior, a pattern emerges: we tend to hold situational factors responsible for bad outcomes that happen to us or to those we perceive to be part of our group, while we hold dispositional factors responsible for bad outcomes that happen to others and to those whom we regard as outsiders.[26] Thus, we are more likely to blame the victim when we are not the victim or believe that we are not "like" the victim.

Reviewing the psychological studies, Linda Krieger explains how the content of group stereotypes can affect the causal attribution process.[27] Krieger tells us that when an actor's behavior appears to confirm a stereotype about the actor's group, we tend to attribute that behavior to a dispositional factor within the control of the actor. If, however, the behavior is inconsistent with our stereotype of the actor's group, we are apt to seek out an external explanation and attribute the behavior to situational factors. She describes experiments in which subjects were asked to predict whether a person's behavioral transgression was likely to recur in one of three possible situations: where the transgression reflected stereotypes of the person's ethnic group; where the transgression was inconsistent with stereotypes of the person's ethnic group; and where no stereotype was activated. In the first situation, in which the stereotype was activated, the observers tended to attribute the behavior to stable, stereotypic, character-like traits, without searching further for causal explanations in the surrounding circumstances. Krieger indicates that, in such situations, "the stereotype operate[d] as a kind of cognitive shortcut, bringing the search for additional causal antecedents to a screeching halt."[28] In contrast, in the counter-stereotypical situation and in the situation in which no stereotypes were activated, observers more easily recalled other causally relevant circumstances of the case, apparently because they were more willing to search for outside causes beyond the actor's character that might explain the transgressive behavior.

In such contexts, the fundamental attribution error can operate to introduce bias that, by playing into unconscious group-based stereotypes, may distort judgments about blame and responsibility. Thus, for example, if a black student gives a poor response to a question in class, a white professor might unconsciously attribute his poor performance to the black student's lack of ability or to his lack of commitment, in line with negative stereotypes of blacks as unintelligent and lazy. However, if a white student seems unprepared and responds poorly, the same white professor may also wonder whether the student is ill or whether she had a family emergency that prevented her from preparing. Because the white student's poor response does not activate negative stereotypes associated with whites as a group, the professor may be more inclined to search for situational factors that arguably "caused" the lack of preparation and thus may be more likely to excuse the student's poor performance.

The important point about the fundamental attribution error for our purposes is that, because of the widespread nature of gender and racial stereotypes, we can expect that the causal attribution process as it is engaged in by judges and jurors will at times also be distorted by stereotyping. Causal explanations that are consistent with stereotypes linked to a party's gender or racial group will more readily come to the mind and will be more likely to stick when decision makers in personal injury cases decide issues of liability.

Related to the fundamental attribution error and of particular significance to determinations of factual causation is the phenomenon known as "normality bias." Psychologists explain that the "normality bias" makes it easier for people to imagine a different result when an event is considered to be unusual than when the event is regarded as normal.[29] In tort cases, the normality bias has the potential to affect the framing steps that Robertson sees as integral to the legal analysis of causation. As mentioned earlier, to answer the "but-for" question, the judge or jury must "mentally correct" the defendant's conduct in order to frame the counterfactual question of whether the injury would still have occurred if defendant had acted reasonably or "correctly." This judgment requires an exercise of imagination, specifically imagining whether and how events could have unfolded differently. The "normality bias" comes into play at this point, as Professor Lu-in Wang explains it, because we have "difficulty imagining alternatives to scenarios that we perceive as normal, routine, or unexceptional, but can easily recast events that strike us as surprising or unusual."[30]

In this connection, psychologists refer to the "mutability" of events, meaning the ease with which we can mentally alter a factual event. Simply put, an event that strikes us as abnormal is more mutable than one that seems unexceptional. And, most important, the more mutable an event, the more likely people will be to identify the event as "causal."[31] The normality bias means that when a legal decision maker sees harm arising in the presence of abnormal conditions, there is a greater tendency to "lock in on those conditions as causal, and the agent who brought about those abnormal conditions . . . [as] responsible for the harm."[32]

Not surprisingly, in some cases, the normality bias may play into well-entrenched ideas and expectations about the likelihood of suffering experienced by members of different social groups. Critical race scholar Richard Delgado gives the example of the response to the eviction of an upper-class white family from a suburban home and compares it to the response to the suffering of starving Biafran children as seen on television.[33] In part because the eviction of the affluent, white family is such a rarity and violates norms about the type of families that end up on the street, that family's predicament is apt to elicit greater sympathy from an observer than that of the African children, whose plight we have come to associate with starvation and death. As Wang sees it, the normality bias "predisposes us to sympathize more with those who typically suffer less and inures us to the pain of hardships we expect."[34]

In the torts context, the normality bias can mean that judges and jurors might find it harder to imagine negative events turning out differently when those events correspond to the hardship and suffering we have come to associate with plaintiff's social group. This "failure of imagination" in turn may affect judgments about causation, insofar as decision makers are not predisposed to look for causes outside the victim's own conduct for an understanding of what happened. Like the tendency to ascribe the behavior of an outsider to his character or disposition, rather than to scrutinize the situation to see how it may have contributed to the outcome, the normality bias has the potential to discourage jurors or judges from considering causes for a plaintiff's injury other than the conduct of the victim herself.

Finally, a well-documented psychological tendency to attribute the cause of events to precipitating actions, rather than to inaction, may reinforce the normality bias in particular cases, further discouraging the search for outside causes. This "omission bias" describes the tendency of people to place blame on actions for bad results, rather than on otherwise equivalent omissions. [35] Actions speak louder than failures to act, psychologists suggest, because it is easier mentally to "undo" an action, thus facilitating the counterfactual reasoning process. Behavioral scientists Robert Prentice and Jonathan Koehler note how the omission and normality biases often work in tandem in a typical situation in which inaction and omission serve to preserve a normal state of affairs.[36] In such a case, it may be particularly difficult for a judge or jury to ascribe causal significance to a defendant's failure to act when the bad outcome is considered normal, in part because of the social identity of the plaintiff.

Wrongful Birth Cases

Cultural shifts in understandings of causation are most often gradual and hard to detect. In one genre of cases, however, it is quite easy to trace marked changes in causal attribution, linked to the rapid medical, scientific, and cultural developments related to gender and reproduction. The "wrongful birth" tort claim is a product of the late 1960s and 1970s, arising on the heels of the women's liberation movement and closely aligned with *Roe v. Wade*,[37] the 1973 decision of the U.S. Supreme Court that afforded women a constitutional right to seek abortion during the early stages of pregnancy. Wrongful birth claims are typically malpractice claims, in which a woman—and often a couple—alleges that the doctor was negligent in failing to provide her with adequate prenatal treatment or advice. In most wrongful birth cases, the woman claims that she gave birth to a child with serious genetic disorders and was never warned by her doctor of such a risk. What makes the wrongful birth claim distinctive is that the crux of the case turns on plaintiff's causal assertion that she would have chosen to terminate the pregnancy if she had been properly advised or treated. Indeed, the name of the tort tracks the causal dimension of the claim: presumably, the birth is considered "wrongful" because it was avoidable and traceable to defendant's negligence.

Prior to the late 1960s, claims for wrongful birth were virtually unknown. There were a few cases in which plaintiffs succeeded in recovering damages when physicians negligently performed sterilization procedures and plaintiffs alleged that their malpractice resulted in unwanted pregnancies and births.[38] These "wrongful conception" cases, however, did not implicate the decision to abort and did not do very much to change the legal landscape.

By the 1980s, however, two powerful forces combined to increase the chances that wrongful birth claims would be filed and would be more palatable to judges and juries, although the claim still remains controversial and is far from universally recognized.[39] On the medical front, advances in scientific knowledge about genetic and other risks to fetuses made it possible to predict which women were at a higher risk of giving birth to children with serious disabilities, developments that rendered the reproductive process less mysterious and inevitable. On the cultural side, the women's movement and its influence on the law made it possible for tort plaintiffs to articulate and assert a right to control their own reproduction and to place responsibility on doctors who allegedly interfered with such right.

Many of the early wrongful birth cases involved women who had contracted rubella (German measles) during the first months of pregnancy. The connection between rubella and prenatal injury had become widely known since 1964, when a rubella epidemic in the United States resulted in 20,000 fetal deaths and 30,000 cases of severe birth defects.[40] The science indicated that the risks of rubella to women in their first trimester of pregnancy were especially high: approximately 25 percent of infants born to women in this group had congenital rubella syndrome, which included such serious effects as microcephaly, mental retardation, and congenital heart defects.[41] Given the severity of these risks, a strong case could be made that physicians owed a duty to counsel their patients about the dangers of rubella, in line with norms of "informed consent" that were also being developed at the time.

By the mid-1970s, a new crop of wrongful birth cases appeared, centering on a physician's failure to recommend amniocentesis, a test that could be used to detect the presence of Down Syndrome in a fetus.[42] Down Syndrome is a nonhereditary genetic disorder characterized by mental retardation and a constellation of physical abnormalities. Physicians began to recommend the amniocentesis procedure for women over age thirty-five at the date of delivery, the age at which the risk of carrying a child with Down Syndrome is roughly equal to the risk of miscarriage caused by the procedure itself, approximately .5 percent.[43] These wrongful birth cases, often involving older mothers and less severely disabled children, formed the backdrop against which sharply contested views about the desirability of the new cause of action and the assignment of cause and responsibility played out as the tort was introduced in the various states.

By the late 1990s, the potential for wrongful birth suits in diverse contexts grew considerably. By that time, there were at least 800 tests available to diagnose risks to a fetus, including tests for hereditary disorders such as Tay-Sachs disease, sickle cell anemia, hemophilia, muscular dystrophy, and cystic fibrosis.[44] One common test that emerged in this period, for example, is an AFP blood test, typically conducted in the fifteenth week of pregnancy, that detects certain abnormal levels of protein associated with birth defects.[45] Because the AFP test has a high rate of false positives, however, physicians often must also decide whether to recommend amniocentesis for pregnant women who "fail" the AFP test, at the risk of being charged with negligence if they unreasonably fail to order the test.

The scientific and medical developments of the era were matched in significance and scope by changing cultural attitudes and social practices related to reproduction. Reproductive rights were high on the agenda of women's rights organizations, whose members sought to transform the ways physicians, employers, and governmental institutions approached pregnancy, motherhood, and the intersection of work and family. Second-wave feminists of the late 1960s and 1970s pushed against prevailing cultural norms, which had defined women in terms of their reproductive capacity and assigned to women the primary burden of caring for children and maintaining a household.[46] In several important "equal protection" victories in the U.S. Supreme Court, for example, feminists persuaded the Court to hold gender-based laws unconstitutional because they were premised on antiquated "breadwinner/homemaker" assumptions about the roles of husbands and wives that tended to reinforce stereotypes of women as naturally domestic and disadvantage "nontraditional" women in the workplace.[47] The precarious status of pregnant women in the workplace was also ameliorated by judicial and congressional action that made it illegal to force pregnant women to quit their jobs and equated discrimination on the basis of pregnancy to discrimination on the basis of sex.[48]

Most important for our purposes, through a variety of legal doctrines, the law began to recognize a right of self-determination in matters of reproduction and to conceptualize reproduction as a choice subject to individual control, rather than as a natural, inevitable process. Even prior to *Roe v. Wade*, major Supreme Court precedents established a right of access to contraceptives for both married and unmarried persons, which allowed women to take advantage of the birth control pill and other new methods to control their fertility and to plan for parenthood in ways not heretofore possible.[49] The constitutional "privacy" rationale for protecting reproductive rights shifted the locus of decision making from the state, with its enforcement of community standards of morality, to the individual and, in the process, built up an expectation of individual control over reproduction. As Justice Brennan famously observed in *Eisenstadt v. Baird*, "if the right of privacy means anything, it is the right of the individual, married or single, to be free from unwanted governmental intrusion into matters so fundamentally affecting a person as the decision whether to bear or beget a child."[50]

Cumulatively, these rapid changes in public policy affecting pregnancy, contraception, and abortion were quite dramatic: reproduction was revealed to be a human activity and squarely placed within the social realm. To be sure, the changes in thinking and policy were partial and highly contested, as the newer, more egalitarian conception of women and reproduction competed with traditional views of women solely as wives and mothers. When the first wrongful birth cases emerged in the courts, the contending views were vividly on display, producing sharply differing judicial opinions that map quite closely onto the "pro-choice" or the "pro-life" perspective.

The initial battles over recognition of a cause of action for wrongful birth were fought in large part over the terrain of causation. Courts first tended to dismiss claims for wrongful birth, citing lack of proof of causation. The most famous wrongful birth case, *Gleitman v. Cosgrove*, decided prior to *Roe*, was a 1967 decision by the Supreme Court of New Jersey denying a cause of action.[51] In a sharply split 4-3 decision, the majority in *Gleitman* denied recovery to a woman who had contracted rubella while pregnant and who claimed that her physician had falsely represented that the disease would have no effect on her child. When she gave birth to a son who was partially blind and deaf and suffered other serious disabilities, she and her husband sued, on their own behalf and on behalf of the child, to recover a host of damages stemming from the doctor's negligence, including the extraordinary expenses associated with the child's special needs. Although most abortions were illegal in New Jersey at that time, plaintiff alleged that she would have been able to secure a lawful abortion elsewhere if she had been correctly apprised of the risks.

Presaging what would become the consensus position, the New Jersey court held that the child, as a plaintiff in his own right, had no cognizable legal claim against the doctor. According to the court, the child's so-called wrongful life claim could not be brought because it would require the court to compare the value of an impaired life against the value of no life at all (or, as the court put it, "the utter void of nonexistence"), a comparison the court was unwilling to make.

When it came to the mother's and father's claim for wrongful birth, however, the court acknowledged the doctor's breach of duty toward his patient but nevertheless ruled that a crucial element of the claim was lacking. According to the court, "[i]n the present case there is no contention that anything the defendants could have done would have decreased the likelihood that the infant would be born with defects." For this reason, it flatly declared that "[t]he conduct of defendants was not the cause of the infant plaintiff's condition."

Even after *Roe* was decided, several states continued to refuse to recognize the claim and continued to dispute causation.[52] An influential opinion turned out to be a dissenting opinion from Justice Sol Wachtler, who then sat on the Court of Appeals of New York, the state's highest court.[53] The case involved a child born with Down Syndrome to a woman over age thirty-five who was never advised about the availability of amniocentesis. Justice Wachtler thought it clear that the doctor should escape liability, concluding that "the heart of the problem in these cases is that the physician cannot be said to have caused the defect." He drew a sharp contrast between wrongful birth cases involving the failure of a physician to detect a birth defect during a prenatal examination and other malpractice cases in which "the doctor has failed to make a timely diagnosis of a curable disease." For Wachtler, the wrongful birth cases stood out as distinctive because "[t]he child's handicap is an inexorable result of conception and birth." In his estimation, holding the physician liable was tantamount to recognizing a "medical paternity suit," in which the physician would be forced to take on the father's traditional role of financially supporting the child.[54] Justice Wachtler's position on causation found favor in socially conservative states and was subsequently endorsed by the highest courts in Georgia, North Carolina, and Missouri, which all rejected the wrongful birth claim.[55]

By the 1980s, the tide began to turn as several courts began to recognize a right to sue for wrongful birth.[56] In endorsing the claim, the Supreme Court of New Hampshire, for example, pointed to recent scientific developments, most notably amniocentesis, which had increased the ability of health-care professionals to predict and detect the presence of fetal defects.[57] The New Hampshire court also felt bound by *Roe* to use tort law to protect a woman's right to terminate her pregnancy. For these courts, proof of causation was no longer considered an insuperable obstacle, even though they frequently set limits on the types of damages plaintiffs could recover in such cases.[58] Instead, the courts had little trouble with cause-in-fact and simply applied the "but-for" test in a straightforward fashion. They reasoned that if the mother had been properly counseled by her physician, she would have secured an abortion and would not have incurred the emotional and financial expenses of raising an impaired child.

Put in those terms, the causation issue seemed simple and made it appear surprising that there would be a split in the jurisdictions on this fundamental issue. By the 1990s, some courts were willing to trace the causal chain out even further. An appellate court in Maryland, for example, ruled that parents of a child born with spina bifida could recover for a physician's failure to inform them of the existence of AFP testing, used to detect elevated levels of protein, arguing that the results of such test would have caused the physician to order further diagnostic tests, which ultimately would have led to the parents' decision to abort the child.[59]

It is telling that these sharply differing approaches to causation occurred in the wrongful birth cases, despite the fact that all courts embraced the "but-for" test and applied a counterfactual analytical framework. The critical difference between the two lines of cases, however, lies not in the choice of a legal standard but rather relates to how the causation issue was framed. The courts that allowed the wrongful birth claim did not ask whether the child's disabilities could have been avoided if the physician acted correctly. Rather, they centered their analysis on the mother's right to reproductive choice and informed consent. For these courts, the injury stemmed from the denial of individual choice and self-determination, the constitutional right guaranteed by *Roe*. The courts receptive to claims of wrongful birth opened up the causation question to permit plaintiffs to argue that their doctor's negligence had led to serious injury, even if it did not produce the medical condition that affected the child. In contrast, the courts that continued to disallow the claim clung to a narrower, more traditional view of causation that required the plaintiff to show a link between the doctor's action and the child's illness or disease.

It seems clear that changing social practices relating to abortion and reproductive choice affected how courts and litigators framed the causation inquiry. Once reproduction was seen as a mutable process—a process that could be halted by human choice—it was far easier to attribute the injury to sources beyond the body of the woman herself and to place some responsibility on the treating physician. Applying Robertson's causation analysis, what was really at stake in these cases was a struggle to define the injury and thereby set the frame for the causation inquiry. The courts that allowed the claim saw the injury as a dignitary harm to the parents that deprived them of the opportunity to make a critical personal choice.

In the wrongful birth cases, the shift in causation analysis in the 1980s was propelled by a shift in public policy relating to women's rights, as the new politics of reproductive rights found its way into "neutral" causation analysis. Moreover, it is not surprising that the status of the wrongful birth claim never totally stabilized, given the volatility and ferocity of opinion surrounding abortion in the larger culture. Significantly, as part of the wave of antichoice legislation in the 1990s, some states enacted statutes abolishing the wrongful birth claim, making protection against physician negligence depend on the particular jurisdiction.[60]

In retrospect, the pivotal issue in the wrongful birth cases seemed to boil down to whether the courts and legislatures would allow a new conception of reproduction to influence the shape of tort claims. The courts that permitted wrongful birth claims regarded them as integral to more general protection against medical malpractice and as simply a species of informed-consent litigation. As one court explained, to deny a claim would create a "void in recovery for medical malpractice," leaving pregnant patients with less protection against physician negligence than patients who had other medical conditions.[61] Under this view, recognition of the claim of wrongful birth "normalized" pregnancy by treating it on a par with other medical conditions. The wrongful birth claims thus directly responded to feminist arguments of the day that reproduction and women's reproductive health should not be excised from the duties of due care owed by physicians to their patients and that patient self-determination should not be diminished by the fact of a woman's pregnancy.[62]

The shift in causal thinking evident in the wrongful birth cases also suggests how cultural change can influence the counterfactual reasoning process that is so central to application of the "but-for" test. Seen through the lens of cognitive psychology, the wrongful birth cases reflect not simply a change in available medical technologies but also a shift in causal attribution. Put most simply, the early cases tended to locate responsibility for the child's condition "internally," placing blame on the mother and on natural forces. Later cases, however, were willing to extend responsibility to "external" forces, namely the physician and other health-care personnel who provided prenatal advice and care. For the early courts, reproduction was conceptualized as a natural, normal, inexorable process leading to the birth of a child. Some judges, as exemplified in Justice Sol Wachtler's opinion, seemed unable or unwilling to imagine a different result. In contrast, in the decade after *Roe*, courts began to regard reproduction as a mutable process, subject to human intervention. They were able to imagine events unfolding in a different way, perhaps leading to abortion, rather than birth.

In the judicial debate over cause-in-fact in this genre of cases, we can see the operation of each of the three cognitive biases discussed earlier—the fundamental attribution error, the bias toward normality, and the omission bias. The bias toward normality is perhaps most prominent. In the context of wrongful birth, the bias toward normality is likely to come into play when a judge finds it hard to imagine a result other than what actually occurred, largely because what occurred is considered to be normal. Since the normality bias works to make it difficult to even imagine a departure from what is customary, it becomes equally difficult to imagine that such a departure would have made a difference in the outcome. Thus, in the early cases rejecting the wrongful birth claim, judges seemed to regard the live birth of a child as the inevitable and normal result of the reproductive process, even if the child turned out to be impaired in some way.[63] This "fact" about reproduction, with its inalterable nature, drove the courts to conclude that the doctor's role had no causal significance in producing the bad result. Despite plaintiffs' allegations, the courts framed the "but-for" inquiry in a way that refused to regard abortion as a realistic alternative, precisely because such a course of action would not have produced a healthy child. Under this view, it was hard to envision a woman escaping her fate, given that some unfortunate percentage of women invariably gave birth to impaired children. In this pre-*Roe* world view, giving birth to a defective child was something that just happened to some women in the normal course of events that could not be cured by a legal remedy.

In the later wrongful birth cases, courts began to imagine counterfactual scenarios in which pregnant women exercised some control over the reproductive process, including the choice to abort. Legalizing abortion through *Roe* gave force to the physician's duty to give their patients complete information about the risks of carrying a particular pregnancy to term. In a post-*Roe* world, a new norm emerged in which physicians were expected to deploy the new medical technologies in service of their patients' choice. In turn, these social practices made it possible for parties and judges to speculate about "what might have been," had physicians acted differently by, for example, administering an amniocentesis or providing other prenatal tests. In 1973, *Roe* divided up pregnancy into definable trimesters, rather than visualizing it as a continuous, inexorable process. Similarly, by the 1980s, pregnancy began to be viewed as a process involving steps and stages that required distinct actions and decisions. It was this transformation, we believe, that induced judges to reframe the causation inquiry and to find causation present in cases in which the plaintiff convinced the court that, "but-for" the defendant's negligence, she would have exercised her right to terminate the pregnancy.

It is also likely that the omission bias worked in tandem with the normality bias to influence causation judgments in wrongful birth cases. In the early cases, the courts seemed impressed by the fact that the physician did not take any active steps to increase the likelihood that the child would be born with defects.[64] The courts were disinclined to judge the physician's failure to act harshly, especially given that the bad result the plaintiff suffered was considered part of the normal process of reproduction. For these courts, the physician's omissions were judged to be harmless because they did not interrupt the reproductive process in a way that directly injured the developing fetus.

Insofar as they dismissed negligent failures to act on the part of physicians, these early wrongful birth cases presented a curious logic that seems inconsistent with the approach taken in other types of malpractice cases. The courts were undoubtedly familiar with misdiagnosis cases brought against physicians for failing to detect problems that they did not create. Consider a medical malpractice case in which the plaintiff alleges that the doctor failed to read an X-ray correctly and thus failed to detect a bone anomaly that required prompt surgical treatment to correct. In such cases, the gravamen of plaintiff's claim is that the negligent omission by the physician caused the plaintiff's harm, even though the doctor's action did nothing to create the bone anomaly. Indeed, the physician's only breach of duty is the failure to read the X-ray correctly and thus to ensure the best outcome for the patient. Unlike other actors who have no special relationship to their victims, physicians cannot be heard to argue that they have no duty to act, precisely because of the special contractual and professional duties they take on with respect to their patients.

Seen in this light, a doctor's negligent failure to act can be just as harmful and just as causally relevant as active negligence. What differentiates the wrongful birth cases from the X-ray case, however, is that not even the best treatment and advice can cure or ameliorate the child's condition. In the wrongful birth case, the exercise of due care by the physician guarantees only that the plaintiff's choice will be informed and that she will be in the best position to decide whether to have an abortion and thus avoid the subsequent costs of childbearing and childrearing. The courts that have endorsed the wrongful birth claim do their best to value and measure this choice, much in the same way that courts have struggled with setting damages in malpractice and "loss-of-a-chance" cases involving treatment of cancer patients and other patients with terminal illnesses.

Finally, the wrongful birth cases present a good opportunity to reflect on how notions of gender interact with the fundamental attribution error to affect causal judgments. In retrospect, the greatest shift that took place in the wrongful birth cases was a shift in focus: the early cases focused almost exclusively on internal conditions, whereas the later cases also assessed the influence of external conditions. In its simplest form, the causal issue presented in the wrongful birth cases is whether the harm flows from something inside the body of the mother, such as a disease or an abnormality in the fetus, or from external forces, such as the failure of the physician to treat the pregnant woman properly during the initial stages of her pregnancy.

The fundamental attribution error comes into play when the person making the causal judgment fixes on dispositional factors, such as the presence of rubella in the pregnant woman or the age of the pregnant woman at the time she gave birth to a baby with Down syndrome, as the full explanation for the adverse outcome. This tendency to fix on dispositional factors leads to a disinclination to see and assess the causal significance of situational factors, such as the doctor's inadequate prenatal testing and advice. Like lay persons, judges often seek out simple, one-cause explanations for complex events. Rather than viewing a wrongful birth claim as inevitably involving multiple causes, the early courts seemed to ignore the situational factors and focused exclusively on the traits and condition of the pregnant woman and her fetus.

This tendency to fix responsibility solely on the pregnant woman fits with traditional notions of gender and reproduction. Prior to the legal and cultural changes put into place on the heels of the feminist movement in the 1970s, the idea that "biology is woman's destiny" signified a commonly held view that women had a unique role as childbearers and bore primary responsibility for reproduction and the rearing of children.[65] It is thus not surprising that, when something went wrong in connection with childbirth, judges and other decision makers would fix on the dispositional traits and condition of the pregnant woman as the prime causal agent, in line with stereotypes of women as naturally responsible for their children.

Equally as important is the fact that wrongful birth litigation took place in a highly gendered setting. When the cases were first brought in the 1970s and

1980s, they pitted pregnant women, as the primary plaintiffs, against medical professionals, who were overwhelming male. Because the courts were also heavily male-dominated at that time, the judge was also likely to be male. In assessing causation, it is quite possible that a judge would think of the plaintiff and her predicament as foreign to his personal experience and would more readily empathize with the defendant physician, a professional whose judgment and action were being subjected to close scrutiny. Without being conscious of gender bias, if a judge regarded the female plaintiff in the case as the "other," the fundamental attribution error might come into play to point to the dispositional traits of the "outsider" as the likely cause of the bad outcome and away from the situational encounter with the physician.

In particular, Justice Wachtler's opinion sharply disputing causation in an amniocentesis/Down Syndrome case seems tinged with gender. As mentioned earlier, Wachtler analogized the plaintiff's claim to a "medical paternity suit" as part of his argument that it would be unjust to hold the doctor responsible for this failure to order the test, even though that failure constituted negligence by prevailing professional standards. At first blush, the analogy seems odd because, unlike paternity suits, wrongful birth claims have nothing to do with determining the identity of the biological father of the child. However, from a distinctively male point of view, the two types of suits might appear to have one thing in common: in each, a woman attempts to force a man to take on financial responsibility for her child, against the man's protests. By choosing this strained analogy, Wachtler signaled his concern for such a shifting of responsibility for children onto men and rhetorically aligned himself with the interests of men who resist claims by pregnant women. From the plaintiff's perspective, the analogy could readily be seen as insulting and as activating damaging stereotypes of women as dependent and irresponsible. Wachtler's rhetoric thus subtly reinforced his causal judgment, allowing gender to shade into his opinion, without expressly mentioning gender roles or gender politics.

Lead Paint Cases

Compared to the wrongful birth cases, it is harder to isolate the cultural aspects of causal judgments made by courts in cases brought by children exposed to lead paint. In this new genre of cases, considerations of race and gender are hidden in low-profile pretrial procedural rulings and bound up in scientific questions relating to the origins of complex cognitive impairments, such as learning disabilities, lowered IQs, attention-deficit hyperactivity disorder (ADHD), and mental retardation. Specifically, race and gender enter into the equation when courts exercise their discretion about the proper scope of discovery and are called upon to judge the plausibility of counterfactual scenarios posed by lead paint litigants.

At bottom, the lead paint cases present a battle over legal responsibility in a "multiple-cause" context. Most of the cases have involved a parent or guardian who sues a landlord on behalf of a child, alleging that the child suffered cognitive injuries as a result of the landlord's negligence in failing to eliminate or abate hazards from lead paint in their dwellings.[66] The plaintiff's case rests on proving that a source of the child's injury was external, that is, caused at least in part by exposure to the lead paint, rather than stemming exclusively from internal sources, such as the child's heredity or family environment.

Today, the most common source of high-dose lead exposure in young children comes from lead-based paint and lead-contaminated house dust and soil.[67] Although lead paint was banned for residential use in the 1970s, hazardous conditions can still be found in old, poorly maintained, apartments and houses, usually in urban dwellings built before 1950, where there is peeling, flaking, and chipping paint.[68] This deteriorating housing is occupied predominantly by racial minorities who have low incomes.[69] In such residences, children are at higher risk for lead exposure than adults, simply because children more often put their fingers in their mouths and because they absorb lead more readily than do adults. Additionally, exposure to lead can be long-lasting: once a child's lead level is elevated, it may take years before the level can be lowered.

Exposure to lead paint has a strong racial correlation in that elevated blood lead levels are more commonly found among African American and Hispanic children than among white children. According to survey data published in 2003, fully 76 percent of children with elevated blood levels are either African American or Hispanic.[70] African African children are especially likely to be exposed: the same survey found that a striking 60 percent of children with elevated blood lead levels were African American. Even within low-income populations, studies have indicated that blood lead levels of African American children are significantly higher than those of similarly situated white children. One survey, for example, indicated that in urban households with income levels between $6,000 and $14,999, approximately 54 percent of black children but only 23 percent of white children had blood lead levels above 15 micrograms per deciliter.[71] The survey's documentation of concentration of lead exposure in minority children—and African American children in particular—has been widely confirmed.[72] Given the exposure to lead paint in properties occupied by racial minorities and the consequent higher rates of elevated blood lead levels in children who are African American or Hispanic, it is not surprising that a large proportion of lawsuits for lead paint poisoning have been brought on behalf of minority children.[73]

Plaintiffs in lead paint litigation have had little trouble proving general causation, which requires proof that the substance in question (i.e., lead) is capable of causing the disease from which the plaintiff suffers.[74] It is significant that lead is the "most extensively studied environmental neurotoxicant."[75] It is now well established that exposure to lead causes permanent harm to the central nervous systems of children and that, in high enough doses, lead can lead to severe brain injury or even death. Most important for lead litigation, dozens of epidemiological studies have shown that exposure to lead can result in a lowering of IQ in exposed children.[76] In this respect, expert testimony about the numerous harms of lead is on a surer footing than expert testimony in other toxic-tort cases in which the scientific evidence is more recent and less certain.

In a 2005 report, the Centers for Disease Control cautioned that there is no safe threshold level of exposure to lead.[77] Since 1991, however, the CDC has set the "level of concern" at 10 micrograms per deciliter of blood when assessing blood lead levels in children.[78] Scientific studies of the effects of lead on children at these relatively low levels, and even at lower levels, conclude that exposure to lead is linked to lowered IQs, to poor performance on tests of attention, and to ADHD. Additionally, lead-poisoned children are more likely to have learning disabilities and to make slow progress in school than other children. As with many other toxic-related injuries, however, the exact biological mechanism through which lead causes harm is not yet known.

In addition to proving general causation, plaintiffs in lead paint cases have likewise generally had little difficulty proving that they have been exposed to lead from a source under control of the defendant landlord. As proof of such exposure, plaintiffs typically point to medical records of lead levels in the child plaintiff's blood and to inspection reports of lead paint in the child's dwelling. To date, there has been little dispute that the source of the elevated lead levels in plaintiff's blood was the apartment or other dwelling owned by the defendant, except in cases in which plaintiffs resided in more than one dwelling containing a lead paint hazard.

In virtually all the cases, moreover, plaintiffs have been prepared to offer expert testimony to demonstrate specific injury or harm to the plaintiff child.[79] This showing is typically made through expert review of the child's medical and educational records, examination of the child, and the conducting of a battery of tests. In one case, for example, plaintiff presented testimony from a pediatrician and a neuropsychologist who diagnosed the child as suffering from ADHD, oppositional defiant disorder, a reading disorder, and other cognitive disorders, all described as "permanent conditions."[80] In combination with testimony from the school psychologist and plaintiff's mother, the experts painted a grim portrait of plaintiff's prospects as being severely hampered by "lifelong difficulties" that made her a "social pariah" at school and significantly depressed her future capacity to earn a living.

The precise issue on which the heated debate in the lead paint cases has centered is specific causation, namely tying the individual plaintiff's injury to exposure to the toxic substance. This aspect of proof essentially requires plaintiff to link the lead exposure to his or her individual cognitive deficits—in the "but-for" sense of factual causation—by arguing that, absent such exposure, the injuries would not have occurred or would not have been as severe. It is important to note here that, in line with the limited role for factual causation and the "eggshell plaintiff" rule, a plaintiff in such a case need not prove that lead exposure was the sole cause of the injuries. It should be enough for the plaintiff to prove that lead was one of multiple causes of the injuries or that the exposure to lead aggravated or precipitated those injuries.

The principal defense strategy in lead paint litigation has been to attempt to negate specific causation by offering an alternative theory of plaintiff's injury, namely that plaintiff's disability was caused by genetic factors or by the plaintiff's family environment. As one litigator wrote in 2006, "[t]ypically, defense attorneys will argue that a lead exposed child's deficits and behavioral problems are due to environmental or inherited physiological or psychological factors."[81] In its simplest form, the typical defense argument is that plaintiffs' cognitive deficits were "passed on" to them by their parents or were a result of harmful parenting practices, most often fixing on the behavior of the child's mother during pregnancy and thereafter. In essence, this alternative causation argument attempts to show that, in the specific case, the child's exposure to lead was harmless, despite the general tendency of lead poisoning to cause the type of harm suffered by the child. The basic claim is that the child would have experienced the same cognitive deficits even absent the exposure to lead.

In crafting their alternative causation arguments, defendants have benefited from the fact that, in contrast to injuries caused by toxic substances such as asbestos, exposure to lead does not produce a "signature" injury that indisputably links the harm exclusively to exposure to the toxin. Instead, the cognitive injuries of which plaintiffs complain in lead paint cases can be produced by a number of other sources, in addition to toxic exposure. Thus, in a 2004 article in the *Defense Counsel Journal*, an author explained why, in his view, lead paint litigation has not been a "gold mine" for plaintiffs, comparable to tobacco or asbestos litigation.[82] The author observed that

> [I]n most childhood lead poisoning cases, the claimed injuries are most often cognitive or behavioral in nature—diminished intellectual capacity, poor school performance, attentional disorders, even juvenile delinquency . . . [these conditions] also have a myriad of other potential causes, including maternal and paternal intelligence, low birth weight, prenatal alcohol and drug exposure, poor nutrition, inadequate or inferior schools, single-parent families, lower socio-economic status and many other variables. Childhood lead poisoning is today most prevalent in *urban, low-income areas where many of these variables come into play.* Separating the effects of lead exposure on a child's intellectual and cognitive status from the effects of these other variables is a hugely difficult, if not impossible task for most childhood lead poisoning plaintiffs.[83]

As the article suggests, counsel for landlords in lead paint litigation have taken advantage of the lack of a signature injury to seize upon the cultural and racial context in which childhood lead poisoning occurs as a way to shift attention away from the external hazard present in the dwelling and to scrutinize the child's background and family situation. Although the author does not specifically mention the race or ethnic membership of the prototypical plaintiff in lead paint litigation, his use of the code words "urban, low-income area" easily conjure up an image of an inner-city inhabitant who is a member of a racial or ethnic minority group. Additionally, the author's recitation of the myriad social problems cognitively associated with the brand of racialized poverty commonly found in the United States—namely drug and alcohol addiction, single-parent households, inferior schools—reinforces the idea that the problem of lead paint poisoning is inseparable from the problems facing low-income minorities generally and suggests that it is unfair to attribute cognitive deficits to exposure to lead. In an unsubtle way, this shift in emphasis highlights the racial and socioeconomic component of childhood lead exposure cases in a way that overshadows the causal effects of exposure to lead.

As discussed earlier, the victims of lead poisoning are disproportionately minority children from lower-income families. Their exposure to lead stems from the fact that such children are more likely to live in deteriorating dwellings where lead hazards have not been abated. The gender effect comes into play in childhood lead-poisoning cases through the demographic fact that most cases of exposure occur in households headed by women. In this area, the focus in the scientific research and in the cases tends to be on the role of mothers, rather than fathers, whether in assessing the child's heredity or family upbringing. As one neuropsychologist explained:

> [M]ost of the discussion has focused upon mothers. . . . First, mothers are typically more available than fathers to participate in long term research projects. Second, in lead paint litigation the majority of children come from single parent homes headed by the mother and information regarding the father is unavailable. Third, even in homes in which both parents are present and share responsibilities for child rearing, the mother typically controls the environment.[84]

Some of the arguments presented by defendants have quite explicitly traded on popular conceptions of personal responsibility that tend to blame genetics and poor mothering for the behavioral and psychological problems of children, especially poor, minority children. For example, in a 2006 oral argument before a New York trial judge, the lawyer for the plaintiff resisted discovery of a mother's educational records dating from the 1970s, contending that they did not have the tendency to prove that her child's ADHD was genetic in origin.[85] Especially because ADHD was not a documented diagnosis until the 1980s, plaintiff argued that, even if the mother's educational records showed that she had performed poorly in school, it would not tend to prove the origin of child's ADHD but would only generate additional questions as to why the mother had done poorly in school. Plaintiff expressed concern that the defendant would attempt to use the records to "prejudice a jury" by saying that "we all know the apple doesn't fall far from the tree," hoping to convince the jury that "if this kid is doing poorly in school, that's not a result of lead, it's because he's the son of the mother." The defense counsel responded that, aside from the question of whether the child's condition was genetically based, the mother's educational records should be discoverable, claiming that "the fact that mom was doing poorly in school is, in and of itself relevant, in diagnosing the child . . . if mom's doing poorly in school, it sort of reflects on the home environment and whether or not the child at issue in this case is at home listening to Shakespeare being read to him or her, or in front of a video game eight hours out of the day."

What is most striking about the argument in this case is how defense counsel used both genetics and home environment to suggest that, under the circumstances, the child's impairments were normal, that they were simply a part of the child's ordinary lot in life. The rhetorical contrast between the (presumably middle- or upper-class) child who spends time listening to Shakespeare and the (presumably lower-class) child who spends eight hours a day playing video games works well to activate stereotypes of poor children as slow and lacking in intellectual curiosity, even absent exposure to lead paint. This portrait of the low-income child suggests that it is poverty—and neglectful parenting supposedly associated with poverty—that should be the key variable of interest, deflecting attention from the contribution of exposure to lead.

In the past decade, these variables of race, poverty, and gender have surfaced primarily in the pretrial legal skirmishes in lead paint litigation. For the most part, courts have not yet ruled on ultimate questions of causation, nor have they decided whether defendants' attempts to avoid liability by pointing to genetics and family environment as causal factors should succeed. Instead, the controversy has involved the scope of discovery and has engaged causal issues only preliminarily and indirectly. Specifically, in an effort to delve into family history, counsel representing landlords in lead paint litigation have sought to require production of medical, educational, and other personal records of the child's mother and sometimes siblings and half-siblings. Additionally, in many cases, defendants have gone beyond seeking existing records and have sought an order requiring the child's mother to submit to IQ and other psychological testing.[86]

In these cases, the defense strategy has been to open up the causation inquiry to investigate the psychological and medical condition of family members in an effort to establish a possible alternative causation theory for plaintiff's cognitive injuries. In support of their requests, defendants have typically stressed that the legal standard for granting discovery requests is quite lenient: material is discoverable if it has a tendency to prove or disprove a matter that is properly at issue in the case. In the context of lead paint litigation, defendants assert that material relating to family members is discoverable because it will aid in the resolution of the issue of causation.

In resisting defendants' discovery requests, plaintiffs have maintained that requests for discovery of personal records of individuals other than the parties to the litigation are on an entirely different footing than requests to the parties themselves and that, in particular, intrusive psychological testing of nonparties should be ordered only in extraordinary cases. They have argued that, in contrast to the child plaintiff, the mothers in lead paint cases have not put their mental states in issue and should not be subject to burdensome and potentially embarrassing discovery relating to their health, intelligence, and personal habits. At this early stage in the litigation, the strategy of plaintiffs has been to limit discovery to ascertainable facts relating to the child's own condition and his or her exposure to lead. They maintain that defendants are able to mount an adequate defense by gaining access to all the medical, educational, and other records pertaining specifically to the lead-exposed child and by having the defendant's own experts administer whatever psychological and other tests they wish to the child.

The discovery requests have required trial courts to evaluate competing concerns. They must analyze the potential relevance of the requested records and sought-after IQ test results in light of the hardship caused to family members and administrative concerns that overbroad discovery will lead to delay and confusion. In addition to raising issues of medical privilege, confidentiality of educational and other personal records of nonparties, and the rights of individuals to be free from compelled psychological testing, the discovery requests force litigants to address the difficult question of the etiology of cognitive disorders. In essence, plaintiffs contend that data on family members is of no relevance or of such marginal relevance that discovery requests to nonparties should generally be denied.

To date, the decisions on the permissible scope of discovery have been split, with variations both from state to state and even within states. The most prominent decision, *Andon v. 302-304 Mott Street Associates*, was issued in 2000 by the New York Court of Appeals, a state with a high number of lead paint cases.[87] *Andon* dealt exclusively with whether a mother could be compelled to submit to an IQ examination conducted by defendant's expert. In that case, Prudencia Andon, a Mexican American woman, resisted a trial court's order requiring her to submit to an IQ examination in connection with a suit for damages she brought on behalf of her son. The defendant claimed that the IQ test was needed to determine whether her son's alleged cognitive disabilities were genetic. In support of its motion, defendant relied on an affidavit from a pediatrician who cited "unidentified studies" for the proposition that maternal IQ was "extremely relevant" in assessing a child's potential cognitive development. The high court affirmed the lower appellate court's decision not to order the test, relying heavily on that court's broad discretion in ruling on discovery matters. The court below had determined that allowing the request would "hardly aid in the resolution of the question of causality" and that it would "dramatically broaden the scope of the litigation," turning the factfinding process into a "series of mini-trials regarding at a minimum, the factors contributing to the mother's IQ and possibly, that of other family members."[88] It cited the point made by one of us in a prior article that "[t]here is no logical end to the litigation inquiry once individual boundaries have been crossed."[89]

Significantly, however, even though the court ruled for the plaintiff, *Andon* emphasized that it was not creating a blanket rule prohibiting discovery and that lower courts should evaluate each discovery request on a case-by-case basis. This has meant that in New York there is still much variation in the rulings. Recent cases have both denied and allowed discovery requests, with no discernible difference in the facts of the cases. Additionally, one New York judge exercised his discretion by allowing the discovery of the academic records of the plaintiff's two nonparty siblings but denying requests to subject the parents to IQ testing.[90]

Outside New York, there is no clear trend. More courts have denied requests than have approved them. But the only other high court to rule on the issue—the Iowa Supreme Court—held that educational records of siblings of an African American child were admissible and affirmed a trial court's ruling of no liability for the defendant landlord.[91] As the issue percolates through the lower courts, however, the social significance of the discovery rulings is beginning to be appreciated. For example, one influential District of Columbia judge, who had issued the most comprehensive opinion in 1994 allowing IQ testing of a mother, subsequently changed his mind and began consistently to rule against ordering IQ examinations of nonparty family members in 2000, citing Jennifer Wriggins's scholarship discussing the race and gender impacts of this practice.[92]

One major reason that the cases have not yet produced a uniform position is that the science relating to the etiology of cognitive disorders is both difficult to understand and contested. It is well established that exposure to lead is linked to cognitive disorders. It is also clear that cognitive disorders are often produced by sources other than lead. Unfortunately, there is no foolproof scientific test to determine the source of a disorder in an individual case. Except for rare instances in which a child suffers an exceptionally serious, near-fatal exposure to lead, there will necessarily be some uncertainty as to specific causation, leaving room for a defendant to argue that the exposure did not produce the child's injury.

As in many other kinds of toxic tort cases, courts are called to determine whether the existing science relating to the disorder plausibly supports a party's causation or alternative-causation theory. It is important to note that most of the epidemiological studies on the harmful effects of lead exposure relied on by plaintiffs have controlled for a variety of factors (known as "confounding" variables) that might plausibly account for the incidence of the disease. A confounding variable is "an extraneous factor that independently associates with a higher or lower disease rate, but which is differentially present in the exposed [group]."[93] Thus, many of the lead studies of effects of relatively low levels of lead exposure on children have taken into account such variables as parents' educational level, family socioeconomic status, and mothers' IQ. Despite these controls, however, the studies continue to find harmful effects from lead. The repeated and consistent nature of the epidemiological studies strengthens the case for plaintiffs and makes it plausible that an exposed child's condition, at least in part, was traceable to lead, even in cases of children from poor families whose mothers have relatively low IQs. One court, for example, in denying defendant's requests for family medical and educational records, justified its ruling by noting that "[s]tudies of lead poisoning in children support that lead causes the same pro rata permanent cognitive damages in children regardless of the IQ and socioeconomic levels of the parents."[94]

In contrast, the science on which the defendants have relied to support their alternative-causation arguments based on heredity and family environment is speculative and seems largely designed to raise doubts about the validity of the studies relied upon by the plaintiff, without discrediting them directly. Defendants typically cite scientific evidence that finds that socioeconomic status is related to measures of intelligence—whether through nutrition, parental stimulation, or resources available in the home—and studies of identical twins raised by different families to argue that conditions such as ADHD have a genetic component.[95] In litigation, defendants' experts have emphasized that the scientific studies have not "definitively" shown a causal relationship between lead and cognitive disorders at lower blood-lead levels, exploiting lingering doubts that socioeconomic factors may play a more significant role than is currently believed. The basic strategy is to present expert testimony to minimize the role of lead as a causative agent in cognitive disorders and lowered IQ.[96] In one case, for example, to support its ruling ordering the production of a mother's educational records, a judge noted the defendant's expert opinion that "lead poisoning is at the bottom of the list of factors affecting causation for a plaintiff's deficits."[97] Perhaps because of the pretrial context in which these controversies have emerged, however, the cases lack detailed discussion about the crucial issue of precisely how and why these studies would serve to undercut plaintiff's epidemiological evidence that already controls for many of the variables that defendants cite as potentially causative agents.

Some of the confusion in the case law may stem from a failure to specify the precise causal burden plaintiff shoulders in lead paint litigation. Language in some cases suggests that plaintiff must show that lead is the sole cause of the child's injuries in order to prevail. In one Virginia case, for example, the court required plaintiff's mother to submit to an examination to assist defendant's expert in "determining whether any deficits the plaintiff may have are solely the result of lead poisoning or whether other factors, such as his mother's intelligence and education, are contributing factors."[98] Similarly, in the 2004 article in the *Defense Counsel Journal*, quoted earlier, the author assumed that plaintiff had the burden of "separating the effects of lead exposure on a child's intellectual and cognitive status from other variables," a task he described as "hugely difficult."[99] The courts and the litigants do not always approach the case as a "multiple-cause" situation in which defendant might be held responsible, even if other contributing causes are also found to be present. Rather, the debate in discovery often follows an "either-or" structure, implying that proof of the existence of other plausible causative agents automatically disproves plaintiff's case on causation.

Indeed, the interplay among potential multiple causative agents is itself a complex subject and subject to debate. In an article on genetic testing in toxic injury litigation, Professor Susan Poulter explains that even in cases of diseases with genetic components, exposure to toxic agents may nevertheless contribute to the harm.[100] The reason for this is that the genetic component may operate in one of two ways: it may predispose the plaintiff to injury, regardless of toxic exposure, or it may operate to "facilitate toxic injury by making an affected cell more or less susceptible to toxic insult." Tellingly, only in the first scenario, as Poulter explains, will arguments about alternative cause have any validity. In the second "susceptibility-to-toxic-insult" situation, the toxic substance continues to play a causal role in the injury.

Using the example of lead paint litigation, Poulter asserts that arguments predicated on an alternative-causation theory are problematic because they overlook the possibility that a genetic predisposition may actually operate in conjunction with exposure to lead, rather than instead of it, to produce cognitive disorders. Without a scientific basis for determining which of the two models is appropriate, Poulter concludes that there is no sound basis for treating genetic and toxic causes as mutually exclusive and thereby tacitly endorsing an alternative cause model, especially given that "current knowledge about how genetic variations predispose individuals to disease suggests that most commonly both genetics and toxic insult combine to produce disease."[101]

Given the difficulties with mounting an alternative cause defense, it is telling that defendants have nonetheless had some success in convincing courts to order production of sensitive records of nonparties and to compel mothers to submit to IQ testing. The defense strategy of attempting to extend discovery to nonparties and to prove the cause of plaintiff's injury by investigating medical histories of family members marks a radical departure from ordinary cases.[102] Traditionally, the procedural rules governing tort litigation have respected the boundary between plaintiffs and other persons, reflecting the tort system's focus on the individual. The common law's strong tradition of protecting the inviolability of the body has meant that only parties who have waived their objections to such intrusions by filing suit and putting their mental states in controversy must submit to medical examinations by defense experts.

To compel a mother who is not claiming injury on her own behalf to submit to IQ testing is not just an inconvenience. The information obtained through an IQ test involves access to one's mind and information about oneself that can profoundly affect a person's self-image and public image. Understandably, many persons have a strong interest in not knowing their IQ and in keeping it private, particularly if they fear that disclosure of test results to third parties, such as employers or government officials, might have adverse consequences. Moreover, given that test results can fluctuate depending on the conditions under which the test is given, mothers tested under the pressure of litigation have a justifiable concern that their test scores might be inaccurate. The practical impact of such wide-ranging discovery is to raise the cost of litigation for the plaintiff, both financially and emotionally. Attorneys representing plaintiffs on a contingency-fee basis may be more reluctant to pursue litigation with high discovery costs. A mother may well be deterred from filing suit if she is advised by her lawyer that the medical and educational records of her other children will be scrutinized by strangers and that her own intelligence will be measured by a test administered by the defendant.

In analyzing the costs and benefits of such discovery, some courts have overestimated the potential relevance of the information that might be gleaned from family members. The courts that have ordered IQ testing of mothers and required that confidential records of siblings be produced have tacitly raised the threshold needed to prove cause-in-fact, proceeding as if plaintiff had to dispel all scientific uncertainty as to the origin of the child's condition to prevail, despite the fact that the science of toxins is continually evolving and rarely yields definitive answers. More important, courts that endorse wide-reaching discovery seem not to display that "rightful impatien[ce]"[103] with defense arguments of lack of causation that courts traditionally have shown in cases when defendant's wrongful conduct is known to produce the very type of harm that plaintiff alleges. An interesting question then becomes why there might be more skepticism about plaintiff's causal assertions in lead paint cases than in the classic case of the stout woman who falls down an unlighted stairway.

We contend that part of the explanation lies in the social identities of plaintiffs and their families in lead paint litigation. The backdrop of race, poverty, and gender helps to explain the willingness of defense lawyers to raise counterfactual causal arguments based on heredity and upbringing in plaintiffs' families and some courts' willingness to accept them. When defendants assert that genetics, not lead exposure, is responsible for a child's cognitive deficits, they present arguments that resonate with a historical use of "science" to establish that racial minorities—and particularly African Americans—are intellectually inferior and that intelligence is genetically inherited. Arguments based on the inherent inferiority of African Americans have been a cornerstone of the ideology of white supremacy in the United States and were deployed in the early 20th century, in combination with the eugenics movement, to support a number of now-discredited laws, including antimiscegenation legislation and laws providing for mandatory sterilization.

In the contemporary era, there is still a widespread popular belief that IQ is inherited, as evidenced by the popularity of the 1994 book *The Bell Curve*, which revived the debate about race and intelligence.[104] The authors of *The Bell Curve* claimed that intelligence was 40 to 80 percent "heritable," suggesting to many that it was possible to quantify the degree to which an individual's intellectual capacity was genetically based. What gets lost in the popular reception of such claims of "heritability," however, is that they invariably describe observations about a population of people and cannot be used to predict the intelligence level of any given individual. Despite warnings by the authors of the *Bell Curve* that "it makes no more sense to talk about the heritability of an individual's IQ than it does to talk about his birthrate," disclosure of a parent's IQ still often leads to the belief that the child's IQ will necessarily be similar.[105] In the racialized context of lead paint cases, requests for documents relating to the mothers' and siblings' IQs recapitulate these deterministic arguments about the passing down of intelligence and lay the groundwork for a defense that trades on commonly held but unscientific notions about the origins of systemic problems in the minority community.

Additionally, the narrative evoked by defendants' alternative causation arguments echoes familiar stereotypes about poor, unmarried, black mothers and gains credence by drawing upon these popular notions of responsibility and blame. Particularly in the policy debates about welfare, a prototype of the "welfare mother" has emerged; in the public's imagination, she is often an unmarried black mother who is dependent on the state, has several children, and has never held a job.[106] This racialized image defines dependency and deviance in our culture and is often linked to what is called a "culture of poverty" through which welfare mothers transmit bad values to their children and reproduce dependency in the next generation.[107]

Scholars such as Dorothy Roberts assert that this pathological model associated with poor minority mothers contributes to the belief that such mothers have nothing positive to offer to their children and are more likely to be a source of injury, thereby deflecting responsibility for poverty-linked harms away from structural features of the U.S. economy.[108] The negative prototype of the welfare mother has justified programs that invade the privacy of such women to a far greater degree than that of their middle-class counterparts. Welfare mothers have been required by the state to reveal their sex lives as part of paternity proceedings designed to seek reimbursement to the state for welfare expenditures by extracting child support from biological fathers, and they have been subjected to supervision and regular visits by bureaucrats and social workers. The surveillance of welfare mothers and their families is so prominent a feature of such programs that these families are sometimes referred to as "public families," making it seem appropriate for the state to intervene in family matters.[109] Against this backdrop, the compelled testing of a mother's IQ in a tort suit resembles the kinds of intrusion on privacy imposed in other encounters with the state and the legal system.

Despite studies that show that the prototype of the welfare mother is inaccurate—that the typical mother receiving welfare payments is not African American, has fewer than three children, and frequently engages in paid employment[110]—the negative prototype has proved especially resilient. Thus, as they make their arguments about causation, lead paint plaintiffs must confront and counter a background expectation that traces the cognitive deficits of child plaintiffs to the inadequacies of their mothers and tolerates a high degree of governmental intrusion.

Finally, in the debate over alternative causation in lead paint cases, cognitive biases likely operate to magnify racial and gender impacts. Given the general preference for simple, one-cause explanations over multiple-cause theories, it is not surprising that some courts and litigants have displayed a tendency to slip into either/or thinking in lead paint cases and to proceed as if genetics (or genetics and upbringing) and exposure to lead paint were mutually exclusive causes of injury. At this point, the legal implications of the eggshell plaintiff rule—which imposes liability when external forces affect a preexisting vulnerability—are easily forgotten.

The cultural context of lead paint cases is also ripe for operation of the fundamental attribution error. The lead paint cases require the factfinder to sift through complex medical evidence to decide whether to place responsibility externally—on a landlord's failure to abate a lead paint hazard—or internally—on the victim's own psychological makeup, as uncovered through an investigation of family traits and histories. Recall that the fundamental attribution error comes into play when a decision maker is more likely to be satisfied with a dispositional, internal explanation for a harm that occurs to an "outsider" than if the harm had befallen himself or a member of his social group. In the racialized context of lead paint litigation, a "dispositional" explanation for cognitive disorders, and in particular for low IQs of exposed children, is readily activated by stereotypes about poor minority families headed by women. Especially when a trial judge is called upon to determine whether a defendant's alternative causation theory is plausible enough to warrant further discovery, the attributional bias toward internal explanations might well tip the balance.

Perhaps even more striking, the normality bias can operate in lead paint cases to dispose a factfinder toward genetic and socioeconomic explanations for the plaintiffs' harms, despite strong scientific evidence linking cognitive injuries to lead paint exposure. As discussed earlier, the normality bias makes it harder for people to imagine a different result when the outcome is regarded as normal than when it is deemed unusual or extraordinary. That a poor minority child from a "bad" neighborhood would experience problems in school and behavioral and learning disorders is regarded as a normal, if regrettable, state of affairs. Despite the fact that exposure to lead is entirely preventable, judges and jurors may find it difficult to believe that such a child's difficulties were not inevitable and to imagine events turning out differently. Professor Wang notes that "[e]ven the same, equally appalling forms of victimization can elicit different degrees of concern depending on race and class."[111] To explain the disparate media coverage given to missing white children, as compared to missing African American children, for example, Wang observes that more attention is paid to the case of a white child from an affluent family, such as Elizabeth Smart, largely because that case is regarded as unusual. In contrast, the public is conditioned to expect that bad things will happen in black neighborhoods and therefore tends to approach the suffering of black families as "normal and unremarkable." Similarly, the cognitive injuries and loss of potential alleged by plaintiffs in lead paint cases can more readily be seen as simply part of "Black people's rough road in life,"[112] particularly in cases in which the legal standard merely asks whether such an explanation is plausible.

In some respects, the interplay of cultural factors—race, poverty, and gender—is so close to the surface in the lead paint cases that it is hard to imagine that they have no effects on litigation. However, the precise cultural impact is more difficult to capture than in the wrongful birth cases. Unlike the wrongful birth context, there has not yet been a discernible shift in causal thinking in lead paint cases—no before-and-after cases—through which we see can the difference over time that gender and racial attitudes play in generating counterfactual scenarios and in making such scenarios more or less plausible. Instead, the lead paint cases require us to imagine whether courts would be as willing to delve into personal records of family members and to order psychological testing of parents in recurring cases involving white middle-class or affluent children alleging similar cognitive disorders. Imagine, for example, a case of an automobile accident in which an infant plaintiff from an affluent white family suffers a head injury that is commonly linked to long-term cognitive injury. We doubt that, in such a case, a defendant's alternative causation argument that the child might well have suffered cognitive deficits from genetics and upbringing, even absent the head injury, would be persuasive enough to warrant extensive discovery of personal records of family members, although, even in such a case, there may still be some uncertainty about causation. The lead paint cases serve as a warning that, in making difficult but crucial determinations of causal attribution, there is a risk that judges and jurors will employ variables, such as race and gender, as a way to tip the balance, resolve nagging uncertainties, and reinforce cultural expectations and norms that disadvantage social minorities.

6

Damages

Proof of damages is an essential element of most tort actions. Except for some intentional torts in which plaintiffs are entitled to recover nominal damages once they establish their cause of action, in all other cases plaintiffs are required to demonstrate actual harm and to provide individualized evidence of the extent of their loss. Despite the importance of the damages element, however, the subject of damages was much neglected in the torts curriculum and in torts scholarship until quite recently.[1] This technical, practically oriented corner of the law was generally left to upper-class courses on remedies and rarely was the focus of appellate court opinions typically selected for inclusion in first-year torts casebooks. Even the leading hornbook on torts, *Prosser on Torts* (and, later, *Prosser and Keeton on Torts*),[2] had no separate section on damages and paid little attention to the justifications for awarding damages or to the measures and methods of computing compensation, save for some discussion of the exceptional case of punitive damages.

This pattern of neglect began to change, however, starting in the mid-1980s.[3] A major impetus for the shift has been the "tort reform" movement, which has made "out-of-control" damage awards one of its principal targets. Much of the recent empirical scholarship in torts has been undertaken in response to charges and critiques made by these business-oriented tort reformers. The relentless push for tort reform has encouraged academics to pay closer attention to damages and to theorize more about the connection between damages and the general objectives of tort law. On the legislative front, states have enacted a wide array of damage caps and other measures aimed at reducing awards and limiting liability. These tort reform statutes have raised new questions about the disproportionate impact of such measures on women and less affluent social groups.

More recently, two important developments have highlighted the connections between race and gender and the calculation of damage awards. In October 2008, a well-known federal judge, Judge Jack Weinstein from the Eastern District of New York, issued an opinion barring the use of race-based life-expectancy calculations in a tort case brought by an African American victim of the 2003 Staten Island ferry crash. His landmark ruling in *McMillan v. City of New York*[4] was the first to hold that the use of race to determine tort damages violates the equal protection and due process guarantees of the U.S. Constitution. If followed by other courts, *McMillan* could significantly alter the valuation of tort claims for plaintiffs in a wide variety of cases.

Weinstein's ruling was foreshadowed by the approach taken by Kenneth Feinberg, the Special Master of the federal September 11 Victim Compensation Fund.[5] In devising a grid for determining the amount of damages to be awarded to families of the 9/11 victims, Feinberg made a choice to ignore race and to reject the use of gender-based statistics that would have lowered awards for families of female victims.[6] Feinberg did not rely directly on the Constitution but based his decision on considerations of public policy and equity. Because of their high-profile nature, these two decisions have the potential to call into question the widespread use of race-based and gender-based methods of damage computation in tort litigation and to stimulate a broader debate about the connection between concepts of civil rights and civil damages.

It goes without saying that damages are important to tort victims because they determine the degree to which such victims will be able to ameliorate the harmful consequences of their injuries, even if money damages cannot totally recreate the lives they led before the injury. Damages are also crucially important to plaintiffs' attorneys, who decide whether potential cases are worth taking under a contingency fee system in which the lawyer's share is typically one-third of the plaintiff's recovery. Additionally, damages are important because they are widely thought to create incentives for actors to avoid dangerous conduct and thus are key to whether and how tort law deters and prevents injuries.

In this chapter we highlight the expressive as well as the material importance of damages. From this perspective, damages are important because they signal how injuries are valued by the legal system, beyond simply whether a plaintiff has a legally recognized claim. In the realm of torts, courts and juries do more than determine liability; they are required to measure injuries, as well. Not unlike sentences meted out in criminal cases,[7] tort measurements of lost earnings potential, pain and suffering, and other types of damages can be affected by negative attitudes toward social groups and are not immune to conscious and unconscious gender and race bias. Thus, close scrutiny of the rules and methods that govern damage awards is a chief way to protect against the devaluation of individuals and social groups and to ensure basic equity in the torts system of compensation.

When we look at the overall picture, the broadest division of tort damages consists of two categories: compensatory damages and punitive damages. Compensatory damages are routinely awarded and are considered the "normal" remedy in tort cases.[8] Their main function is most often described as "repairing" the plaintiff's injury or "making the plaintiff whole." The animating idea behind compensatory damages is to restore the plaintiff to the status quo ante, to the condition the plaintiff would have occupied absent the accident. Of course, the "make-whole" purpose of compensatory damages must be understood as a metaphor, since the award of money cannot literally restore the plaintiff to a pre-accident state; once a limb is severed or a family member has died, for example, such a loss is irretrievable and cannot be recaptured through money alone.

To accomplish the restorative function of tort law to the widest extent possible, however, compensatory damages are awarded to cover a wide variety of losses. They include economic damages, such as lost wages, loss of future income capacity, and past and future medical and rehabilitative expenses. They also include noneconomic harms, such as pain and suffering, loss of enjoyment of life, and damages for physical impairment, disfigurement, and relational losses. It is this last category of damage awards for noneconomic losses, often described in shorthand as "pain and suffering," that has generated the most controversy and has most frequently been the target of damage caps, particularly in medical malpractice cases.

It is common to contrast compensatory damages to punitive damages. Unlike the routine award of compensatory damages, punitive damage awards are rare—they are awarded in roughly only 5 percent of tort cases[9]—and require a showing that the defendant acted with malice or conscious indifference to the risks posed by his conduct. Most courts maintain that the main function of punitive damages is to punish the defendant for reprehensible conduct and to deter such behavior in the future. This retributive function suggests that the nature and quality of defendant's behavior plays a more prominent role in setting punitive damages than it does in measuring compensatory damages.

However, the conventional wisdom that tightly links compensatory damages to the "make-whole" or compensation purpose of tort law, while tying punitive damages exclusively to retribution and deterrence, can be misleading. Historically, the "make-whole" principle has not been the complete rationale for compensatory damages.[10] Juries have awarded compensatory damages not only with an eye to restoring plaintiff to a pre-accident condition but also to accomplish other objectives. Thus, in addition to indemnifying a plaintiff for her losses, an award of compensatory damages may represent a desire to deter conduct, to articulate a norm of social disapproval of undesirable conduct, or to fix damages at the level that vindicates the invasion of plaintiff's rights. Particularly in a system in which juries have traditionally been accorded considerable discretion to determine the amount of compensation, it makes sense to view damage awards as furthering a mix of objectives besides the "make-whole" principle. As we shall argue in more depth later in this chapter, considerations of race and gender equity—as expressions of important social norms—are properly taken into account in setting damage awards and should not be ruled out of bounds as foreign to the enterprise of measuring damages.

In this chapter, we look at the two main components of compensatory damages—economic and noneconomic damages—and discuss the gender and race impact of specific doctrines and reforms relating to the computation and amount of such damages. Specifically, our treatment of economic damages critiques the use of gender- and race-based tables to calculate awards for loss of future income capacity, an important component of personal injury and wrongful death recoveries. With respect to noneconomic loss, we discuss the contemporary assault on the legitimacy of noneconomic damages and recent scholarship documenting the harsh impact of damage caps on marginalized groups, principally women, children, the elderly, and minorities.

Gender- and Race-Based Tables and the Calculation of Lost Income

Economic and pecuniary damages are often characterized as objective, capable of precise measurement, and less susceptible to manipulation by the parties than noneconomic damages. Indeed, some calculations of economic losses are relatively straightforward, such as the calculation of past medical expenses. However, when it comes to calculations involving future economic losses, the task is quite different, in large part because the future is so notoriously hard to predict. Predictions about the future are more than simple determinations of historical fact; they involve complex, policy-laden inquiries about the likely influence of social forces and the direction and rate of social change, matters on which there is no societal or professional consensus. It is at this point that the relevance of gender and race often comes into play and affects judgments about the economic value of the lives of tort victims.

Hidden race and gender bias are present in the standards currently used to calculate loss of future income or, more precisely, loss of future earning capacity, often a big-ticket item in fixing damages in cases of permanent injury or wrongful death. Loss of future earning capacity is largely a function of two variables: the number of years a person would likely have worked (worklife expectancy) and the likely yearly income the plaintiff would have earned each year, discounted to present value.[11] It is interesting to note that even in the contemporary era, when explicit gender and race classifications have largely disappeared from statutes and regulations, expert witnesses continue to rely on gender-based and race-based tables to calculate both of these variables: to determine worklife expectancy and to estimate yearly earnings.[12] Particularly now that many states have placed a cap on noneconomic damages in certain classes of tort actions, loss of future income capacity represents an increasingly important component of a damage award. It is also of great social importance because it is a measure of a person's potential.

Gender- and race-based tables are in effect gender-specific and race-specific comparisons, comparing women only to other women, blacks to blacks, or men to men. The use of gender- and race-based tables saddles nonconforming individuals with generalizations about their group, a kind of stereotyping generally prohibited by the constitutional guarantees of equal protection and statutory antidiscrimination laws. Gender- and race-based worklife expectancy tables are used to predict the number of years a plaintiff would likely have remained in the workforce. They may be used in cases of injured children and even in cases involving adult plaintiffs, if there is uncertainty about the longevity and continuity of the plaintiff's career. For example, if in the past women have taken several years out of the labor market to raise children, gender-based worklife tables predict that they will continue to do so in the future. If black men have been incarcerated at a much higher rate than white men, resulting in lower labor-force participation rates for black men, race-based worklife estimates predict that they will continue to work fewer years than whites.

Gender- and race-based earnings tables are of particular importance in cases involving severe injuries to persons who have not yet established an individual track record of employment and earnings, notably children. In such cases, courts are forced to rely on statistics, rather than judgments about the individual plaintiff, to gauge the likely earning power such a child would have had, absent the disabling injury. When courts rely on gender- and race-based earnings tables, it means that historical patterns of wage discrimination in the labor market are replicated in tort awards, even though the labor-force participation of social groups may be changing rapidly.

As a practical matter, the use of race-based and gender-based tables results in significantly lower awards for minority men and women of all races. For example, in *U.S. v. Bedonie*, a 2004 decision determining damages for two homicide victims, an expert testified that one decedent, a young Native American man who had graduated from high school, would have earned approximately $433,000 in his lifetime.[13] The expert arrived at this figure by first estimating what the average high school graduate earns and then multiplying that amount by 58 percent, because 58 percent was the average ratio of the wages of Native American males to those of white males. On his own motion, the judge asked the expert to calculate the amount the deceased would have earned without making any racial adjustment. That figure was approximately $744,000. In the same case, a calculation using a race and gender adjustment for lost earning potential made a huge difference when the decedent was a Native American female infant. Unadjusted, her earnings potential was estimated to be approximately $308,000, versus only $171,000 when the calculation was based on gender and race. Significantly, although the expert had performed thousands of lost-income analyses, he testified that he had never before been asked to provide race- and sex-neutral calculations in a wrongful death case. It appears that the lawyers had relied on the economists to construct economic loss appraisals, and neither the economists nor the lawyers ever questioned the appropriateness of using race and sex to predict earning power.

In some contexts, the use of race- and gender-based economic data can result in the systematic undervaluation of recurring types of injuries. For example, legal commentators have analyzed the impact of race-based calculations in lead paint litigation.[14] As discussed in chapter 5, lead poisoning is typically caused by the ingestion of paint chips or dust, likely to be found in older, deteriorating buildings in low-income neighborhoods. Depressed awards for plaintiffs derive from the fact that the population of lead paint victims contains a disproportionate number of young, typically poor, African American or Hispanic children. When lost earning capacity is calculated using race-based tables, the awards are considerably lower than they would be for comparably injured white children. Landlords and government housing authorities—the typical defendants in lead paint cases—thus have less incentive to take measures to clean up toxic hazards in the neighborhoods most affected by lead paint.

The reliance on race- and sex-based tables is not subtle discrimination but overt discrimination of the kind that the U.S. Constitution and statutory antidiscrimination laws have long outlawed or at least have made very hard to justify. It is well established in constitutional law that race-based classifications are suspect and trigger strict scrutiny and that gender-based classifications are disfavored and trigger a stringent intermediate scrutiny.[15] In cases of employment discrimination governed by Title VII of the Civil Rights Act of 1964, virtually all race-based classifications are prohibited, while sex-based classifications are allowed only in the rarest of cases in which sex is a bona fide occupational qualification for a particular job. Notably, in *City of Los Angeles Department of Water and Power v. Manhart*,[16] the U.S. Supreme Court in 1978 held that sex-based actuarial tables could not be used to justify requiring female employees to pay higher monthly contributions to an employer-run retirement fund,[17] despite the fact that women as a group live longer than men. This strong distaste for explicit race and sex classifications, however, did not immediately carry over into ordinary tort cases. Instead, when the gender and race classifications were embedded in statistical tables and used by experts to construct loss appraisals, the discrimination tended not to be noticed and was accepted as natural and unproblematic.

The illegitimacy of using gender- and race-based tables to calculate loss of future earning capacity is most evident when we consider the difficulty courts and juries face when the injured party is biracial or multiracial. In his ruling barring the use of race to determine the life expectancy of an African American plaintiff, Judge Weinstein stressed that it was "not scientifically acceptable" to hinge damage awards on ascriptions of a plaintiff's race, given the history of racial mixing in U.S. society.[18] Weinstein viewed "race" largely as a social construct and remarked that most Americans would consider it "absurd" to attempt to categorize a person such as Barack Obama as either "white" or "black" for purposes of determining damages. As precedent, he cited the 1991 case of *Wheeler Tarpeh-Doe v. United States*,[19] a case involving the categorization of a biracial male child whose father was Liberian and whose white mother lived in the United States. In that case, the court was confronted with the uncomfortable question of whether it should select the "white" tables or the "black" tables to determine lost earning capacity. The opinion was notable for its time because the court refused to decide whether the child was black or white for purposes of choosing the appropriate statistic. Instead, the court decided to use blended earnings tables combining persons of all races.

Until Judge Weinstein's ruling, however, the proper use of statistical tables to calculate future economic losses had been a low-visibility issue, even though courts had struggled with the problem for more than 100 years. One notable early discussion can be found in *The Saginaw and the Hamilton*, a 1905 admiralty case involving wrongful death on the high seas, decided in the Southern District of New York.[20] In that case, the admiralty commissioner was called upon to calculate the economic losses stemming from the drowning death of eight passengers and crew members. The court described two of the deceased as "white" and six as "colored." To arrive at an estimate of life expectancies for the victims—before the invention of worklife expectancy tables—the commissioner consulted race-neutral (i.e., blended) mortality tables, in line with the common practice at that time of using such tables to estimate how long a person would have lived and worked. In an extraordinary opinion, the district court faulted the commissioner for using the neutral data, claiming that the data were particularly inaccurate "where colored persons are concerned." Relying on data provided by Frederick Hoffman in his 1896 book *Race Traits and Tendencies of the American Negro*, the court took judicial notice of the lower life expectancy of blacks and of a marked "difference in the vitality of the races." He consequently lowered the amounts awarded to the victims using his own sense of how much each of the victims would have contributed to his family had he lived.[21]

Frederick Hoffman's book would later be remembered for his attempt to prove "scientifically" that the black population would eventually die out because of the race's purportedly immoral traits and tendencies. The racist foundation for the *Saginaw* court's method of calculating damages, however, largely went unnoticed and unquestioned. Even though the case eventually reached the U.S. Supreme Court, and resulted in an opinion by Oliver Wendell Holmes, commentators generally fixed on other issues in the case and did not discuss the significance of race in calculating damages.

Race was similarly taken in account to lower damage awards for black plaintiffs in Louisiana in the 1930s, again without debate.[22] As discussed in chapter 2, Louisiana appellate courts in several cases awarded reduced amounts for black victims by comparing their awards to amounts other *black* victims had previously recovered. Similar cases of whites who suffered injury were not included in the courts' comparisons. For these courts, obvious—but unspoken—differences between the races apparently justified the race-based comparisons, despite the likely devaluation of the awards for the black plaintiffs. The practice reflected the segregationist mindset in the Deep South at the time and was not challenged as illegitimate.

Today, we would likely regard such explicit segregation in setting awards as clearly inappropriate and a relic of a pre-civil rights era. But in one key respect, the contemporary reliance on gender- and race-based tables amounts to an updated version of the old discriminatory practice. Importantly, both techniques use the depressed social and economic status of a racial group as the benchmark for an award to an individual plaintiff.

Before Judge Weinstein's opinion, a few courts in the United States had rejected race- and gender-based calculations on public-policy grounds,[23] without reaching the issue of whether such a practice was unconstitutional. In one notable case, a federal district judge in Utah refused to use race- and gender-based estimates to determine a compensation award for family members of two homicide victims under the Mandatory Victims Restitution Act.[24] As mentioned earlier, the homicide victims in *U.S. v. Bedonie*, one male, one female, were both Native American. The judge decided that, as a matter of public policy, no downward adjustments for either race or sex should be made to the awards. He instead elected to rely on blended, race- and gender-neutral tables to determine lost earnings.

Outside the United States, some courts have been less hesitant to rely on considerations of equality and social justice to reject use of gender- or ethnic-based statistics. For example, an important decision in 2005 by the Israeli Supreme Court, *Migdal Ins. v. Rim Abu Hanna*,[25] assessed the appropriate statistical basis for computing an award to an Arab girl from a poor village who was injured in a road accident when she was five months old. The defendant noted that women living in the child's village generally were not employed outside the home and sought to base damages on those local conditions. In a sweeping decision, the Israeli court ruled that the appropriate standard for computing future loss of earnings should be based on tables for the average wage throughout the country. The court ruled that it was not enough to restore the plaintiff to the status quo ante but reached to determine a "just and fair" status that would not reproduce past inequalities among social groups. For the Israeli court, this more egalitarian measure of the child's potential was necessary to ensure that "every child of whatever sex, origin, race or religion" is treated in accordance with a "conception of universal justice, the justice that requires equality, that requires recognition of the right to autonomy, and that nourishes hope."[26]

Additionally, for quite some time, courts in Canada have grappled with the legitimacy of using gender-based calculations in tort cases. Starting first in British Columbia, in 1998,[27] and then spreading to Ontario,[28] some courts have rejected the use of gender-based estimates of lost earning capacity, generally agreeing with plaintiffs' arguments that expert calculations of economic loss should be scrutinized to ensure that they are not based on assumptions or tables that are unfair to individual women or that serve to perpetuate patterns of inequality. In one prominent case, for example, the court's decision to use blended tables meant a difference of approximately $600,000 for a seventeen-year-old girl seriously injured in a car crash, an amount more than double the amount that the victim received for noneconomic damages ($250,000) under Canada's capped-recovery scheme for noneconomic damages.[29] Canadian courts have employed a variety of approaches to infuse gender equity into damage awards for female tort victims, sometimes using blended tables, sometimes relying on male tables to calculate awards for female victims, and sometimes "grossing up" awards based on female-specific actuarial tables to reflect the court's view that the amount underestimated what the female plaintiff would likely have earned.[30]

Prior to *McMillan*, however, probably the most significant event in the United States was the decision by Special Master Kenneth Feinberg to reject the use of "female" worklife tables to determine economic damage awards for the families of female victims who died in the September 11 terrorist attacks.[31] Initially, Feinberg had indicated that in calculating awards under the September 11 Compensation Fund, he planned to rely on separate gender-based tables for male and female victims to estimate how many years the victims would have worked. During the comment period before adoption of the final rule governing distribution under the Fund, however, the NOW Legal Defense Fund objected to the use of gender-based worklife expectancy tables and urged Feinberg to reconsider his methodology. Feinberg ultimately agreed with NOW Legal Defense that the awards should not disadvantage the families of women. In keeping with the Fund's policy of being generous to 9/11 families, he decided to use the "male" worklife expectancy tables for all victims. His remedy thus had the effect of raising the awards for families of female victims without lowering awards for families of male victims.

These developments set the stage for Judge Weinstein's ruling in *McMillan*. Interestingly, in contrast to the prior cases, the debate in *McMillan* centered not on loss of future earning capacity but on the amount that should be awarded to James McMillan for future medical expenses. His case, however, still required the judge to determine how many more years McMillan likely would live and be in need of medical care, a calculation similar to the estimations of worklife expectancy courts or juries make when they calculate loss of future income. McMillan's injuries were catastrophic: when the Staten Island ferry ran into a pier, McMillan suffered a spinal cord injury that left him completely paralyzed in the legs and partly paralyzed in the arms. On the critical issue of McMillan's estimated life expectancy, the City introduced statistical evidence suggesting that African Americans with spinal cord injuries lived for fewer years than persons of other races with similar spinal cord injuries.

Judge Weinstein rejected the City's race-based data and declared that, in setting the award, he would rely only on race-neutral estimations. His opinion rested both on the factual unreliability of racial categories and on the constitutional infirmity of using race to measure the value of a tort plaintiff's recovery. First and foremost, Weinstein repudiated the notion that "race" is a simple biological fact and that a tort plaintiff may reliably be placed into a discrete racial category. As mentioned earlier, the judge emphasized the mixed racial heritage of Americans, many of whom are nevertheless bluntly categorized as either "white" or "black," and the lingering effect of the "one-drop-of-blood rule" that once defined as "black" anyone who was known to have African ancestors. For Weinstein, to treat all "dark-skinned" Americans as completely different from "light-skinned" Americans was the built-in "fallacy" of race-based statistics. Next, Weinstein stressed the strong tendency in U.S. culture to accept apparent racial differences uncritically when such differences could better be explained by socioeconomic factors and geography. In this respect, reliance on race to predict life expectancy was misleading because it masked the effect of other, more situational factors that might change over the course of a person's life. Weinstein concluded that "by allowing the use of 'race'-based life expectancy tables, which are based on historical data, courts are essentially reinforcing the underlying social inequalities of our society rather than describing a significant biological difference."

Weinstein's conclusion that race-based statistics were factually unreliable laid a crucial foundation for his legal ruling that the use of race-based data violates constitutional guarantees of equal protection and due process. He first cited a long line of U.S. Supreme Court cases holding that government may not rely on explicit racial classifications, absent compelling justification for their use. He reasoned that because judicial reliance on race-based statistics constituted "state action," it triggered strict scrutiny and a subsequent need for justification. Although Weinstein did not supply the next step in the analysis explicitly, it was abundantly clear from the structure of his main argument: he determined that no such justification was possible in this case because the race-based statistics offered by the City were unreliable and could not enhance the accuracy of the estimation of McMillan's life expectancy or his damage award. He finally concluded that "equal protection in this context demands that the claimant not be subjected to a disadvantageous life expectancy estimate solely on the basis of a 'racial' classification."

The unreliability of race-based statistics was also at the heart of Weinstein's due process analysis. He started from the proposition that under state and federal law there was a "right—in effect a property right—to compensation in cases of negligently caused damage to the person." He then reasoned that allowing the use of race-based statistics would create "arbitrary and irrational state action" and would impose an automatic and undue burden on a class of litigants who seek compensation, resulting in a denial of due process.

Despite the breadth and sophistication of Weinstein's decision, he did not tackle all issues related to race and gender in the setting of economic damages. In particular, his analysis of the legitimacy of using gender to calculate future losses was somewhat confusing. He cited with approval those cases that had rejected gender-based data in the calculation of worklife expectancy and lost future earnings and also relied on our prior scholarship that advocated gender and race neutrality in the calculation of damage awards. However, Weinstein noted that, in McMillan's case, he "disregarded all 'race'-based computations for life expectancy and applied predictions for the general male population, and particularly those suffering from quadriplegia." He gave no reason why he chose to rely on "male" tables in this case; nor did he indicate whether he regarded the calculation of life expectancy in estimating future medical costs as raising different issues than the estimation of worklife expectancy used to compute loss of future earning capacity. Thus, in the end, Weinstein's ruling squarely dealt only with race and did not specifically address the use of gender-based data. Although highly significant, it represents the beginning, rather than the end, of the debate over gender and race and the calculation of economic damages in tort cases.

What is most significant about these developments is that, after years of neglecting the issue, some courts are finally expressing doubts about the legality and fairness of gender- and race-based assessments and are reaching to reform damage calculations in a manner consistent with constitutional principles and civil rights norms. However, no court in the United States has yet thoroughly analyzed what such reform might mean for tort law. In particular, U.S. courts have not explained how rejection of gender and race data fits within traditional tort notions of compensation, particularly the "make-whole" principle that seeks to restore an individual victim to his or her pre-accident condition.[32]

The most familiar objection to eliminating the use of gender- and race-based tables and data is generally couched in terms of "accuracy." In its starkest form, the objection based on accuracy starts from the premise that the only legitimate goal of tort law is to restore the victim to the status quo ante. The next step in the argument is to assert that gender- and race-based disparities are located in the larger society (e.g., prevailing wage rates) and that accident victims should not seek compensation from defendants to make up for societal inequities. Thus, the argument goes, if the statistics show that women and minorities work fewer years than white men and/or make lower average wages, tort damages based on those statistics are a fair and accurate measurement of what the victim likely lost as a result of the accident. As one recent commentator put it, looking at the race and gender of the victim seems to fit with the bedrock notion that the defendant "takes the victim as he find him," whether that constitutes a preexisting condition or membership in a particular racial group.[33]

However, both the starting premises of this argument and the conclusion that purportedly follow from it do not hold up under scrutiny. It is perhaps easiest to see the flaws in the conclusion that use of race- and gender-based statistics increases accuracy. Even some critics of reform acknowledge that current practices are deficient insofar as they rely upon race- and gender-based statistical estimates that do not accurately mirror current or future realities. With respect to race, Judge Weinstein pointed out the fallacy of relying on crude race-based statistics that do not take into account the multiracial heritage of many Americans. Even though it is easier to classify most tort plaintiffs as either men or women, many of the gender-based worklife and earnings tables used in litigation are simply outdated and do not even accurately describe the status quo at the time of trial.

Another difficult problem in calculating loss of future income capacity derives from the fact that it is necessary not simply to have a reliable picture of the past but to predict the future. Yet, there is no unfailingly accurate way to predict the future. One astute commentator has described the process of determining future economic losses as "a crystal ball exercise that's as much art as science."[34] For example, worklife expectancy tables admittedly can tell us about workforce participation rates for men and women in the past. However, they are not good predictors of the workforce participation rates for those groups in the future, unless they are refined to take into account social change and employment trends, such as changes in the pattern of women's working lives or a narrowing of the gender wage gap. If historical data are not refined to take account of such future trends, the effect is to saddle historically disadvantaged groups with the burdens of the past and to compensate them at a below-market rate, simply because they were unlucky enough to become tort victims.[35]

Once we acknowledge that the tables must be refined and cannot be "used off the shelf," as it were, we have passed imperceptibly from a discussion about historical fact to a debate about the likely influence of social forces in the future, a debate that often takes on a normative cast and is difficult to separate from political judgment. Thus, although most people seem to think that the gender wage gap will narrow in the future, there is no agreement about whether and when gender parity will occur.[36] Likewise, no confident judgment can be made about how much time women will take away from the paid workforce twenty or thirty years from now to raise children.

More fundamental, objections about accuracy often fail to appreciate that predictions about the future have a way of simultaneously affecting the present and constructing the future. Consider an example relating to the narrowing of the gender wage gap. Some Canadian courts have noted that the size of the gender gap in wages depends in part on the sector in which the plaintiff would have been employed, given that pay equity initiatives in public employment and in organized workplaces have served to narrow the gap in these sectors.[37] However, predicting the degree to which the pay equity movement will spread to the private sector in the future is not wholly removed from the debate over whether gender equity should be infused into the process of computing tort damages. Because tort law does not exist separate and apart from the larger culture, the two domains are invariably intertwined and mutually constitutive.[38] As many commentators have noted, tort law has an expressive or aspirational dimension.[39] Compensating men and women on the same basis in tort law thus makes a statement about the type of equality the culture embraces. In turn, the example set by tort law might well generate additional pressure for pay equity in the workplace, similar to the effect that the equal pay movement and other sex-equality initiatives had in stimulating proposals for gender fairness in tort law when they first appeared in the 1970s.

The main point is that the line between accuracy and aspiration becomes blurred once it is recognized that it is possible to shape the future in a certain way in part by predicting that it will take that shape. When courts award damages for loss of earning capacity in tort litigation, they do more than passively pass on the market price of plaintiff's labor; they express a view about the future and should not be oblivious to their own role in constructing that future.

The willingness of economists and judges to rely on sex and race as a measure of an individual's future earning potential may have as much to do with habit as it does with strict fidelity to the "make-whole" principle. The choice to rely on race and gender over other possible predictors of future earning potential may be affected by cognitive habits and biases that overstate the importance of these highly salient personal characteristics. Thus, we suspect that even if the data clearly indicated, for example, that Catholics earned higher average incomes than Baptists, courts nevertheless would be reluctant to predict an individual's future earning capacity on the basis of his religious affiliation.[40] In such cases, there would likely be a sense that using religion as a variable was inappropriate, even if it seemed to have predictive value. The objection to using religion would be based on a judgment that any past disparity in income between Catholics and Baptists was not a function of persistent differences in the character or abilities of the two social groups but more likely explainable in terms of greater opportunities historically that may have been available to the higher-earning Catholics. Thus, using religion to predict an individual's future income not only would be distasteful but likely would be inaccurate, because, as opportunities and situations changed over time, religion would cease to be a valid predictor.

By contrast, what likely lies behind the willingness to use race and gender to predict future income is the assumption that race and gender will continue to be powerful predictors of income, regardless of future equal opportunity programs, stepped up enforcement of antidiscrimination laws, or broader cultural change. The unspoken premise is that, in the final analysis, women and racial minorities will continue to lack the character, ability, or commitment to compete successfully with white men in the workplace. This selective use of race and gender over other predictive variables has the effect of naturalizing racial and gender differences and eclipsing the role that lack of opportunities and the persistence of race and sex discrimination play in producing pay disparities. It also reinforces the view that race and gender differences are inevitable and enduring, rather than a product of political and social arrangements that are subject to change. Such a dispositional explanation for the lower wage levels of "outsider" groups may well reflect the operation of the fundamental attribution error, as discussed in chapter 5. As Judge Weinstein noted in *McMillan*, the presence of a powerfully salient factor such as race has the effect of masking the impact of other factors. In the context of calculations of future earning capacity, the effect is to shut off the search for more situational explanations for persistent pay gaps. Ultimately, what looks on the surface to be a hard-boiled objection to change centering on accuracy turns out to implicate the politically charged debate about the sources of gender and racial disparities in our society and the role of courts and law in reproducing patterns of inequality. Thus, even if the only concern of tort law was to accurately measure losses and restore the victim to the status quo ante, continued reliance on race- and gender-based tables would not achieve that objective.

Moreover, we also challenge as flawed the starting assumption that the only legitimate concern in calculating compensatory damages is accuracy. As mentioned earlier, the "make-whole" principle is an inadequate description of the mix of objectives behind the award of compensatory damages. Some tort doctrines are best understood not only as a means of restoring victims to their pre-accident condition but also as an expression and reinforcement of ideals of social justice and civil rights. In chapter 3, for example, we discussed how many state courts have permitted harassment victims to sue for intentional infliction of mental distress because providing such a tort claim for workplace harassment reinforces the state's public policy against discrimination. Additionally, the development of the "public policy" tort in the 1970s by which employees were afforded a right to challenge wrongful discharges by their employers is a prominent example of using tort law to achieve both "make-whole" and social justice objectives.[41] The "public policy" tort was designed not only to provide financial compensation for unemployed plaintiffs but to send a message that employers were no longer free to use their power to terminate workers in ways that undermined larger societal goals.

Because social justice considerations have affected the shape of tort law, the key question is not whether it is proper to "deviate" from tort law principles to interject civil right norms but whether social justice concerns ought to influence the shape of the particular tort rule in question. The methods used to compute lost earning capacity have enormous practical significance and represent concrete expressions of the differing values tort law places on human life and potential. The elimination of race-based and gender-based computations—and the substitution of blended tables representing the composite experiences of men and women of diverse races—is a tort reform that would infuse a much-needed equality dimension into basic tort concepts of value and compensation.

Caps on Noneconomic Compensatory Damages

The drive to impose caps on the recovery of noneconomic damages has been the centerpiece of the most recent tort reform movement. The movement has targeted both punitive damages and the noneconomic portion of compensatory damages. Although both kinds of damages are important to plaintiffs—particularly because each can be used as a fund to defray attorney's fees and other costs of litigation—in this section we focus on restrictions placed on noneconomic compensatory damages. In many respects, the assault on noneconomic compensatory damages is more controversial and more fundamental than the heated debate over punitive damages. This is because damage caps on pain and suffering and other intangible injuries potentially affect a broader range of ordinary tort cases and represent a challenge to traditional tort notions of cognizable injury and adequate compensation. Most important, like caps on punitive damages,[42] their effects are felt unequally: caps have the most negative impact on those persons whose injuries defy monetization and disproportionately affect women, children, the elderly, and minorities, who are unable to prove the value of their loss in market-based terms.

Twenty-nine states currently have some form of cap on noneconomic compensatory damages.[43] In seventeen of these states, the caps on noneconomic damages apply exclusively to medical liability actions,[44] while in seven of these states, the caps on noneconomic damages apply to all tort actions. In contrast, only six states have imposed caps on the total amount of compensatory damages, reaching both the economic and noneconomic components of an award. So far, the campaign to curb damage awards has centered mostly on noneconomic damages and has not questioned the wisdom of using tort law to replace even extremely large economic losses sustained by the most affluent tort victims.[45]

The California legislature set the precedent for capping noneconomic damages in medical malpractice awards in 1975 with the enactment of the Medical Injury Compensation Reform Act (MICRA), which capped noneconomic damages at $250,000, a fixed sum that was not indexed to the cost of living or other adjustments for inflation.[46] Several states followed suit, imposing the same $250,000 limit in medical liability actions, while others enacted somewhat higher caps, ranging up to $500,000 in such actions. Some of the recent statutes are more complex than MICRA, allowing for higher caps in some cases of serious injuries or disfigurement or capping noneconomic damages at a multiple (e.g., two or three times) of economic damages, typically coupled with an upper dollar limit. Such multiplier caps have the effect of depressing even small awards of noneconomic damages in those cases in which economic damages are also low.

The caps on noneconomic damages in medical liability cases do more than signal disapproval of high malpractice awards and a desire to lower costs to medical professionals and their insurers. Instead, the selective imposition of caps on noneconomic damages is part of a larger assault on the legitimacy of such damages that has begun to spill over into other areas of tort law. This recent assault has solidified a structural feature of contemporary tort law that surfaced earlier but was much less defined prior to the widespread adoption of caps on noneconomic damages. It is now increasingly clear that there is an implicit hierarchy of value in tort law that ranks economic damages higher than noneconomic damages. As Lucinda Finley explains, the hierarchy rests on "the assumption that the wage earning and economic aspects of human life are more important and worth protecting than emotional, relational, dignitary, and other whole person aspects of life."[47]

This hierarchy resembles—but does not duplicate—the hierarchy, discussed in chapter 4, that privileges physical harm over emotional or relational injury. Although they operate in tandem and are mutually reinforcing, the two hierarchies are conceptually distinct. It is important to recognize that both physical and emotional injuries give rise to both economic and noneconomic damages. Thus, for example, plaintiffs who suffer physical injury seek not only recovery for economic damages consisting of medical expenses, lost wages, and loss of future income capacity but also noneconomic damages for pain and suffering and loss of enjoyment of life. Similarly, plaintiffs suing for negligent infliction of emotional distress are also likely to have medical expenses and loss of income, in addition to noneconomic damages. The hierarchy of damages thus operates within claims for different types of harm to give higher priority to the pecuniary or economic aspects of the damage claim.

In contrast to the historical privileging of physical harm over emotional and relational claims, the hierarchy of types of damages is not a creature of the common law. Instead, it has largely been created by statutory changes in tort recovery. Beginning with the early-20th-century movement for workers' compensation,[48] tort reform has often targeted noneconomic damages for elimination, suggesting that these damages are somehow less essential to a fair system of compensation than are damages for economic loss. One crucial difference between these early reforms and contemporary tort reform measures, however, is that plaintiffs are no longer accorded a quid pro quo for giving up their claim of noneconomic damages. Importantly, the considerable advantages of workers' compensation and automobile no-fault schemes, such as quicker recoveries for plaintiffs and the elimination of the need to prove fault, are not features of the one-sided tort reforms of the past twenty-five years.

In the abstract, noneconomic losses appear gender-neutral, in that both men and women can suffer pain, grieve over the loss of a child, or experience fright or terror at the prospect of impending death. However, in practice, noneconomic damages are critical for female tort plaintiffs for a variety of reasons linked to gender. The privileging of economic over noneconomic losses turns out to be a very powerful way in which tort law devalues recurring injuries that happen mostly to women and delivers an unequal measure of protection to female litigants.

Historically and culturally, noneconomic damages have been cognitively associated with women and women's injuries. As discussed in chapter 2, the association was first forged in "nervous-shock" cases in the early 20th century in which women plaintiffs sought recovery against railroads for miscarriages, stillbirth, and other fright-based injuries that caused both physical and mental harms. The judicial response to these early cases was complex and contradictory. Although some courts allowed recovery—particularly when the plaintiff was a white woman—they tended to classify such cases as "mental distress" cases, regardless of their physical consequences, and to subject them to more stringent requirements than were applied to ordinary cases of physical injury. In this way, the gender of the prototypical plaintiff served to overwhelm the other features of the case and to mark the case as different, calling attention to the emotional aspects of the claim. Although both men and women had long been permitted to recover money for pain and suffering in ordinary physical harm cases, the nervous-shock cases cemented the links that connected women, emotional harm, and noneconomic loss.

The updated versions of the nervous-shock cases are contemporary cases, brought disproportionately by women plaintiffs, that allege sexual or reproductive injury. The list includes intentional tort claims for domestic violence, claims for sexual harassment or sexual abuse, and claims brought by women seeking recovery for infertility and other reproductive harms produced by dangerous drugs and medical devices. Tort recovery for these sexual and reproductive injuries still largely depends on the award of noneconomic damages.

Although the injuries plaintiffs have sustained in these contexts vary considerably and defy categorization, these cases are most often approached and tried as cases involving noneconomic loss. For example, Professor Finley explains that the plaintiffs in high-profile DES and Dalkon Shield cases experienced tangible and observable harms, such as misshapen uteruses and cervixes, miscarriages, septic abortions, and pelvic inflammatory disease.[49] However, because the full measure of these losses could not be expressed in market-based terms, they tended not to count as economic losses, save for the relatively small portion attributable to medical bills for short-term treatment. Lost in the crude dichotomy of economic versus noneconomic damage is the longer-term impact of infertility and reproductive injuries, which may profoundly change the way a woman regards herself, approaches life, and interacts with family, intimates, and the larger community. Reducing reproductive injury to either economic or noneconomic loss tends to blunt the life-altering dimension of such harms and to focus our attention away from its particularized impact on the individual plaintiff. Especially when a loss is classified as "noneconomic," there is a danger that it will be assimilated to hurt feelings and negative emotions and regarded as ephemeral and insubstantial. Like most dichotomies, the economic/noneconomic divide not only differentiates between two types of damage awards but privileges one type of damage award over the other.

Feminist theorists have long recognized that harms typically associated with women—for which there is no common male analogue—are often the most difficult to articulate and value in the law.[50] They tend to fall through the cracks of the available categories and get lost in translation from social injury to legal harm. Part of the problem lies in the fact that the economic dimension of injuries experienced disproportionately by members of subordinated groups may go unnoticed or be regarded as too remote for the law to redress. For example, studies reveal that workplace harassment lowers productivity on the job and prevents victims from seeking transfers or promotions, particularly if they face increased hostility in the new setting.[51] The claim of hostile environment harassment, however, is regarded mainly as a claim for noneconomic loss. The U.S. Supreme Court underscored this point in a 2004 constructive discharge case in which it held that claims of workers forced to quit because of sexual harassment would be treated differently and less favorably than claims of workers forced to quit because of a demotion or other tangible action.[52] Although the harm was the same in each situation—the unemployment of the target of discrimination—the Court fixed on what it regarded as the intangible, noneconomic character of sexual harassment to single out such claims for less favorable treatment. Similarly, Lucinda Finley reports on an interview with a plaintiff who suffered severe injury to her bladder and reproductive system from DES-caused cancer.[53] She told Finley that she was embarrassed by having to empty her catheter frequently and, for that reason, decided to forgo promotions that involved travel and client contact. Her attorneys, however, proceeded on the assumption that her medical bills were the only economic losses she had suffered and never inquired about other consequential economic damages, apparently because these damages had escaped their notice or were regarded as too attenuated to claim.

From a gender perspective, the chief dangers of bluntly classifying damages as either economic or noneconomic are invisibility and minimization. The dichotomy suggests that we already know the character of the two types of losses and discourages investigation into the specifics of injuries. Particularly because of the highly disparate nature of what are now regarded as noneconomic losses—ranging from devastation and stigma at being unable to bear children to decreased prospects for advancement on the job—it is hard to resist the temptation to simplify a case and proceed as if all intangible harm were basically the same. If injured parties are not allowed to tell the whole story of their injury to a jury, their harm can become invisible, defeating the important narrative function of tort law. Most important, unless the full effect of injuries are articulated and explained, they can more easily be minimized. The infelicitous label "noneconomic loss" signals a lack of substance and makes noneconomic damages a prime target for cutbacks in liability.

It is not surprising that caps directed at noneconomic damages disparately impact specific segments of the population. Researchers are now beginning to document the effects of such caps on women, children, the elderly, and minorities. At first blush, caps would seem solely to affect the amount of recovery some plaintiffs receive, for example, those injured seriously enough to allege noneconomic losses that exceed the cap. Thus, by their very nature, caps have the perverse effect of targeting the most severely injured plaintiffs, the subgroup of injured persons long known to be relatively undercompensated compared to victims with less serious injuries. However, what is not always recognized is that caps affect not only the amount of damages but also the number and kind of cases that plaintiffs' attorneys are willing to accept. This screening effect is particularly significant for social groups that discover that after tort reform they cannot secure representation because their cases are no longer worth filing.

One reason that noneconomic damages loom so large in tort recoveries for female victims is that, as a group, women still earn far less money than men, and thus their economic losses tend to be lower. Simply stated, noneconomic losses mean more to women because they form a higher proportion of women's overall damage awards. For example, a 2004 study of jury verdicts in medical malpractice cases in California found that noneconomic damages represented 78 percent of total damages for female plaintiffs but only 48 percent for male plaintiffs.[54] The study also compared awards before and after the imposition of the $250,000 MICRA cap on noneconomic damages and found that application of the caps exacerbated the gender disparity in damage awards. Before the cap was applied, women's median jury award was 94 percent of the men's median; after application of the cap, women's median was only 58.6 percent of the male median.

Damage caps are particularly harsh in cases involving gender-specific injuries or sexualized injuries that disproportionately affect women. Tellingly, the California malpractice data showed that in gynecological cases—a subset of cases with all-female plaintiffs—the proportion of damages represented by noneconomic damages (median 92.5%) was even greater than for female plaintiffs in non-gender-specific types of injuries (median 78%).[55] Gynecological injuries typically involve "impaired fertility, impaired sexual functioning, incontinence, miscarriage, and scarring in personally sensitive body areas."[56] These harms are frequently serious but are not likely to transform into significant loss of wages, at least in the short term. Additionally, with respect to sexual assault victims, data from Florida cases generated two important conclusions: that women were overrepresented in such cases (95% of the total) and that awards for female sexual assault victims were more heavily concentrated in noneconomic damages (91.7%) than were those for male assault victims (66%).[57] These data confirm that noneconomic damages are especially important for women because they compensate for the kinds of injuries women are likely to incur and often represent the bulk of recovery in such cases.

Empirical research also indicates that subgroups other than women are penalized by damage caps through the operation of similar dynamics. For each of these subgroups, noneconomic damages are disproportionately important because the victims suffer a relatively low level of economic damages and because courts are unable to recognize the serious nature of their injuries except through an award of noneconomic damages. Noneconomic damages can be crucially important in cases involving injury to children. Particularly in cases of wrongful death of children, noneconomic damages are essential to ensure that awards are not trivial, given that children in today's culture are more likely to be financial liabilities to their parents than financial assets. In malpractice cases in which a child died, for example, application of the MICRA damages cap reduced the median wrongful death award by a stunning 79 percent, whereas in cases involving the injury of children the reduction was only 11 percent.[58] The combined effect of the damages hierarchy and the application of the cap substantially reduced the value of a child's life, largely because there is no market price for the lost companionship and grief suffered by surviving parents.

Similarly, there is evidence that damage caps have had a devastating effect on nursing home litigation, in which the plaintiffs are most often elderly women. In a recent article, titled *Heart of Stone*, Michael Rustad posited a prototypical victim in a nursing home case—a woman in her late 80s who dies in the nursing home of sepsis, a bacterial infection that poisons the blood.[59] In such cases, the victims' families often charge that negligence on the part of the nursing home staff caused the elderly woman to develop painful pressure sores, which eventually produced an infection in her bones, hastening her death. Rustad discovered that more than half of nursing home cases consisted of death cases involving allegations of pressure sores, malnutrition, and emotional distress. In many of these cases, there was an allegation that the resident was given insufficient pain medication over a period of weeks or months prior to her death. In short, the prototypical nursing home case seeks recovery for a painful, undignified, and premature death. It is the kind of injury that is undeniably serious, whether we contemplate our own quality of life at the end of our lives or the quality of life for our elderly parents living in nursing homes.

Since the imposition of damage caps, however, many plaintiffs' attorneys have decided that nursing home cases are no longer worth bringing. An article published in the *ABA Journal* in October 2006, titled *Tort Reform Texas Style*,[60] indicated that a $250,000 cap on noneconomic damages enacted in 2003 had the effect of forcing most nursing home litigators to relocate out of state or to switch their practice to concentrate on other types of cases, for example, intellectual property disputes. The available data showed a sharp drop in medical malpractice cases after tort reform, down more than 40 percent in the Houston area.[61] These lawyers realized that in prototypical nursing home cases there will be minimal economic losses because the residents are no longer in the workforce and their life expectancy is very limited. Importantly, the kind of harms suffered in these cases—the pain and suffering that accompany bed sores, malnutrition, lack of pain medication, and shortened life—will likely fall under the category of noneconomic loss, subject to the caps.[62]

With respect to the impact of damage caps on racial minorities, the empirical evidence is less extensive. Researchers do generally agree, however, that, because racial minorities earn less on average than whites, more of their total awards is likely to be in the form of noneconomic damages. Capping noneconomic damages thus tends to reduce compensation to minorities disproportionately.[63] Additionally, in the medical malpractice context—the kind of case in which caps on noneconomic damages are frequently imposed—there is evidence that minorities are exposed to medical mistakes more frequently than whites.[64] Minorities are more often uninsured than whites and are commonly treated in emergency rooms, the hospital location with the highest proportion of negligent adverse events. Capping damages in medical malpractice cases therefore tends to target the types of injury that minorities are disproportionately likely to experience.

Damage caps on noneconomic damages also likely have a screening effect that discourages plaintiffs' attorneys from taking cases involving minority plaintiffs. Because caps on noneconomic damages reduce plaintiffs' recoveries, lawyers are less likely to represent minority and other low-income plaintiffs when a contingency fee is the only avenue for attorney compensation. Interviews with plaintiffs' attorneys in Texas, for example, revealed that, after imposition of damage caps, lawyers screened cases not only for the level of injury but also for characteristics of the potential client. One attorney admitted that "across the board the credibility of your client is ever, ever more important in these times." He stressed that, in assessing the value of the case, "[y]ou have to have a client that has a good work history, a client who has never been in trouble with the law."[65]

While such stringent screening criteria are racially neutral on their face, it is highly likely that they disparately impact racial minorities, given that unemployment rates, conviction rates, and arrest rates are higher for African Americans and Hispanics than for whites.[66] Such screening criteria echo the kind of "morality" or "character" factors that insurance underwriters have historically relied upon to screen out unacceptable risks, making it more difficult for minorities and other nonmiddle-class groups to obtain insurance.[67] Thus, in the same way that caps make it harder for elderly victims in nursing homes to find lawyers to take their cases, the racial impact of caps likely surfaces even before cases are filed, settled, or tried. Moreover, because of its embedded character, such racial bias is hard to detect and does not show up in empirical studies of damage awards in litigated cases or settlements.[68] Damage caps thus appear to exacerbate the tendency of attorneys, claims adjusters, and judges to factor in the race of the injured party as one of the "potential risks" in tort cases.[69]

Given the negative distributional impact of caps on noneconomic damages, one might question why they have been such a prime target of tort reform. The main thrust of the tort reformers' general critique of noneconomic damages is that noneconomic damages are excessive and unpredictable. They seek to discredit pain and suffering awards by portraying them as irrational jury responses to sympathetic victims as constructed by skillful plaintiffs' attorneys.[70] The more theoretical claim of the tort reformers is that intangible harms, such as pain and mental trauma, are incapable of being fixed or repaired by money. They argue that awarding compensation for such harms—at least without strict limits—gives juries free rein to exercise their subjective judgment in an erratic fashion that often turns compensation into punishment.[71] Importantly, the arguments against noneconomic damages all presuppose that tort awards not tied to precise market valuations are inherently suspect and lead to abuse.

At its most basic level, the controversy over noneconomic compensatory damages rests on whether recovery for such losses is regarded as an essential feature of the torts system. Proponents of noneconomic damages point out that noneconomic losses are often the most serious harms a person can suffer and therefore deserve to be compensated in tort. The importance of noneconomic losses can perhaps best be appreciated by contemplating the high value people place on the nonpecuniary aspects of their everyday existence. As Neil Komesar observes, the significance of noneconomic losses can be seen by "asking yourself whether you would be indifferent or even nearly indifferent between an uninjured state and a severely injured state, such as paraplegia, blindness, or severe brain damage, so long as your income and wealth remained constant." For Komesar, the answer to such a question "reveals the depth of nonpecuniary components captured roughly under the rubric of pain and suffering." He contends that these noneconomic elements are "primary elements of life" and that it "turns reality on its head to give transcendence to the pecuniary."[72]

Once it is accepted that noneconomic losses are genuine and serious, the next step to consider is whether any distinctive feature of noneconomic damages justifies treating them less favorably than economic damages. In our view, the distinction drawn between economic and noneconomic damages is a false dichotomy. The oft-stated reason that economic damages, unlike noneconomic damages, can be precisely measured has been unmasked as an "illusion" that obscures the fact that many types of economic damages are also notoriously hard to measure. This is particularly true for calculations of future economic losses, such as future medical expenses and loss of future earning capacity, discussed in the previous section. Robert Rabin, for example, asserts that "every tort scholar recognizes that there is frequently extraordinary uncertainty and imprecision involved in recovery of pecuniary loss in serious injury cases of the sort that generate high intangible-loss awards."[73]

At the other end of the spectrum, it is not always understood that damages for pain and suffering are not wholly unpredictable but rather depend to a significant degree on the severity of the injury. The current system achieves some degree of "vertical equity" in that it awards higher damages to those who suffer the most severe types of injuries.[74] The variation in awards is said to result in a lack of "horizontal equity," however, because different juries give widely varying amounts for injuries judged by researchers to be of comparable severity. Such variation is not surprising, however, once it is recognized that an individual who suffers a certain type of bodily injury, of a specified severity, will not or should not necessarily experience the same type or degree of pain and suffering as another individual who sustains a similar injury. Looked at from this perspective, the failure to achieve precision in the evaluation of similar injuries is not a major flaw in the system but a refined response to highly individuated injuries. It must be remembered that plaintiffs who suffer similar injuries can also receive widely varying amounts for economic damages, because of the large differences in wages and future earning capacity of victims from different socioeconomic classes. Unless we are to fault plaintiffs for not experiencing the modal amount of pain and suffering—that is, for being individuals—there is nothing particularly troubling about variations in pain and suffering awards, except for cases in which there is reason to believe that the jury has awarded an unconscionably high or low award.[75]

The more potent argument against awarding noneconomic damages is what is known as the incommensurability argument: the claim that because money damages cannot repair intangible harms, they should not be awarded simply to give victims something tangible to recognize their loss. Richard Abel, for example, believes that noneconomic damages have a corrupting influence, in large part because they reduce human experience to money. He argues that awarding noneconomic damages violates "our essential humanity" by attempting to price bodily integrity, emotional well-being, and relationships.[76]

Much like the claims about imprecision, however, the incommensurability objection is flawed because it fails to differentiate between economic and noneconomic damages and applies with some force to both types of damages. To make this point, Lucinda Finley notes that a money award does not repair a broken spine or restore the injured person to his or her pre-accident state. It simply allows the injured person to obtain medical treatment and other assistance, often by reimbursing "substitute ways of functioning, such as wheel chairs." Additionally, when a person is so severely injured that she cannot return to work, she loses more than simply lost wages. The disability also brings the loss of crucial nonmonetary aspects of employment, including "self-esteem, status, place in the community, and social networks," aspects of a person's identity that may be as important as the income generated by the job.[77] Because neither type of damage award literally makes the victim whole or restores the victim to the status quo ante, selective elimination or curtailment of noneconomic damages cannot be expected to cure the problems of imprecision and incommensurability that inhere in the tort system of money damages generally.

So far, however, the academic defense of noneconomic damages has not stopped the legislative assault against noneconomic damages and the reinforcement of the damages hierarchy. In part, the political success of the tort reform movement stems from the seductive familiarity of the labels themselves. Labeling damages "economic versus noneconomic" tacitly erects economic damages as the baseline and trades on the positive valence generally attached to economic measures. Compared to the term "general damages," used historically to encompass compensatory awards for nonpecuniary losses, the term "noneconomic" damages sounds like it describes a more marginal classification. For many, the category of economic damages seems more objective and measurable, in line with prevailing notions of market-based measures as neutral and scientific. In contrast, the category of noneconomic damages lumps together a wide variety of losses, presumably sharing the negative feature of not being based on economics.

These labels, however, are deceiving. Heidi Li Feldman points out that the legal distinction between economic and noneconomic damages did not originate in the discipline of economics and cannot be justified by commonly accepted economic principles.[78] Feldman explains that, for economists, any diminution in human welfare counts as a loss to that individual. She asserts that "nowhere in the entire history of modern economics, starting with the classical economists of the 18th century, does one find economists arguing that some reductions in welfare are peculiarly economic and others are not."[79] Rather than employing a narrow definition of human welfare centered on monetary gains and losses, modern economics presupposes that individuals choose to enhance their personal welfare in a variety of different ways and that they place different values on the losses they suffer. Interestingly enough, the wide array of terms used in the law to express noneconomic losses—including not only physical pain and suffering but also "fright, nervousness, grief, anxiety, worry, mortification, shock, humiliation, indignity, embarrassment, apprehension, terror or ordeal"[80]—fits well with the broad conception of loss of welfare as used by economists. Feldman concludes that there is no support in economics for privileging economic loss over noneconomic loss and insists that the distinction is best understood as a "rhetorical invention" of tort reformers.

As the research on damage caps becomes more sophisticated, it will undoubtedly refine and complicate the picture of the impact of damage caps on specific social groups, particularly as some of the unintended effects of such legislation are identified and analyzed. Catherine Sharkey's empirical study of medical malpractice caps, for example, has indicated that plaintiffs' attorneys and juries may be able to offset the effect of damage caps to some extent by recharacterizing a plaintiff's loss as economic, particularly with the aid of expert witnesses.[81] This "crossover effect," however, may not be feasible in several types of cases. For example, we suspect that even if jurors have the impulse to award fuller compensation in nursing-home cases, they will have less flexibility to do so because it is just too much of a stretch to recharacterize an elderly female plaintiff's injury as economic. The same is likely to hold true for valuations of loss of fertility or other reproductive harms, which are generally regarded as intimate, rather than economic, injuries. Moreover, before such a crossover effect can occur, cases must be filed and litigated. As the Texas nursing home example shows, damage caps not only limit the amount of recovery but can also substantially reduce the number of cases brought in particular jurisdictions.

In the final analysis, the most enduring lesson of the controversy surrounding damage caps on noneconomic compensatory damages is the importance of assessing the gender, racial, and other distributional effects of damage rules. Before the debate on damage caps, tort reform generally proceeded as if the only issue were curbing frivolous lawsuits and excessive awards, oblivious to the social justice impact of revisions in damage rules. The extensive debate about caps has deepened our understanding of the ways gender-linked harms are devalued, fastened scholars' attention on the bias that can result from uncritical acceptance of legal dichotomies, and begun to unearth how racial minorities can be denied access to the civil justice system. By bringing the law of damages more into the mainstream, it has also positioned the measure of injuries—and not just the recognition of injuries—as a central feature of tort law.

Conclusion

Tort law is most often thought of as individualistic and universal, as the area of law that defines private rights and obligations between individuals apart from contract. Despite the singular importance of the individual to tort law, however, tort doctrines do not generally approach the individual as an actual person. Instead, the individual of tort law has largely been an abstraction, disembodied and living outside of society. Historically, this creature of legal theory had no name and fittingly appeared in the examples of the First and Second Restatement of Torts as simply A, B, or C.

This book has offered a picture of tort law that departs from idealized accounts of the field most often provided by torts theorists. Traditionally, the prototypical torts claim is envisioned as arising between strangers, with the success of a claim rarely dependent on the identity of the parties or the particular context in which the injury arose. What distinguishes our critical approach to tort law from these more standard accounts is the attention we have paid to the social identity of tort victims and to the context of their injuries. In analyzing claims for intentional wrongs and negligently caused injuries, we have started from the premise that the individuals who pursue such claims have a race and a gender. In various contexts, we have tracked the connection between a victim's race and gender and the legal response to her injuries.

Beyond the social identity of individual plaintiffs, moreover, in this book we have recognized that tort claims themselves are not always neutral. Specific kinds of claims often have a racial or gendered character or arise in contexts that are cognitively associated with women or racial minorities. We have focused in on these special kinds of cases—whether claims for domestic violence, workplace harassment, or wrongful birth—to present a deep and nuanced view of how tort law treats the variables of gender and race and to assess developments in cases of distinctive importance to women and racial minorities.

In the 21st century, most legal scholars, including tort scholars, have rejected stark versions of legal formalism and have acknowledged that tort law does not exist in isolation from the larger culture. Because tort law is neither self-contained nor autonomous, many scholars also aspire to examine tort doctrines not simply as abstract principles and rules but as they operate in social context. However, in our view, there is still too little discussion of how gender and race have shaped current tort rules or the degree to which tort doctrines might be fashioned to promote gender or race equity. In contrast to its predecessors, the Third Restatement of Torts does now provide first names for the hypothetical individuals used in the examples of tort principles—subtly introducing gender into some situations—but there is still scant commentary on the distributional effects of particular rules on different social groups or the extent to which considerations of social justice inform notions of the “fairness” of tort rules.

In this book we have identified six different pathways by which considerations of race and gender—connected either to the identity of tort victims or to the nature of their claims—have influenced contemporary U.S. tort law. To a certain extent, the six pathways we identify overlap with different types of gender and race bias described and analyzed by scholars in antidiscrimination and constitutional law. However, in this book, our objective has been not only to scan tort law for concrete instances of gender and race bias but also to canvass the field more broadly to seek out the less obvious links between tort doctrine and race and gender, even when they do not clearly amount to bias or injustice.

As a matter of formal law and doctrine, contemporary tort law is largely gender and race neutral. However, on rare occasions, the gender and race of plaintiffs are explicitly taken into account and can alter the outcome of torts cases or the value of cases. Thus, the first pathway by which race and gender enter tort law is through the front door, in the form of *explicit gender and race classifications and categories.* The most important—and most pernicious—example of such explicit reliance on gender and race is the use of gender- and race-based tables, discussed in chapter 6, to predict the amount of economic damages a tort victim may receive in personal injury and death cases. We have argued that resort to race and gender as a shortcut to assessing an individual’s future earning capacity is inaccurate and unfair and a throwback to earlier days when race and gender were uncritically relied upon to award lower amounts for injuries to women and minorities than to similarly situated white male victims.

In other contexts, the gender and race of plaintiffs have been noticed explicitly and have influenced tort judgments in a nonstereotyped manner that tends to promote equality of marginalized social groups, rather than retard it. In chapter 3, we examined the approach of a minority of courts that have declared that discriminatory racial and sexual harassment is more likely to qualify as "outrageous" behavior under the tort of intentional infliction of emotional distress. Such courts have been willing to use tort law to reinforce the state's public policy against discrimination and have treated the racial or gender identity of the plaintiff as relevant both to an assessment of the inappropriateness of defendant's conduct and the serious nature of plaintiff's injury.

More often, considerations of gender and race are covert, resulting in disparate treatment of certain individuals and certain types of claims, in nonobvious and hidden ways. The second pathway by which gender and race enter tort law is through the phenomenon of *devaluation of plaintiffs and their interests because of race or gender*. In some cases, deep-seated negative attitudes toward social groups have resulted in a failure to see and to value their pain and suffering in a manner comparable to the way similar injuries suffered by dominant groups are viewed and valued. In chapter 2, we recounted a pattern in the first half of the 20th century of devaluation of claims for injury brought by black families in Louisiana in cases of wrongful death. Similar racial devaluation of noneconomic losses is likely to be compounded under current law in jurisdictions that impose a "multiplier" cap on noneconomic damages, thereby depressing awards of noneconomic damages for low-income plaintiffs with minimal economic damages.

In some cases, devaluation attaches to the type of interest sought to be vindicated, rather than to the individual plaintiff. In chapter 4, for example, we examined the devaluation of "feminine" interests and activities related to childbearing and childrearing. In numerous cases of negligently caused miscarriages and stillbirths, coerced sterilizations of African American women, and "bystander" claims in which mothers have witnessed their child's serious injury or death, courts have struggled to comprehend the nature of the harm and have often been reluctant to regard the interest at stake as worthy of legal protection. In such cases, we saw that, because the process of gender devaluation infects whole categories of claims, individual men who suffer similar "feminine" injuries are also disadvantaged.

The third pathway by which gender and race considerations enter tort law is through *unconscious stereotyping and cognitive biases* that affect judgments about causation and blame in certain types of tort cases. In chapter 5, we explored principles of cognitive psychology to understand why judges and jurors might be more willing to attribute negative outcomes to a plaintiff's internal traits than to impose responsibility on external forces connected to defendant's behavior. In cases of wrongful birth, we traced the willingness of courts to regard physician negligence as a cause of plaintiffs' harm only after *Roe v. Wade* was decided and related cultural developments supporting women's reproductive autonomy made it possible to imagine an interruption of the birth process. In lead paint cases, we exposed the danger of racial stereotyping infecting causal judgments when judges considered the likely origin of cognitive injuries to minority children exposed to toxic substances. In such gendered and racialized contexts, plaintiffs suffer the risk that legal decision makers will regard their injuries as normal for their group and will not be predisposed to entertain other explanations for the harm.

The remaining three pathways by which gender and race enter tort law relate more to structural features of contemporary tort law than to psychological processes such as the stereotyping, disparate treatment, selective sympathy, and failures of imagination that characterize the three pathways already discussed. Because gender and race equity have not been articulated as a specific goal of tort law, tort doctrines and reforms are not often thoroughly examined for their *disparate effects on marginalized groups*. In some instances, lawmakers and courts may be oblivious to the harmful impacts that neutral policies have on women and on low-income groups, especially minorities. We analyzed the most dramatic example of the disparate social impact of tort reform in chapter 6 in our review of empirical research on legislative caps imposed on noneconomic damages. The larger political debate about caps has not centered on gender and race but has been preoccupied with concerns about runaway verdicts, excessive damages, and disproportionate liability for tort defendants generally. We discussed how the harsh impact of caps, however, has nevertheless been felt selectively by female plaintiffs who suffer nonmonetizeable injuries, such as loss of fertility, by elderly residents of nursing homes, by families of children wrongfully killed, and by low-income minority plaintiffs who are unable to secure legal representation without the prospect of a sizeable award of noneconomic damages. Additionally, in chapter 3 we analyze how seemingly neutral features, such as short statutes of limitations and exclusions in insurance law, operate to disproportionately bar women's claims for injuries from domestic violence.

Perhaps the most important structural feature of contemporary tort law—and the fifth pathway of entry for considerations of gender and race—is the existence of seemingly neutral *dichotomies describing types of injuries and types of damages* that privilege certain tort claims and recoveries and impose special restrictions on others. In chapters 2 and 4, we explained how, historically and at present, claims of negligent infliction of mental distress have been approached skeptically by courts, resulting in precarious recovery for a group made up largely of female plaintiffs who seek recovery for gender-related injuries resulting from sexual exploitation, reproductive injury, and injury to intimate family relationships. This well-entrenched hierarchy in tort law that positions physical injury above injury to emotions and relationships has been remarkably effective in making it more difficult to secure legal protection for many of the serious recurring injuries in women's lives, while appearing evenhanded and gender-neutral. In chapter 6, we described how the recent "tort reform" assault on noneconomic damages has supplemented and reinforced the physical/emotional harm dichotomy by making it more difficult for plaintiffs to recover for injuries that have no market value, adding to the widespread belief that economic harm is somehow more important and more genuine than noneconomic harm. Throughout the book, we have maintained that this is a false dichotomy that harms women by subtly shifting attention away from the negative gender effects of the hierarchy it constructs.

Finally, in chapter 3, we focused on *domain disputes* as the sixth and final pathway through which gender and race connect to tort law. We explained how tort law has never provided a secure remedy for harms, notably domestic violence and workplace harassment, that rank among the most serious forms of abuse affecting women and racial minorities. This enormous gap in protection is no longer justified by denying or failing to recognize the widespread existence of abuse. Rather, similar to the construction of implicit hierarchies of value within tort law, a conceptual boundary has been drawn between the domain of tort law and that of other bodies of law—principally family law and civil rights law—that pushes out claims of gender and race abuse from the mainstream of torts. We have argued against such artificial boundaries and expressed concerns that cordoning off gender- and race-related injuries from tort law severely undercuts its claim to universal protection against wrongful behavior.

The six pathways we describe are not completely separate avenues but are interrelated and often mutually reinforcing. When an explicit racial classification in the form of a "black" earnings table is used to determine an injured child's earning capacity, for example, those tables are partly a product of a history of racial stereotyping and covert disparate treatment of minorities in the workplace. When suits for sexual exploitation and racial harassment are devalued within tort law and categorized as emotional distress claims, it is easier to declare that they are best handled outside the domain of torts, in areas regarded as more suitable for addressing gender and minority interests. Likewise, when injuries from domestic violence are defined as outside the mainstream of torts, we can more readily ignore structural mechanisms, such as insurance exclusions, that burden victims of domestic violence and prevent their claims from being heard. And when there is little inclination to examine tort doctrines or reforms for their disparate effects on marginalized social groups, it is unlikely that judges or jurors will take special care not to allow the racial or gendered context of a controversy to influence their judgments about causation and blame.

The upside potential of the interrelated character of the pathways we describe, however, is that it is also possible to intervene at multiple points to guide tort law in a progressive direction that promotes gender and race equity. As a dynamic body of common law, tort law already contains many progressive cases and doctrinal strands that have allowed us to envision what a more egalitarian approach might look like and how these progressive strands in the law might be organized to make them more visible and influential. In this book, we have offered a variety of specific suggestions to reform current law, such as eliminating the use of gender- and race-based tables and permitting tort claims for workplace harassment to supplement and strengthen the protection offered by statutory civil rights law. Aside from specific proposals attached to distinct claims, however, we have also formulated three general prescriptions for progressive change that we regard as central to making tort law more equitable and more responsive to the interests of women and racial minorities.

The first prescription for change builds on the willingness of some courts to allow principles and norms from statutory civil rights law and constitutional law to migrate into torts. This development has been most pronounced in intentional torts when courts have imported concepts from Title VII hostile workplace environment law to provide a basis for recovery for tort claims for intentional infliction of emotional distress. We have also seen the migration phenomenon at work, however, when courts have cited statutes against sexual exploitation and constitutional rulings protecting a woman's right to procreative choice as a reason for imposing a duty of due care on physicians and other actors whose conduct impairs a plaintiff's interest in sexual autonomy or reproduction. And, most directly, we have witnessed the intersection of civil rights, constitutional law, and tort law in Judge Weinstein's 2008 declaration that the use of race-based tables to calculate a tort victim's damage award was unconstitutional.

Our first prescription for change is to increase and accelerate the migration of these civil rights principles and norms into tort law in a self-conscious effort to weave gender and race equality into basic tort law principles. We advocate connecting civil rights and civil wrongs so that violations of civil rights will no longer be approached solely as public law infractions, insulated from tort liability. So far, this course has been taken only outside the United States. In chapter 3, we explained how the Canadian Supreme Court defined human dignity as intertwined with social equality and considered devaluation and marginalization of social groups to be an affront to human dignity. Fusing dignity and equality in this fashion would make it far less likely that discriminatory behavior could continue to fall below the threshold of "outrageous" conduct actionable under U.S. tort law. Additionally, in chapter 6, we discussed the approach of the Israeli Supreme Court, which rejected the use of ethnic-based statistics to lower an award of damages to an Arab child. The Israeli court made the significant determination that an award of tort damages should strive to return tort victims not simply to the status quo ante but to a "just and fair" status, one that does not reproduce past inequalities among social groups. We urge that U.S. courts move in a similar direction—not to replace or displace established tort principles—but to reframe them in accord with contemporary understandings of civil rights norms and principles.

In line with these developments, our second prescription for change likewise draws upon sex discrimination and constitutional law but is directed more specifically to the important issue of deciding when to impose a duty of due care in negligence cases. Our study of the tort of negligent infliction of emotional distress reveals that this corner of the law is saturated with gender-related issues, full of cases dealing with sexual exploitation, pregnancy, reproductive choice, and intimate family relationships. Despite liberalization in some jurisdictions of the rules governing liability, recovery in negligent infliction cases is still precarious and is hampered by a variety of special restrictions and doctrinal hurdles. A critical feature of so many of these negligent infliction cases is that a defendant's conduct has damaged a plaintiff's well-being in contexts central to her identity as a woman, mother, or family member. Often at stake is the right of the plaintiff to control her own sexuality or to make decisions about bearing and nurturing children. We have made the case for prioritizing plaintiffs' interests in sexual integrity and reproduction as interests worthy of heightened protection in tort law. These interests not only are of crucial importance for women's equality but have attained the status of fundamental rights under the U.S. Constitution. Taking the simple but important step of naming sexual autonomy and reproduction as special interests that trigger a duty of care in negligence law would bring the domain of torts and constitutional law closer together and provide much needed protection for liberty and equality in the private realm.

Our third prescription for change relates to the structure and core of tort law as it is generally conceived. Throughout our study, we have noticed that the areas of tort law of particular importance to women and minorities are most often located at the margins of the field, at some distance from the negligence claims for physical injury situated at the center. Thus, this book devotes far more attention to intentional torts, emotional distress, and damages than would a conventional treatise on torts. The conventional way of thinking about torts, moreover, has the effect of erasing issues of equality and social justice from the core of the field and convincing us that tort law is all about accidents and incidents unrelated to the social identities of victims and the nature of their claims. We have resisted this configuration and have argued that if domestic violence and sexual and reproductive harms were afforded greater protection in torts, the shape of the field would change dramatically, pushing intentional torts and nonphysical harms toward the center. The important point here is that the "core" and "margins" of tort law are not natural or fixed but are dynamic social constructions that are tools of persuasion as well as organization.

Relatedly, we have questioned the boundaries drawn between torts and other fields of law because such boundaries are also social constructions that tend to elide important debates over the degree of protection that should be afforded to persons who suffer recurring types of systemic harm. When domestic violence victims are relegated exclusively to family law or to criminal law to seek redress for their injuries, they are denied the measure of compensation and deterrence that comes only from torts. Taking domestic violence harms out of tort law also takes away the opportunity for private enforcement of equality norms and the occasion to treat domestic violence as a universal injury, instead of a women's issue. Accordingly, our third prescription for change calls for demarginalizing claims of particular importance to women and minorities and reconceptualizing the core of tort law.

It is worth pointing out that beneath each of our prescriptions for change lies the conviction that promoting equality and social justice through tort law is a legitimate enterprise. We recognize that this proposition is not uncontroversial and that arguments for changing tort law are generally couched solely in terms of compensation and deterrence. However, we believe there is room in tort law for equality. Our study of race, gender, and tort law convinces us that race and gender considerations have already significantly influenced tort doctrines. Our critical take on tort law suggests that disregarding gender and race will not ensure equality, but only increases the chances that tort law will reproduce inequities of the past and project them onto the future. The measure of injury is a telling expression of a culture's deeply held values. Gender and race equity should not be left out.

Notes

CHAPTER 1

1. *See* Martha Chamallas, *Vanished from the First Year: Lost Torts and Deep Structures in Tort Law*, *in* Legal Canons 104 (J.M. Balkin & Sanford Levinson eds., NYU Press 2000).

2. *See* Gary T. Schwartz, *Mixed Theories of Tort Law: Affirming Both Deterrence and Corrective Justice*, 75 Tex. L. Rev. 1801, 1802 (1997) (scholarly situation changed dramatically starting in early 1970s).

3. Although we describe our approach as a "critical" approach to tort law, it might just as easily be classified as a progressive approach to tort law, thereby aligning us with such scholars as Michael Rustad, Tsachi Keren-Paz, and Richard Abel. *See e.g.*, the classification scheme used by Tsachi Keren-Paz, Torts, Egalitarianism and Distributive Justice 2 (Ashgate Press 2007) (combining feminists and social justice scholars into a "progressive" camp that aims "to employ tort law progressively, with an ambition to be sensitive to the demands of equality and the interests of disadvantaged groups in society").

4. For example, John Goldberg excluded "feminist theories" altogether from his taxonomy of tort theories, choosing not to include feminist torts scholarship within his category of "social justice" theories. John C. P. Goldberg, *Twentieth Century Tort Theories*, 91 Geo. L.J. 513, 514 n.2, 560–63 (2003).

5. Our description of law and economics pertains only to the neoclassical "Chicago school" style of law and economics and does not cover the newer behavioral economics that questions many of the fundamental assumptions of the Chicago school. *See* Anita Bernstein, *Whatever Happened to Law and Economics?*, 64 Md. L. Rev. 303, 306–07 (2005). Likewise, we make no attempt to describe the details of various brands of corrective justice theory, such as Benjamin Zipursky's civil recourse theory. *See* Benjamin C. Zipursky, *Civil Recourse Not Corrective Justice*, 91 Geo. L.J. 695 (2003).

6. Jon Hanson & David Yosifon, *The Situation: An Introduction to the Situational Character, Critical Realism, Power Economics and Deep Capture*, 152 U. Pa. L. Rev. 129 (2003). See also Marc Galanter, *Introduction: The Path of the Law Ands*, 1997 Wis. L. Rev. 375 (describing law and economics as "a success story in terms of its institutionalization of economic analysis within law schools").

7. *See e.g.*, R. H. Coase, *The Problem of Social Cost*, 3 J. L. & Econ (1960); William A. Landes & Richard A. Posner, The Economic Structure of Tort Law (Harv. Univ. Press 1987); Richard A. Posner, The Economic Analysis of Law (7th ed. 2007). Others such as Judge Guido Calabresi, have also been tremendously influential. See, e.g, Guido Calabresi, The Cost of Accidents: A Legal and Economic Analysis (Yale Univ. Press 1970).

8. David W. Barnes & Lynn A. Stout, The Economic Analysis of Tort Law 27 (1992).

9. *See* Marshall Shapo, Tort Law and Culture 143–44 (Carolina Academic Press 2003) (distinguishing between a "moralizing" sense of deterrence that determines whether an activity injures an "unacceptably large number of people from a social point of view" and the economic concept of optimal deterrence); Richard L. Abel, *A Critique of Torts*, 37 UCLA L. Rev. 785, 806–19 (1990) (critiquing tort law's ability to promote future safety). *See also* Dan B. Dobbs, The Law of Torts 14 (2000) (" a corrective justice approach . . . asks whether the defendant wronged the plaintiff and how to right that wrong, even if righting the wrong turns out to cost more than the plaintiff lost").

10. Some key early texts on corrective justice theory are George P. Fletcher, *Fairness and Utility in Tort Theory*, 85 Harv. L. Rev. 537 (1972); Richard A. Epstein, *A Theory of Strict Liability*, 2 J. Legal Stud. 151 (1973); Jules L. Coleman, *Moral Theories of Torts: Their Scope and Limits*, 1 Law & Phil. 371 (1983); Ernest J. Weinrib, *Toward a Moral Theory of Negligence Law*, 2 Law & Phil. 37 (1983). Two oft-cited collections devoted to the work of corrective justice theorists are Philosophical Foundations of Tort Law (David G. Owen ed., 1995); Symposium, *Corrective Justice and Formalism: The Care One Owes to One's Neighbors*, 77 Iowa L. Rev. 403 (1992).

11. Distributive justice, by contrast, deals with "how the benefits of an organized society should be distributed among its members." Catherine Pierce Wells, *Tort Law as Corrective Justice: A Pragmatic Justification for Jury Adjudication*, 88 Mich. L. Rev. 2348, 2350 (1990).

12. *See e.g.*, Robert Cooter & Thomas Ulen, Law and Economics 289 (3d ed. 2000) (intentional torts are so much like crimes that economic analysis of each is identical).

13. *See* William Landes & Richard Posner, *The Influence of Economics on Law: A Quantitative Study*, 36 J. L. & Econ. 385, 424 (1993) (citational analysis of influence of law and economics movement from 1976 to 1990, concluding that growth of law and economics exceeded that of other interdisciplinary approaches); Robert C. Ellickson, *Trends in Legal Scholarship: A Statistical Study*, 29 J. Legal Stud. 517 (2000) (modest rise in law and economics scholarship from 1982 to 1996); Henry G. Manne, *How Law and Economics Was Marketed to a Hostile World: A Very Personal History, in* The Origins of Law and Economics: Essays by the Founding Fathers 314–25 (Francisco Parisi & Charles Kershaw Rowley eds., 2005) (describing economics summer camps, law and economics center and Liberty Fund seminars, economic institute for judges, Olin Fellowship program and economic institute for law professors); Martha McCluskey, *Thinking with Wolves: Left Legal Theory after the Right's Rise*, 54 Buff. L. Rev. 1191, 1213–33 (2007) (describing material support for law and economics scholarship).

14. *See* Fred R. Shapiro, *The Most-Cited Law Review Articles Revisited*, 71 Chi-Kent L. Rev. 751 (1996) (very high percentage of most-cited articles written between 1982 and 1991 are by women, feminists, minority scholars, critical race theorists, critical legal studies scholars, and other "outsider" scholars).

15. See Garry Minda, *Neal Gotanda and the Critical Legal Studies Movement*, 4 Asian L.J. 7 (1997).

16. *See* Judith Butler, Gender Trouble: Feminism and the Subversion of Identity (2d ed. 1999); Mary Jo Frug, *A Postmodern Feminist Manifesto (An Unfinished Draft)*, 105 Harv. L. Rev. 1045 (1992); Maxine Eichner, *On Postmodern Feminist Theory*, 36 Harv. C.R.-C.L. Rev. 1 (2001). For a general discussion of the links between postmodernism and critical theory, see Simon Malpas, The Postmodern: The New Critical Idiom (Routledge 2005).

17. *Compare* Left Legalism/Left Critique (Wendy Brown & Janet Halley eds., Duke Univ. Press 2002) *with* Catharine A. MacKinnon, *Points against Postmodernism*, 75 Chi. Kent L. Rev. 687 (2000).

18. *See e.g.*, Cornel West, *Forward*, Critical Race Theory: The Key Writings That Formed the Movement (Kimberlé Crenshaw et al. eds., 1995); Symposium, *LatCrit Theory: Naming and Launching a New Discourse of Critical Legal Scholarship*, 2 Harv. Latino L. Rev. 1(1997); Robert B. Chang, *Toward an Asian American Legal Scholarship: Critical Race Theory, Post-Structuralism and Narrative Space*, 81 Cal. L. Rev. 1241 (1993); Critical Race Feminism: A Reader (Adrien Katherine Wing ed., NYU Press 1997).

19. *See* Patrick J. Kelley, *Introduction: Did the First Restatement Adopt a Reform Agenda?* 32 S. Ill. U. L.J. 1, 7, 12 (2007) (noting that Francis Bohlen served as Reporter for First Restatement, while William Prosser, followed by John Wade, served as Reporter for Second Restatement).

20. John C. P. Goldberg, *Twentieth Century Tort Theory*, 91 Geo. L.J. 513, 521–32 (2003).

21. *Id.* at 522 ("the only mode of theorizing that has largely been spared the need to explain and justify itself").

22. *Id.* at 524 (citing Leon Green, *Tort Law, Public Law in Disguise (Pts. I & II)*, 38 Tex. L. Rev. 1, 257 (1959 & 1960) and Robert L. Rabin, *Some Thoughts on the Ideology of Enterprise Liability*, 55 Md. L. Rev. 1190, 1193 (1996)).

23. *Id.* at 525.

24. *Id.* at 526.

25. *Id.* at 528.

26. *Id.* at 515.

27. *See* Edward L. Rubin, *The New Legal Process, the Synthesis of Discourse, and the Microanalysis of Institutions*, 109 Harv. L. Rev. 1393 (1996) (asserting that law is "an essentially prescriptive discipline"). *See also* Keren-Paz, *supra* note 3, at 20–21 (expressing skepticism toward descriptive claims because "there is frequent positive correlation between the researcher's normative commitment and his descriptive account of the law").

28. *See* American Law Institute, 2004 Annual Report, *Published Case Citations to the Restatements of the Law as of March 1, 2004*, available at http://www.ali.org/news/ annualreports/2004/AMO4_07-Restatement Citations 04. pdf (showing the Restatement of Torts cited 67,336 times by state and federal courts).

29. *See* Anita Bernstein, *Restatement (Third) of Torts: General Principle and the Prescription of Masculine Order*, 54 Vand. L. Rev. 1367, 1370 (2001) (restaters are "more political intervenors than neutral observers").

30. Thus, despite sharp divisions in the courts whether to retain the traditional categories of entrants in suits against landowners or to allow bystanders to recover for emotional distress, the Third Restatement has taken a position on these matters. *See* Restatement (Third) of Torts: Liability for Physical and Emotional Harm §51 (Tentative Draft No. 6, March 2, 2009) (duty of land possessors); Restatement (Third)§ 47 (Tentative Draft No. 5, April 4, 2007) (bystander recovery). Yet, with respect to whether particular relationships or activities give rise to a duty to protect "direct victims" against emotional distress, the Restatement commentary expresses no opinion, citing a lack of consensus in the case law and lack of case development. *Id.* § 46 cmt. d (Council Draft No. 7, 2007).

31. *See* Mark Kelman, A Guide to Critical Legal Studies 4 (Harv. Univ. Press, 1987) (discussing how mainstream legal thought treats one side of a contrasting set of terms as dominant or privileged).

32. For more thorough descriptions of the key features of Legal Realism, see Joseph William Singer, *Legal Realism Now*, 76 Cal. L. Rev. 465 (1988); American Legal Realism xi–xv (William W. Fisher III et al. eds., Oxford Univ. Press 1993).

33. Milton C. Regan, Jr., *How Does Law Matter?* 1 Green Bag 265, 269 (1998).

34. *See e.g.*, in emotional harm cases, Restatement (Third) § 47 (Tentative Draft No. 5, April 4, 2007) (rejection of danger zone rule); *id.* § 46 (rejection of physical manifestation rule). In other contexts, see Restatement (Third) § 51 (Tentative Draft No. 6, March 2, 2009) (rejection of categorical approach to landowner liability); Restatement (Third) of Torts: Liability for Physical Harm § 7 (Proposed Final Draft No. 1, April 6, 2005) (imposition of duty to protect against physical harm, absent exceptional cases).

35. *See* Leon Green, *The Duty Problem in Negligence Cases, Parts I and II*, 28 Colum. L. Rev. 1014 (1928) ("there is nothing so weighty with court-room government as the *workability* of a rule or process"). For concessions in the Restatement made for administrative purposes, see Restatement (Third) 11(c) (Proposed Final Draft No. 1, April 6, 2005) (disregard of actor's mental disabilities in determining standard of care); *id.* §10(b) (adoption of bright-line rule negating negligence liability for children under age 5).

36. *See* Katherine T. Bartlett, *Feminist Legal Methods*, 103 Harv. L. Rev. 829, 837–49 (1990); Heather Wishik, *To Question Everything: The Inquiries of Feminist Jurisprudence*, 1 Berkeley Women's L.J. 64, 72–77 (1985).

37. *See* Patricia A. Cain, *Feminist Legal Scholarship*, 77 Iowa L. Rev. 19, 20 (1991).

38. Bartlett, *supra* note 36, at 837.

39. The classic article contrasting the "victim" and the "perpetrator" perspectives is Alan D. Freeman, *Antidiscrimination Law: A Critical Review, in* The Politics of Law: A Progressive Critique 96 (David Kairys ed., 1982).

40. *See* Anita Bernstein, *Whatever Happened to Law and Economics?* 64 Md. L. Rev. 303, 324 (2005) (citing Jeanne Schroeder, *Rationality in Law and Economics Scholarship*, 79 Or. L. Rev. 147, 151 (2000)).

41. See Reva B. Siegel, *"The Rule of Love": Wife Beating as Prerogative and Privacy*, 105 Yale L.J. 2117 (1996).

42. Jennifer B. Wriggins, *Interspousal Tort Immunity and Insurance "Family Member Exclusions": Shared Assumptions, Relational and Liberal Feminist Challenges*, 17 Wis. Women's L.J. 251 (2002).

43. On interlocking systems of oppressions, *see e.g.*, Jennifer Wriggins, *Rape, Racism, and the Law*, 6 Harv. Women's L.J. 103 (1983); Mari Matsuda, *When the First Quail Calls: Multiple Consciousness as Jurisprudential Method*, 11 Women's Rts. L Rep. 7 (1989); Trina Grillo & Stephanie Wildman, *Obscuring the Importance of Race: The Implication of Making Comparisons between Racism and Sexism (or Other Isms), in* Stephanie M. Wildman et al., Privilege Revealed: How Invisible Preference Undermines America 85–102 (NYU Press, 1996); on false universalisms and overgeneralization, *see e.g.*, Katherine T. Bartlett, *Gender Law*, 1 Duke J. Gender L. & Pol'y 1 (1994).

44. The classic statement of the meaning of equal protection that requires that "likes be treated alike" is Joseph Tussman & Jacobus tenBroek, *The Equal Protection of the Laws*, 37 Cal. L. Rev. 341 (1949). For an overview of contemporary equal protection law, see Erwin Chemerinsky, Constitutional Law: Principles and Policies §§9.1–§9.7 at 668–789 (3d ed. Aspen 2006).

45. For a brief history of disparate impact theory in employment discrimination law, *see* Charles A. Sullivan, *Disparate Impact: Looking Past the* Desert Palace *Mirage*, 47 Wm. & Mary L. Rev. 911 (2005).

46. For discussion of cognitive bias as it relates to legal categorization and legal decision making, see Martha Chamallas, *Deepening the Legal Understanding of Bias: On Devaluation and Biased Prototypes*, 74 S. Cal. L. Rev. 747 (2001); Linda Hamilton Krieger, *The Content of Our Categories: A Cognitive Bias Approach to Discrimination and Equal Opportunity*, 47 Stan. L. Rev. 1161 (1995); Joan C. Williams, *Litigating the Glass Ceiling and the Maternal Wall: Using Stereotyping and Cognitive Bias Evidence to Prove Gender Discrimination*, 7 Emp. Rts. & Emp. Pol'y J. 287 (2003).

47. For recent taxonomies of brands of feminist legal theory, see Rosalind Dixon, *Feminist Disagreement (Comparatively) Recast*, 31 Harv. J. L. & Gender 277 (2008); Feminist Legal Theory: A Primer 15–44 (Nancy Levit & Robert R. M. Verchick eds., NYU Press 2006).

48. *See* Boyles v. Kerr, 855 S.W. 2d 593 (Tex. 1993).

49. *See e.g.*, Angela P. Harris, *Race and Essentialism in Feminist Legal Theory*, 42 Stan. L. Rev. 581 (1990); Kimberlé Crenshaw, *Demarginalizing the Intersection of Race and Sex: A Black Feminist Critique of Antidiscrimination Doctrine, Feminist Theory and Antiracist Politics*, 1989 U. Chi. Legal F. 139; Elizabeth V. Spelman, Inessential Woman: Problems of Exclusion in Feminist Thought (Beacon Press 1988); Patricia J. Williams, The Alchemy of Race and Rights (Harvard Univ. Press 1991); Martha Minow, *The Supreme Court Term 1986, Forward: Justice Engendered*, 101 Harv. L. Rev. 10 (1987); Wildman et al., *supra* note 43; Feminist Legal Theory: An Anti-essentialist Reader (Nancy E. Dowd & Michelle S. Jacobs eds., NYU Press 2003).

50. *See* Mari Matsuda et al., Words That Wound: Critical Race Theory, Assaultive Speech and the First Amendment 6 (1993); Devon Carbado & Mitu Gulati, *The Law and Economics of Critical Race Theory*, 112 Yale L.J. 1757, 1766 (2003) (discussing central themes in critical race theory).

51. Richard Delgado, *Crossroads and Blind Alleys: A Critical Examination of Recent Writing about Race*, 82 Tex. L. Rev. 121, 136 (2003) (book review).

52. *See* Roy Brooks, *Critical Race Theory: A Proposed Structure and Application to Federal Pleading*, 11 Harv. Blackletter L.J. 85, 88 (1994).

53. Charles R. Lawrence III, *The Id, The Ego, and Equal Protection: Reckoning with Unconscious Racism*, 39 Stan. L. Rev. 317 (1995).

54. *See* Jennifer B. Wriggins, *Torts, Race, and the Value of Injury*, 1900–1949, 49 How. L.J. 99, 101–03 (2005) (discussing tension between individualized determinations in tort cases and equal treatment under the law).

55. *See* Ian Haney Lopez, White by Law: The Legal Construction of Race 118 (NYU Press 1996); Cheryl Harris, *Whiteness as Property*, 106 Harv. L. Rev. 1709 (1993).

56. *See* Jennifer B. Wriggins, *Whiteness, Equal Treatment and the Valuation of Injury in Torts, 1900–1940*, *in* Fault Lines: Tort Law and Cultural Practice (David Engel & Michael McCann eds., Stan. Law Books 2009).

57. 17 Harv. C.R.-C.L. L. Rev. 133 (1982).

58. Leslie Bender, *A Lawyer's Primer on Feminist Theory and Tort*, 38 J. Legal Educ. 3 (1988); Lucinda Finley, *A Break in the Silence: Including Women's Issues in a Torts Class*, 1 Yale J. L. & Feminism 41 (1989).

59. Finley, *supra* note 58, at 44.

60. *See e.g.*, Jody David Armour, *Toward a Tort-Based Theory of Civil Rights, Civil Liberties, and Racial Justice*, 38 Loy. L.A. L. Rev. 1469 (2005) (discussing tort concept of reasonableness, racial profiling and self-defense cases).

61. Regina Austin, *Employer Abuse, Worker Resistance, and the Tort of Intentional Infliction of Emotional Distress*, 41 Stan. L. Rev. 1 (1988). See also Okianer Christian Dark, *Racial Insults: "Keep Thy Tongue from Evil,"* 24 Suffolk U. L. Rev. 559 (1990) (renewing call for recognizing tort of racial insult).

62. *See generally* Leslie Bender, *An Overview of Feminist Torts Scholarship*, 78 Cornell L. Rev. 575 (1993). On the reasonable person standard, see Margo Schlanger, *Injured Women before Common Law Courts, 1860–1930*, 21 Harv. Women's L.J. 79 (1998); *Gender Matters: Teaching a Reasonable Woman Standard in Personal Injury Law*, 45 St. Louis U. L.J. 769 (2001). On providing a tort remedy for sexual harassment, see Cynthia Grant Bowman, *Street Harassment and the Informal Ghettoization of Women*, 106 Harv. L. Rev. 517 (1993); Krista J. Schoenheider, *A Theory of Tort Liability for Sexual Harassment in the Workplace*, 134 U. Pa. L. Rev. 1461 (1986). On interspousal tort immunity and violence against women, see Carl Tobias, *Interspousal Tort Immunity in America*, 23 Ga. L. Rev. 359 (1989).

63. Jane E. Larson, *"Women Understand So Little, They Call My Good Nature 'Deceit'": A Feminist Rethinking of Seduction*, 93 Colum. L. Rev. 374 (1993).

64. Ellen M. Bublick, *Citizen No-Duty Rules: Rape Victims and Comparative Fault*, 99 Colum. L. Rev. 1413 (1999).

65. Frank M. McClellan, *The Dark Side of Tort Reform: Searching for Racial Justice*, 48 Rutgers L. Rev. 761 (1996).

66. Regina Austin, *"Black People's Money": An Essay on the Interaction of Law, Economics, and Culture in the Context of Race, Gender, and Class* (draft, March 21 2008).

67. Wright v. CTL Distribution, Inc., 650 So.2d 641 (Fla. Dist. Ct. App. 1995); 679 So. 2d 1233 (Fla. Dist. Ct. App. 1996). The first jury reduced the award by 70 percent; the second jury found plaintiff 90 percent at fault and reduced the award accordingly.

68. *See* Christopher J. Robinette, *Can There Be a Unified Theory of Torts? A Pluralist Suggestion from History and Doctrine*, 43 Brandeis L.J. 369 (2005); Keren-Paz, *supra* note 3, at 14–17; Dobbs, *supra* note 9, at 12–21 (discussing corrective justice, social policy, and process aims of tort law).

69. On the importance of factual context for Legal Realists, see Laura Kalman, Legal Realism at Yale, 1927–1960 29 (UNC Press 1986); for contemporary scholars, see Christopher J. Robinette, *Torts Rationales, Pluralism, and Isaiah Berlin*, 14 Geo. Mason L. Rev. 329, 359–60 (2007); Keren-Paz, *supra* note 3, at 15.

70. Robinette, *supra* note 68.

71. G. Edward White, Tort Law in America 291 (expanded ed., Oxford Univ. Press 2003).

72. Robinette, *supra* note 68, at 390.

CHAPTER 2

1. Thomas D. Morris, Southern Slavery and the Law 1619–1860 65 (Univ. of N.C. Press 1996); Jenny Bourne Wahl, The Bondsman's Burden: An Economic Analysis of the Common Law of Southern Slavery 121–22 (Cambridge Univ. Press 1998).

2. There were three waves of statutes: a narrow Mississippi law in 1835 that freed women's property from their husband's debts; a separate wave in the 1840s that established separate estates for women; and broader post–Civil War enactments that protected women's earnings from coverture and allowed wives the capacity to contract and sue in court. *See* Richard H. Chused, *Married Women's Property Law: 1800–1850*, 71 Geo. L.J. 1359, 1398 (1983); Reva B. Siegel, *Home as Work: The First Woman's Rights Claims Concerning Wives' Household Labor, 1850–1880*, 103 Yale L.J. 1073, 1082–83 (1994); Norma Basch, In the Eyes of the Law: Women, Marriage and Property in Nineteenth Century New York 17–21 (Cornell Univ. Press 1982).

3. Katharine Silbaugh, *Turning Labor into Love: Housework and the Law*, 91 Nw. U. L. Rev. 1, 41 (1996).

4. Claims are generally labeled as "negligent infliction of mental distress" claims when the defendant's negligent conduct causes "stand-alone" mental disturbance, that is, mental disturbance unaccompanied by physical injury. A related claim is the claim for "intentional infliction of mental distress" brought by claimants who have suffered severe mental anguish as a result of defendant's intentional and outrageous action. *See* Dan B. Dobbs, The Law of Torts 826, 836 (2000).

5. Gulf C. & S. F. Ry. Co. v. Luther, 90 S.W. 44 (Tex. Civ. App. 1905). For further discussion, see Jennifer B. Wriggins, *Toward a Feminist Revision of Torts*, 13 Am. U. J. Gender, Soc. Pol'y & L. 139 (2005).

6. This discussion of nervous-shock cases incorporates and builds upon one of the author's prior research with the historian Linda K. Kerber. Martha Chamallas with Linda K. Kerber, *Women, Mothers and the Law of Fright: A History*, 88 Mich. L. Rev. 814 (1990).

7. *See* Lynch v. Knight, (1861) 11 Eng. Rep. 854, 863 (H.L.) ("mental pain or anxiety the law cannot value, and does not pretend to redress, when the unlawful act complained of causes that alone"); W. Union Tel. Co. v. Rogers, 9 So. 823 (Miss. 1891); Chapman v. W. Union Tel. Co., 15 S.E. 901 (Ga. 1892).

8. *See* Restatement (First) of Torts §47 cmt. b (1934). To be actionable, there is no need for physical injury. *See* W. Page Keeton et al., Prosser and Keeton on the Law of Torts 291 (5th ed. 1984) ("It is as if a magic circle were drawn about the person, and the one who breaks it, even by so much as a cut on the finger, becomes liable for all resulting harm to the person").

9. *See* William L. Prosser, Handbook on the Law of Torts 57–58, 213 (1st ed. 1941).

10. *See* Rachel F. Moran, *Law and Emotion, Love and Hate*, 11 J. Contemp. Legal Issues 747, 775 (2001); Prosser, *supra* note 9, at 918–19.

11. Today, only a few states allow spouses to sue for damages resulting from adultery. *See* William R. Corbett, *A Somewhat Modest Proposal to Prevent Adultery and Save Families: Two Old Torts Looking for a New Career*, 33 Ariz. St. L.J. 985, 989 (2001).

12. *See* Laura Hanft Korobkin, Criminal Conversations: Sentimentality and Nineteenth-Century Legal Stories of Adultery 122–58 (Columbia Univ. Press 1998) (describing early female-plaintiff criminal conversation lawsuits).

13. *See* Lynch v. Knight, (1861) 11 Eng. Rep. 854, 859–60, 863 (H.L.).

14. Mitchell v. Rochester Ry. Co., 45 N.E. 35 (N.Y. 1896).

15. *See* G. Edward White, Tort Law in America: An Intellectual History 16 (Oxford Univ. Press, expanded ed. 2003); John Fabian Witt, The Accidental Republic: Crippled Workingmen, Destitute Widows, and the Remaking of American Law 24–27, 51–52 (Harv.

Univ. Press 2004); Randolf E. Bergstrom, Courting Danger: Injury and Law in New York City, 1870–1910 (Cornell Univ. Press 1992).

16. Barbara Young Welke, Recasting American Liberty: Gender, Race, Law, and the Railroad Revolution, 1865–1920, 189 (Cambridge Univ. Press 2001) ("That a severe fright or shock could produce miscarriage was a given in medical and lay understanding of the time").

17. Francis H. Bohlen, *Right to Recover for Injury Resulting from Negligence without Impact*, 50 Am. L. Reg. 141,172 (1902).

18. 47 N.E. 88 (Mass. 1897). The case was retried and a second jury verdict for the plaintiff was overruled by the appellate court in an opinion by Justice Holmes. Spade v. Lynn & Boston R.R., 52 N.E. 747 (Mass. 1899).

19. 62 N.E. 737 (Mass. 1902).

20. *Note on Damages for Nervous Shock Sustained in Consequence of a Negligent Act, Unaccompanied by Physical Injury*, 50 Am. Neg. Rep. 2d, Vol. XI 250 (1902).

21. By the late 19th century, neurologists had begun to legitimate diagnoses of hysterical illnesses in women, sometimes under the heading of a condition called "neurasthenia," a disease characterized by profound mental and physical exhaustion. What was once dismissed as hypochondria began to be treated as real illness, although many in the medical profession and elsewhere still doubted its authenticity and regarded female patients as malingerers. *See* George Beard, American Nervousness: Its Causes and Consequences (1881); Barbara Sicherman, *The Uses of a Diagnosis: Doctors, Patients, and Neurasthenia, in* Sickness and Health in America: Readings in the History of Medicine and Public Health 22, 23–24, 26, 32 (Judith Walzer Leavitt & Ronald L. Numbers eds., Univ. Wisc. Press, 2d ed. 1985); Carroll Smith-Rosenberg, *The Hysterical Woman: Sex Roles and Role Conflict in Nineteenth-Century America, in* Disorderly Conduct: Visions of Gender in Victorian America 197, 203–08 (A.A. Knopf 1985).

22. Victorian Rys. Comm'rs v. Coultas, 3 App. Cas. 222 (P.C. 1888). *See also* Coultas v. Victorian Rys. Comm'rs., 12 V.L.S. 895, 895 (1886) (revealing that plaintiff suffered a miscarriage).

23. Prosser, *supra* note 9, at 55.

24. Ewing v. Pittsburgh C. & St. L. Ry. Co., 23 A. 340 (Pa. 1892); Mitchell v. Rochester Ry. Co., 45 N.E. 354 (N.Y. 1898); Spade v. Lynn & B. R. Co., 47 N.E. 88 (Mass. 1897); Braun v. Craven, 51 N.E. 657 (Ill. 1898); Nelson v. Crawford, 81 N.W. 335 (Mich. 1899); Miller v. Baltimore & Ohio Sw. R.R. Co., 85 N.E. 499 (Ohio 1908).

25. 50 N.W. 1034 (Minn. 1892).

26. *See, e.g.*, Simone v. Rhode Island Co., 66 A. 202 (R.I. 1907).

27. Margo Schlanger, *Injured Women before Common Law Courts, 1860–1930*, 21 Harv. Women's L.J. 79, 114–17 (1998).

28. Schlanger, *supra* note 27, at 117–18.

29. By our count, of the twenty-two states that had squarely considered the issue, fourteen states rejected the impact rule by 1925 (Wisconsin, Texas, Minnesota, California, South Carolina, North Carolina, Iowa, Louisiana, Rhode Island, Maryland, Oregon, Washington, Nebraska, and New Hampshire), while eight states endorsed it (Kansas, Pennsylvania, New York, Massachusetts, Illinois, Michigan, Kentucky, Ohio).The historian Barbara Welke reads the cases somewhat differently, counting nineteen states as rejecting the impact rule (Welke, *supra* note 16, at 203 n.1) and listing New York, Massa-

chusetts, Pennsylvania, and "the few states that followed their lead" as endorsing the rule (*id.* at 212). In contrast to Welke, we do not read the cases from Kansas, Alabama, New Jersey, South Dakota, or Tennessee as rejecting the impact rule and interpret the cases from Illinois, Ohio, Michigan, and Kentucky as endorsing the rule. Thus, unlike Welke, we would not say that the "vast majority" of states rejected the impact rule (*id.* at 203, 223), and choose to describe it as rejection by a "clear majority."

30. Battalla v. State, 176 N.E.2d 729 (N.Y. 1961).

31. Niedermann v. Brodsky, 261 A.2d 84 (Pa. 1970). Massachusetts weakened its application of the impact rule in *Freedman v. Eastern Massachusetts State Railway Co.*, 12 N.E.2d 739 (Mass. 1938), before expressly abandoning the requirement in *Payton v. Abbott Labs*, 437 N.E.2d 171 (Mass. 1982). Michigan abandoned the rule in 1970, in *Daley v. La Croix*, 179 N.W.2d 390 (Mich. 1970). Illinois and Ohio followed suit in 1983. Rickey v. Chicago Transit Auth., 457 N.E.2d 1(Ill. 1983); Schultz v. Barberton Glass Co., 447 N.E.2d 109 (Ohio 1983).

32. *See* Porter v. St. Joseph Ry., Light, Heat & Power Co., 277 S.W. 913 (Mo. 1925); Erwin v. Milligan, 67 S.W.2d 592 (Ark. 1934).

33. Tanner v. Hartog, 696 So. 2d 705 (Fla. 1997); Lee v. State Farm Mut.Auto Ins. Co., 533 S.E.2d 82 (Ga. 2000).

34. *See* Catharine A. MacKinnon, Women's Lives, Men's Laws 46 (Harv. Univ. Press 2005) (discussing formal equality principle and its Aristotlean origins).

35. Welke, *supra* note 16, at 196–201.

36. Spohn v. Mo. Pac. Ry. Co., 22 S.W. 690 (Mo. 1893).

37. Gulf, Colo. & S. F. Ry. Co. v. Trott, 25 S.W. 419 (Tex. 1894).

38. *See* Katharine T. Bartlett, Angela P. Harris, & Deborah L. Rhode, Gender and Law: Theory, Doctrine, Commentary 265 (3d ed. 2002) ("[S]ubstantive equality looks to a rule's *results* or *effects* . . . and demand[s] that rules take account of differences to avoid differential impacts that are considered unfair.").

39. *See* Martha Chamallas, Introduction to Feminist Legal Theory 39–60 (2d ed. 2003).

40. *See e.g.*, Boyles v. Kerr, 855 S.W. 2d 593 (Tex. 1993).

41. *See e.g.*, Harnisher v. Univ. of Utah Med. Ctr., 962 P.2d 67 (Utah 1998).

42. For general discussions of the phenomenon of white racial privilege, see Stephanie M. Wildman et al., Privilege Revealed: How Invisible Preference Undermines America (NYU Press 1996); Barbara J. Flagg, Was Blind but Now I See: White Race Consciousness and the Law (NYU Press 1998); Martha R. Mahoney, *Segregation, Whiteness and Transformation*, 143 U. Pa. L. Rev. 1659 (1995).

43. *See e.g.*, S. Ry. Co. v. Norton, 73 So. 1 (Miss. 1916); Shelton v. Chicago Rock Island & Pac. RR. Co., 201 S.W. 521 (Tenn. 1918); Morris v. Ala. & Vicksburg Ry. Co., 60 So. 11 (Miss. 1912); Wyatt v. Adair, 110 So. 801 (Ala. 1926).

44. 90 S. W. 44 (Tex. Civ. App. 1905). This discussion builds upon that in Wriggins, *supra* note 5, at 143–48.

45. Welke, *supra* note 16, at 276–77. *See generally* Catherine A. Barnes, Journey From Jim Crow: The Desegregation of Southern Transit (Columbia Univ. Press 1983).

46. To be precise, the lawsuit was brought by Mr. Luther for his wife's injuries, in accord with the social practice of coverture. Interestingly, at that time in Texas, it appears that Mrs. Luther could have brought suit in her own name. Wriggins, *supra* note 5, at 146.

47. *See* Prosser, *supra* note 9, at 60.

48. Using the Consumer Price index, an award of $2,500 in 1905 would be $51,901.89 today. Economic History Services, What Is Relative Value?, http://eh.net/hmit/compare/.

49. Welke, *supra* note 16, at 289 ("In the wake of the war, white womanhood became a critical bulwark of white supremacy").

50. Quinn v. Louisville & Nashville R. R.Co., 32 S.W. 742 (Ky. Ct.App. 1895). The appellate court in *Quinn* ordered a new trial because of an error in jury instructions. Interestingly, the court was of the view that the train had a duty strictly to enforce the state's segregation mandate and might be liable for allowing white persons to enter colored cars. Thus, at this round of litigation, a black woman prevailed for the sake of strengthening the enforcement of the apartheid system.

51. For more in-depth discussions of devaluation, see Martha Chamallas, *Deepening the Legal Understanding of Bias: On Devaluation and Biased Prototypes*, 74 S. Cal. L. Rev. 747, 755–56 (2001); Martha Chamallas, *The Architecture of Bias: Deep Structures in Tort Law*, 146 U. Pa. L. Rev. 463, 470–71 (1998).

52. The account of the facts of the case is taken largely from the article appearing in the *New York Times, Negro Not Equal to White*, N.Y. Times, May 22, 1909, at 16. On the work and working conditions of Pullman porters, see Larry Tye, Rising from the Rails, Pullman Porters and the Making of the Black Middle Class 88 (Henry Holt 2004). For further discussion of the case, see Jennifer B. Wriggins, *Torts, Race, and the Value of Injury, 1900–1940*, 49 How. L. J. 99, 130–35 (2005).

53. *See* Dobbs, *supra* note 4, §39, at 75 (noting that in most instances false imprisonment "redresses a dignitary or intangible interest, a species of emotional distress or insult that one feels at the loss of freedom and the subjugation to the will of another").

54. *See* Griffin v. Brady, 117 N.Y.S. 1136 (N.Y. App. Div. 1909); 118 N.Y.S. 240 (N.Y. App. Div. 1909); 126 N.Y.S. 1130 (N.Y. App. Div. 1910).

55. Editorial, *No Light on the Main Point*, N.Y. Times, July 16, 1909, at 6.

56. W.E.B. Du Bois, *The Talented Tenth* (1903), *reprinted in* Writings by W.E.B. Du Bois in Non-Periodical Literature Edited by Others (Hebert Aptheker ed., Kraus-Thompson 1982).

57. *See Negroes' Feelings Cheaper*, The Boston Post, May 22, 1909; *A New York Court Draws the Color Line*, 69 Central L.J. 118 (1909); Gilbert Thomas Stephenson, *Race Distinctions in American Law*, 43 Am. L. Rev. 905 (1909).

58. 69 Central L.J. 188, *supra* note 57, at 119.

59. Martha Minow, *Justice Engendered*, 101 Harv. L. Rev. 10 (1987).

60. Martin S. Pernick, A Calculus of Suffering: Pain, Professionalism, and Anesthesia in Nineteenth Century America 6–7, 238–39 (Columbia Univ. Press 1985).

61. *A New York Court Draws the Color* Line, *supra* note 57, quoting Bodrengam v. Arcedekne, Year Book 31, 31, Edw. I 106 (1302). The Oxford English Dictionary defines "buffet" to mean a "blow."

62. Another glaring example of explicit devaluation is *Blackburn v. L.A. Ry. & Navigation Co.*, 54 So. 865 (La. 1910), in which the damages award for a black plaintiff was reduced because of "the well-known improvidence of the colored race and the irregular life these colored brakemen lead."

63. The study of the Louisiana appellate decisions was conducted by Jennifer Wriggins and is more fully discussed in Wriggins, *supra* note 52.

64. *See* Wex S. Malone, Torts in a Nutshell: Injuries to Family, Social and Trade Relations 18–22 (1979) (discussing relationship between wrongful death and survival actions).

65. *See* Frank L. Maraist & Tom C. Galligan, Jr., Louisiana Tort Law 415–426,§§18-1–18-9 (1996); Helmuth Carlyle Voss, *The Recovery of Damages for Wrongful Death at Common Law, at Civil Law and in Louisiana*, 6 Tul. L. Rev. 201, 223 (1932).

66. *See* William E. Crawford, *Life on a Federal Island in the Civilian Sea*, 15 Miss. C. L. Rev. 1, 2 (1994).

67. *See* Arthur Larson & Lex K. Larson, Larson's Workers' Compensation Law (2003); Witt, *supra* note 15, at 173.

68. See Robert L. Rabin, *The Quest for Fairness in Compensating Victims of September 11*, 49 Clev. St. L. Rev. 573, 578 (2001).

69. 189 So. 477, 481 (La. Ct. App. 1939).

70. Shamburg v. Thompson, 186 So. 616 (La. Ct. App. 1939) ($3,200 award); Edwards v. Texas & Pac. Ry. Co., 185 So. 111 (La. Ct. App. 1938) ($3,000 award).

71. Rousseau v. Texas & Pac. Ry. Co., 4 La. App. 691 (La. Ct. App. Orleans 1926) ($6000 award).

72. Boykin v. Plauche, 168 So. 741 (La. Ct. App. 1936); 169 So.131 (La. Ct. App. 1936) ($8780 award). The appellate court originally awarded $9,780 but ultimately decided to reduce that amount by $1,000.

73. The study analyzes all published Louisiana wrongful death and survival cases from 1900 to 1940 that discuss damage amounts. The database was compiled by retrieving cases using two methods. The first method involved reading cases categorized under West Publishing Company's key number system relating to death actions, specifically those cases listed under damages, measure and amount of damages awarded, statutory limits, discretion of jury, inadequate damages, and excessive damages. The cases generally referenced the race of the decedent or his or her family when the decedent was black. The second method involved computer searches of the Westlaw Louisiana Cases database, selecting cases using such relevant terms as "negro," "tort," and names of specific torts, and "colored," "tort," and names of specific torts. If such cases revealed the race of the decedent, they were added to the study's database. Between 1900 and 1940, 124 such cases were decided, of which 26 were brought by blacks. *See* Database (August 24, 2005) on file with Jennifer Wriggins, and Wriggins, *supra* note 52, at 110.

74. For writings on the status and treatment of African Americans in Louisiana during this period, see Henry C. Dethloff & Robert R. Jones, *Race Relations in Louisiana, 1877–98*, *in* The African-American Experience in Louisiana, Part B, From the Civil War to Jim Crow 501–517 (Charles Vincent ed., U. of La. 2000) [hereinafter African-American Experience]; Mark T. Carleton, *"Judicious" State Administration, 1901–1920*, in African-American Experience, Part C , *id.* at 119.

75. Reva B. Siegel, *"The Rule of Love": Wife Beating as Prerogative and Privacy*, 105 Yale L.J. 2117 (1996); Reva B. Siegel, *Home as Work: The First Woman's Rights Claims Concerning Wives' Household Labor, 1850–1880*, 103 Yale L.J. 1073 (1994); Reva B. Siegel, *The Modernization of Marital Status Law: Adjudicating Wives' Rights to Earnings, 1860–1930*, 82 Geo. L.J. 2127 (1994).

CHAPTER 3

1. *See* Martha Chamallas, *Vanished from the First Year: Lost Torts and Deep Structures in Tort Law*, *in* Legal Canons 104–29 (J.M. Balkin & Sanford Levinson eds., NYU Press 2000).

2. Restatement (Third) of Torts: General Principles xxi (Discussion Draft Apr. 5, 1999).

3. Oliver Wendell Holmes, *The Path of the Law,* 10 Harv. L. Rev. 457, 467 (1897).

4. Roscoe Pound, An Introduction to the Philosophy of Law 169–75 (Yale Univ. Press 1922).

5. Richard L. Abel, *Torts, in* The Politics of Law: A Progressive Critique 446–47 (David Kairys ed., Basic Books, 3d ed. 1998).

6. Guido Calabresi, The Costs of Accidents: A Legal and Economic Analysis (Yale Univ. Press 1970).

7. Robert Cooter & Thomas Ulen, Law & Economics 288–89, 429 (3d ed. Addison-Wesley, 3d ed. 2000) (stating that most of tort law concerns accidental harm while criminal law concerns intentional harm).

8. *See generally* Ernest J. Weinrib, The Idea of Private Law (Harv. Univ. Press 2003); Jules L. Coleman, Risks and Wrongs (Camb. Univ. Press 1992).

9. *See* National Violence against Women Survey, discussed in Katharine T. Bartlett & Deborah L. Rhode, Gender & Law: Theory, Doctrine, Commentary 474 (4th ed. 2006).

10. *See* Elizabeth M. Schneider, Battered Women & Feminist Lawmaking 67–69 (Yale Univ. Press 2000) ("[a] theoretical framework that recognizes primacy of gender need not exclude other factors").

11. Bartlett & Rhode, *supra* note 9, at 419.

12. Pat K.Chew & Robert E. Kelley, *Unwrapping Racial Harassment Law*, 27 Berkeley J. Emp. & Lab. L. 49, 63 (2006) (empirical study indicating that men outnumber women plaintiffs in racial harassment suits).

13. Schneider, *supra* note 10, at 5 ("heterosexual intimate violence is part of a larger system of coercive control and subordination . . . based on structural gender inequality").

14. Fredrica L. Lehrman, Domestic Violence Practice and Procedure § 1.3, at 1–7 (1997); *see also* Clare Dalton, *Domestic Violence, Domestic Torts and Divorce: Constraints and Possibilities*, 31 New Eng. L. Rev. 319, 333–34 (1997).

15. Dan B. Dobbs, The Law of Torts §28, at 52–53 (2000).

16. For histories of the marital rape exemption, see Jill Elaine Hasday, *Contest and Consent: A Legal History of the Marital Rape*, 88 Cal. L. Rev. 1373 (2000); Rebecca M. Ryan, *The Sex Right: A Legal History of the Marital Rape Exemption*, 20 Law & Soc. Inquiry 941 (1995).

17. Dobbs, *supra* note 15, §33, at 63–64.

18. *Id.* at §36, at 67–69.

19. *See* Restatement (Second) of Torts §46 (1965); Martha Chamallas, *Discrimination and Outrage: The Migration from Civil Rights to Tort Law*, 48 Wm. & Mary L. Rev. 2115 (2007); Dobbs, *supra* note 15, §304, at 826–29; Daniel Givelber, *The Right to Minimum Social Decency and the Limits of Evenhandedness: Intentional Infliction of Emotional Distress by Outrageous Conduct,* 82 Colum. L. Rev. 42 (1982); William L. Prosser, *Intentional Infliction of Mental Suffering: A New Tort,* 37 Mich. L. Rev. 874 (1939); William L. Prosser, *Insult and Outrage*, 44 Cal. L. Rev. 40 (1956).

20. Restatement (Second) of Torts §46 cmt. d (1965).

21. *See* 29 C.F.R. §1604.11(a) (3) (2009).

22. Douglas D. Scherer, *Tort Remedies for Victims of Domestic Abuse*, 43 S.C. L. Rev. 543, 565 (1992).

23. Jennifer B. Wriggins, *Domestic Violence in the First-Year Torts Curriculum*, 54 J. Legal Educ. 511, 513 n.8 (2004).

24. *See* Centers for Disease Control and Prevention, National Center for Injury Prevention and Control, *Cost of Intimate Partner Violence against Women in the United States*, 1 (2003), http://www.cdc.gov/ncipc/pub-res/ipv_cost/IPVBook-Final-Feb18.pdf (estimates that nearly 2.0 million women incur injuries from intimate partner violence per year, more than 550,000 of which require medical attention).

25. Catherine M. Sharkey, *Dissecting Damages: An Empirical Exploration of Sexual Harassment Awards*, 3 J. Empirical Legal Stud. 1, 38 n.150 (2006).

26. However, race discrimination complaints constitute a significant percentage of the charges filed with the EEOC. Since the EEOC's inception, the majority of charges filed have been for race discrimination. In 2005, 35.5 percent of overall charges were for race discrimination. *See* Remarks of Jocelyn Frye, Commission Meeting on Race and Color Discrimination of April 19, 2006, Washington, D.C., *available at* http://www.eeoc.gov/abouteeoc/meetings/4-19-06/frye.html. Since the early 1990s, racial harassment charge filings with the EEOC have more than doubled, from 3,075 in 1991 to approximately 7,000 in 2007. Race remains the most frequently alleged basis of discrimination in charges brought to the EEOC. *See* EEOC Press Release, *Lockheed Martin to Pay 2.5 Million to Settle Racial Harassment Lawsuit*, http:// www.eeoc.gov/press/1-2-08.html.

27. *See* The Black Worker 2 (Eric Arneson ed.) (2007); Linda Gordon, Heroes of Their Own Lives: Politics and History of Family Violence, Boston 1880–1960 (Viking 1988); Reva B. Siegel, *"The Rule of Love": Wife Beating as Prerogative and Privacy*, 105 Yale L.J. 2117 (1996); Abbott v. Abbott, 67 Me 304 (1877), quoting State v. Oliver, 70 N.C. 60 (1874) (wife should not be able to sue because "it is better to draw the curtain, shut out the public gaze, and allow the parties to forget and forgive").

28. Carl Tobias, *Interspousal Tort Immunity in America*, 23 Ga. L. Rev. 359 (1989); Carl Tobias, *The Imminent Demise of Interspousal Tort Immunity*, 60 Mont. L. Rev. 101(1999).

29. *See* Townsend v. Townsend, 708 S.W. 2d 646 (Mo. 1986) (en banc). *See also* Reva B. Siegel, *The Modernization of Marital Status Law: Adjudicating Wives' Rights to Earnings, 1860–1930*, 82 Geo. L.J. 2127 (1994).

30. Siegel, "*The Rule of Love,*" *supra* note 27.

31. W. Page Keeton et al., Prosser and Keeton on the Law of Torts 291 (5th ed. 1984).

32. *See e.g.*, Am. Law Inst., Principles of the Law of Family Dissolution: Analysis and Recommendations 43 (2002) ("prior to 1968, consideration of fault or misconduct was almost universally allowed"). Fault was relevant, for example, not only to determine the spouse's eligibility for divorce or entitlement to alimony but also in determining the amount of alimony. Ira Mark Ellman et al., Family Law: Cases, Text, Problems 270–71 (2d ed. 1991); Judith Areen, Cases and Materials on Family Law 713–14 (3d ed. 1992).

33. See Catherine F. Klein & Leslye E. Orloff, *Providing Legal Protection for Battered Women: An Analysis of State Statutes and Case Law*, 21 Hofstra L. Rev. 801 (1993).

34. *See* Robert E. Keeton & Alan I. Widiss, Insurance Law: A Guide To Fundamental Principles, Legal Doctrines, and Commercial Practices, §§ 5.3(f), 5.4(d), at 493–94, 518–19 (student ed. 1988); Jennifer Wriggins, *Interspousal Tort Immunity and Insurance 'Family Member Exclusions': Shared Assumptions, Relational and Liberal Feminist Challenges*, 17 Wis. Women's L.J. 251 (2002); Kenneth S. Abraham, The Liability Century: Insurance and Tort Law from the Progressive Era to 9/11 186 (Harv. Univ. Press 2008). Automobile insurance policies contain the same exclusions.

35. Kent D. Syverud, *The Duty to Settle*, 76 Va. L. Rev. 1113, 1114–15 (1990).

36. Tom Baker, *Blood Money, New Money, and the Moral Economy of Tort Law in Action*, 35 Law & Soc'y Rev. 275 (2001).

37. *Compare* Ellen M. Bublick, *Tort Suits Filed By Rape and Sexual Assault Victims in Civil Courts: Lessons for Courts, Classrooms and Constituencies*, 59 SMU L. Rev. 55 (2006) (discussing considerable success of 3d-party tort claims in rape cases) *with* Town of Castle Rock v. Gonzales, 545 U.S. 748 (2005) (refusing to hold municipality liable for failure of police to prevent domestic violence).

38. *See* Tom Baker, *On the Genealogy of Moral Hazard*, 75 Tex. L. Rev. 237 (1996); Cooter & Ulen, *supra* note 7, at 50; Stephen P. Croley & Jon D. Hanson, *The Nonpecuniary Costs of Accidents: Pain-and-Suffering Damages in Tort Law*, 108 Harv. L. Rev. 1785, 1848–50 (1995).

39. Alan I. Widiss, Uninsured and Underinsured Motorist Insurance § 2.5, at 29–30 (2d ed. 1999); Michelle E. Boardman, *Known Unknowns: The Illusion of Terrorism Insurance*, 93 Geo. L.J. 783 (2005).

40. Abraham, *supra* note 34, at 222–23.

41. Jennifer Wriggins, *Domestic Violence Torts*, 75 S. Cal. L. Rev. 121, 139–140, 172–175 (2001).

42. Dalton, *supra* note 14, at 360–62. *See e.g.*, Feltmeier v. Feltmeier, 798 N.E.2d 75 (Ill. 2003).

43. Wriggins, *Domestic Violence Torts*, *supra* note 41, at 173.

44. Dalton, *supra* note 14, at 387.

45. Chen v. Fischer, 843 N.E.2d 723 (N.Y. 2005).

46. Weicker v. Weicker, 237 N.E.2d 876 (N.Y. 1968); Pickering v. Pickering, 434 N.W.2d 758 (S.D. 1988).

47. Twyman v. Twyman, 855 S.W.2d 619, 637 (Tex. 1993) (Hecht, J. concurring and dissenting).

48. Ira Mark Ellman & Stephen D. Sugarman, *Spousal Emotional Abuse as a Tort?* 55 Md. L. Rev. 1268 (1996). Am. Law Inst., Principles of the Law of Family Dissolution: Analysis and Recommendations 54–64 (2002).

49. Restatement (Third) of Torts § 45 cmt. d (Tentative Draft No. 5, 2007) ("[a]lthough an actor exercising legal rights—such as procuring a divorce or dismissing an at-will employee—is not liable . . . merely for exercising those rights, the actor is not immunized from liability if the conduct goes so far beyond what is necessary to exercise the right that it is extreme and outrageous").

50. Civil rights statutes typically allow harassment victims to seek recovery against their employers. In response to this exposure to liability, employers have increasingly purchased Employment Practices Liability Insurance to cover claims of discrimination, sexual harassment or wrongful discharge. *See* Nancy H. Van der Veer, *Employment Practices Liability Insurance: Are EPLI Policies a License to Discriminate? Or Are They a Necessary Reality Check for Employers*, 12 Conn. Ins. L.J. 173 (2005–06); James B. Dolan, Jr., *The Growing Significance of Employment Practices Liability Insurance*, 34 The Brief, Winter 2005, at 32.

51. Sharkey, *supra* note 25, at 39.

52. Although the U.S. Supreme Court opened the door for same-sex harassment claims in *Oncale v. Sundowner Offshore Services, Inc.*, 523 U.S. 75 (1998), there is still great uncertainty as to how plaintiffs in such cases can establish that their harassment was based on sex. *See generally*, David S. Schwartz, *When Is Sex Because of Sex? The Causation Problem in Sexual Harassment Law*, 150 U. Pa. L. Rev. 1697 (2002).

53. Courts often have difficulty dealing with "intersectional" claims in which it is impossible to separate the different strands of discrimination, for example, when an individual experiences distinctive discrimination as a low-income woman of color. *See generally* Kimberlé Crenshaw, *Race, Gender, and Sexual Harassment*, 65 S. Cal. L Rev. 1467 (1992); Regina Austin, *Employer Abuse, Worker Resistance, and the Tort of Intentional Infliction of Emotional Distress*, 41 Stan. L. Rev. 1, 12–15 (1988) (discussing multidimensional discrimination against workers).

54. Early on, the U.S. Supreme Court acknowledged that discrimination against a subgroup of a protected class is actionable under Title VII. *See* Phillips v. Martin Marietta Corp., 400 U.S. 542, 543–44 (1971). However, plaintiffs still have difficulty proving discrimination when other members of the protected class are not targeted. *See* Martha Chamallas, *Feminist Constructions of Objectivity: Multiple Perspectives in Sexual and Racial Harassment Litigation*, 1 Tex. J. Women & L. 95, 132 (1992).

55. See Devon W. Carbado & Mitu Gulati, *Working Identity*, 65 Cornell L. Rev. 1259, 1293–94 (2000); Mary Anne C. Case, *Disaggregating Gender from Sex and Sexual Orientation: The Effeminate Man in the Law and Feminist Jurisprudence*, 105 Yale L.J. 1, 31 (1995).

56. *See* Kenji Yoshino, *Covering*, 11 Yale L.J. 769 (2002); Paulette M. Caldwell, *A Hair Piece: Perspectives on the Intersection of Race and Gender*, 1991 Duke L.J. 365; Angela Onwuachi-Willig & Mario L. Barnes, *By Any Other Name?: On Being "Regarded as" Black and Why Title VII Should Apply Even if Lakisha and Jamal Are White*, 2005 Wis. L. Rev. 1283, 1284 (discussing discrimination against persons with black-sounding names and voices).

57. Intermediate appellate courts in California have taken the position that harassment that violates the state's anti-discrimination law is *per se* outrageous and gives rise to a tort action for intentional infliction of emotional distress. *See* Fisher v. San Pedro Peninsula Hosp., 262 Cal. Rptr. 842, 858 (Cal. Ct. App. 1989); Kovatch v. Cal. Casualty Management Co., 77 Cal. Rptr. 2d 217, 230 (Cal. Ct. App. 1998).

58. Hoy v. Angelone, 720 A.2d 745, 754 (Pa. 1998).

59. 214 F.3d 615 (5th Cir. 2000).

60. See Greenland v. Fairtron Corp., 500 N.W.2d 36, 38 (Iowa 1993); Quantock v. Share Mktg. Serv. Inc., 312 F.3d 899, 905 (7th Cir. 2002) (applying Illinois law); Arthur v. Pierre Ltd., 100 P.3d 987 (Mont. 2004).

61. Jenson v. Employers Mut. Cas. Co., 468 N.W.2d 1,8 (Wis. 1991); Fernandez v. Ramsey County, 495 N.W.2d 859, 862 (Minn. Ct. App. 1993): Konstantopoulos v. Westvaco, 690 A.2d 936, 940 (Del. 1996); Green v. Wyman-Gordon Co., 664 N.E.2d 808, 813 (Mass. 1996); Gordon v. Cummings, 756 A.2d 942, 945 (Me. 2000); Nassa v. Hook-SupeRx, Inc. 790 A.2d 368 (R.I. 2002); Hardebeck v. Warner Jenkinson Co., 108 F. Supp. 2d 1062, 1064–65 (E.D. Mo. 2000); Dickert Metropolitan Life Ins. Co., 428 S.E.2d 700, 701–10 (S.C. 1993).

62. Alcorn v. Anbro Engineering, Inc., 468 P.2d 216 (Cal. 1970) (referring to plaintiff as "[y]ou goddam niggers" and indicating that he was "getting rid of all the niggers").

63. *Id.* at 499 n.2 ("plaintiff's status as employee should entitle him to a greater degree of protection than if he were a stranger to defendants"); *Id.* at 499 n.3 (discussing minority plaintiff's "susceptibility" to emotional distress).

64. Byrd v. Richardson-Greenshields Securities, Inc. 552 So. 2d 1099, 1104 (Fla. 1989).

65. Horodyskyi v. Karanian, 32 P.3d 470, 479 (Colo. 2001).

66. Byrd, 552 So.2d at 1104.

67. *See* Kathryn Abrams, *The New Jurisprudence of Sexual Harassment*, 83 Cornell L. Rev. 1169, 1217–20 (1998); Katherine M. Franke, *What's Wrong with Sexual Harassment?* 49 Stan. L. Rev. 691, 696 (1997); Lu-in Wang, *The Transforming Power of "Hate": Social Cognition Theory and the Harms of Bias-Related Crime*, 71 S. Cal. L. Rev. 47, 119 (1997); R.A. Lenhardt, *Understanding the Mark: Race, Stigma, and Equality in Context*, 79 N.Y.U. L. Rev. 803, 836 (2004).

68. *See* Beth A. Quinn, *The Paradox of Complaining: Law, Humor, and Harassment in the Everyday Work World*, 25 Law & Soc. Inquiry 1151, 1167–71 (2000); Catharine A. MacKinnon, Sexual Harassment of Working Women: A Case of Sex Discrimination 27–28 (Yale Univ. Press 1979).

69. *See e.g.*, Corne v. Bausch & Lomb, 390 F. Supp. 161 (D. Ariz. 1975).

70. Keeton, *supra* note 31, §6, at 29.

71. *See* Chamallas, *Discrimination and Outrage*, *supra* note 19, at 2154–61 (discussing early solicitation cases).

72. Calvert Magruder, *Mental and Emotional Disturbance in the Law of Torts*, 49 Harv. L. Rev. 1033, 1055 (1936).

73. Lisa R. Pruitt,*"On the Chastity of Women All Property in the World Depends": Injury from Sexual Slander in the Nineteenth Century*, 78 Ind. L.J. 965 (2003).

74. Lisa Pruitt, *Her Own Good Name: Two Centuries of Talk about Chastity*, 63 Md. L. Rev. 401, 458–89 (2004).

75. Orit Kamir, Framed: Women in Law and Film 6 (Duke Univ. Press 2006).

76. Law v. Canada (Minster of Employment & Immigration), [1999] 1 S.C. R. 497, 530 (S.C.C Mar. 25, 1999.); Halpern v. Toronto, 36 R.F. L. (5th) 127 (O.C A. June 10, 2003). *See* Ann Scales, Legal Feminism: Activism, Lawyering and Legal Theory 74–76 (NYU Press 2006) (discussing the Canadian vision of equality).

77. *See* Burlington Northern & Santa Fe Ry. Co. v. White, 548 U.S. 53, 71 (2006) (adopting "reasonable person in plaintiff's position" as the standard in retaliation cases); Martha Chamallas, Introduction to Feminist Legal Theory 242–45 (2d ed. 2003) (discussing reasonable woman standard).

CHAPTER 4

1. *See* John C. P. Goldberg & Benjamin C. Zipursky, *The Restatement (Third) and the Place of Duty in Negligence Law*, 54 Vand. L. Rev. 657 (2001); David Owen, *Duty Rules*, 54 Vand. L. Rev. 767 (2001); Robert L. Rabin, *The Duty Concept in Negligence Law: A Comment*, 54 Vand. L. Rev. 787 (2001); Ernest J. Weinrib, *The Passing of* Palsgraf? 54 Vand L. Rev. 803 (2001).

2. Restatement (Third) of Torts: Liability for Physical Harm §7(b) (Proposed Final Draft No. 1, April 6, 2005) (noting that "in exceptional cases, when an articulated countervailing principle or policy warrants denying or limiting liability in a particular class of cases, a court may decide that the defendant has no duty").

3. There is also no general duty to protect against economic loss unaccompanied by physical property loss. The protection of economic interests, however, is principally protected by contract law.

4. *See* Martha Chamallas, *Removing Emotional Harm from the Core of Tort Law*, 54 Vand. L. Rev. 751 (2001).

5. *See* Wex S. Malone, Torts in a Nutshell: Injuries to Family, Social and Trade Relations (1979); Joseph W. Glannon, The Law of Torts: Examples and Explanations 244–45 (3d ed. 2005).

6. *See* Martha Chamallas & Linda K. Kerber, *Women, Mothers and the Law of Fright: A History*, 88 Mich. L Rev. 814, 824–34 (1990) (tracing the rationale for denying recovery in early cases).

7. Restatement (Third) of Torts: Liability for Physical and Emotional Harm 2 (Tentative Draft No. 5, April 4, 2007) (Scope Note).

8. *See e.g.*, Rodrigues v. State, 472 P.2d 509, 519–20 (Haw. 1970); Sinn v. Burd, 404 A.2d 672, 678–79 (Pa. 1979); W. Page Keeton et al., Prosser and Keeton on the Law of Torts, § 54, at 360 (5th student ed. 1984); Peter A. Bell, *The Bell Tolls: Toward a Full Recovery for Psychic Injury*, 36 U. Fla. L. Rev. 333, 351 (1984); Robert J. Rhee, *A Principled Solution for Negligent Infliction of Emotional Distress Claims*, 36 Ariz. St. L. J. 805, 831–36 (2004).

9. It has not been a straight-line trend toward liberalization. Notable plaintiff victories of the 1970s were curbed in the 1980s, when courts and legislatives cut back on liability in the name of tort reform. In the past two decades, there has been some incremental liberalization of recovery, with wide variations in different states.

10. *See e.g.*, Thing v. La Chusa, 771 P.2d 814, 819 (Cal. 1989); Wilder v. City of Keene, 557 A.2d 636, 638 (N.H. 1989); Williams v. Baker, 572 A.2d 1062, 1069 (D.C. 1990); Finnegan *ex rel.* Skoglind v. Wis. Patients Comp. Fund, 666 N.W.2d 797, 802–03 (Wis. 2003). *See* Robert L. Rabin, *Tort Recovery for Negligently Inflicted Economic Loss*, 37 Stan. L. Rev. 1513,1524–26 (1985) (discussing fear of infinite liability in emotional harm cases).

11. *See* Consolidated Rail Corp. v. Gottshall, 512 U.S. 532, 545 (1994) *citing* Richard N. Pearson, *Liability to Bystanders for Negligently Inflicted Emotional Harm—A Comment on the Nature of Arbitrary Rules*, 34 U. Fla. L Rev. 477, 507 (1982).

12. Restatement (Third) at 3 (Tentative Draft No. 5, April 4, 2007) (Scope Note).

13. See Martha Chamallas, *The Architecture of Bias: Deep Structures in Tort Law*, 146 U. Pa. L. Rev. 463 (1998).

14. *See* Restatement (Third) §§45-46 (Tentative Draft No. 5, April 4, 2007) (sections treating liability for emotional disturbance).

15. Chamallas, *supra* note 13, at 510–21 (discussing devaluation of injuries associated with child care, sexual harassment, and gender-linked cases of medical malpractice).

16. *See* Catharine A. MacKinnon, Toward a Feminist Theory of the State 173 (Harvard Univ. Press 1989) (critiquing liberal, male-oriented conception of consent); Martha Chamallas, *Lucky: The Sequel*, 80 Ind. L.J. 441, 461 (2005) (discussing sex/violence dichotomy); Martha Chamallas, *Consent, Equality and the Legal Control of Sexual Conduct*, 61 S. Cal. L. Rev. 777, 814–35 (1988) (reconstructing consent to exclude consent secured through excessive physical, economic, and psychological pressure).

17. Robin West, Caring for Justice 117–118, 127–129 (NYU Press 1997) (analyzing maternal/child relationship and harms of separation); Leslie Bender, *From Gender Difference to Feminist Solidarity: Using Carol Gilligan and an Ethic of Care in Law*, 15 Vt. L. Rev. 1, 41–47 (1990) (emphasizing importance of values of care, cooperation, and nurturing commonly associated with women and women's work).

18. *See* Restatement (Third) at 66 (Tentative Draft No. 5, April 4, 2007) ("The impact requirement has virtually disappeared today."); Florida continues to use the impact rule but does so selectively. Dan B. Dobbs & Paul Hayden, Torts and Compensation 745 (5th ed. 2005) (Teacher's Manual).

19. Restatement (Third) at 113 (Tentative Draft No. 5, April 4, 2007).

20. *See e.g.*, Falzone v. Busch, 214 A.2d 12 (N.J. 1965) (near miss); Williamson v. Waldman, 696 A.2d 14 (N.J. 1997) (fear of AIDS).

21. Restatement (Third) §46 cmt. b (Tentative Draft No. 5, April 4, 2007).

22. Dobbs & Hayden, *supra* note 18, at 752.

23. *See e.g.*, O'Donnell v. HCA Health Serv. of N.H., 883 A.2d 319 (N.H. 2005); Reynolds v. Highland Manor, Inc., 954 P.2d 11 (Kan. App.1998); Reilly v. United States, 547 A.2d 894 (R.I. 1988).

24. There is a debate, for example, as to whether mental illness qualifies as a physical harm. *See* Harnicher v. University of Utah Med. Ctr., 962 P2d 67 (Utah 1998). *See also* Armstrong v. Paoli Memorial Hosp., 633 A.2d 605 (Pa. Super. 1993) (momentary loss of continence, nightmares, and insomnia qualifies as physical injury).

25. Restatement (Third) §46 (b) (Tentative Draft No. 5, April 4, 2007).

26. Larsen v. Banner Health System, 81 P.3d 196 (Wyo. 2003).

27. *See e.g.*, Young v. Western Union Tel. Co., 11 S.E. 1044 (N.C. 1890) (negligent failure to deliver death telegram); Christensen v. Superior Ct., 820 P.2d 181 (Cal. 1991); Whitehair v. Highland Memory Gardens, Inc., 327 S.E. 2d 438 (W. Va. 1985) (mishandling of dead bodies).

28. *See* Oswald v. LeGrand, 453 N.W.2d 634 (Iowa 1990).

29. Restatement (Third) at 59–60 (Tentative Draft No. 5, April 4, 2007).

30. *See generally* Erwin Chemerinsky, Constitutional Law: Principles and Policies §§10.1-5 at 792–855 (3d ed. 2006) (discussing fundamental rights to marry, custody of children, reproductive autonomy and sexual activity). *See e.g.*, Lawrence *v.* Texas, 539 U.S. 558 (2003) (right of sexual intimacy); Roe v. Wade, 410 U.S. 113 (1973) (right to abortion); Eisenstadt v. Baird, 401 U.S. 934 (1972) (right to contraception); Skinner v. Oklahoma, 316 U.S. 535 (1942) (right to procreate); Santosky v. Kramer, 455 U.S. 746 (1982) (parental rights).

31. Boyles v. Kerr, 855 S.W.2d 593 (Tex. 1993); Twyman v. Twyman, 855 S.W. 2d 619 (1993) (companion case) (Justice Spector's dissent).

32. Torts plaintiffs often "underlitigate" their cases, asserting only negligence claims, because of the basic exclusion for intentional harm in standard liability policies. *See* Ellen S. Pryor, *The Stories We Tell: Intentional Harm and the Quest for Insurance Funding*, 75 Tex. L. Rev. 1721 (1997).

33. Boyles v. Kerr, 855 S.W.2d 593, 610 (Doggett, J. dissenting) (citing Amicus Brief of Women's Advocacy Project at iii).

34. *Id.* at 604 (Gonzalez, J. concurring).

35. Twyman v. Twyman, 855 S.W.2d 619, 644 (Tex. 1993) (Spector, J., dissenting) (companion case to Boyles v. Kerr).

36. *See* Mae C. Quinn, *The Garden Path of* Boyles v. Kerr *and* Twyman v. Twyman, 4 Tex. J. Women & L. 247 (1995) (discussing high threshold of proof). Indeed, after the Texas Supreme Court's decision, the case settled for a fraction of the initial verdict without ever litigating the intentional tort claim.

37. Corgan v. Mueling, 574 N.E.2d 602 (Ill.1991).

38. *Id.* at 603.

39. Denise LeBoeuf, *Psychiatric Malpractice: Exploitation of Women Patients*, 11 Harv. Women's L.J. 83 (1988) (Note).

40. Corgan, 574 N.E. 2d at 611 (Heiple, J., dissenting).

41. *See* Catharine A. MacKinnon, Women's Lives, Men's Laws 243 (Harv. Univ. Press 2005).

42. *See* Martha Chamallas, *Discrimination and Outrage: The Migration of Civil Rights to Tort Law*, 48 Wm. & Mary L. Rev. 2115, 2130 n.75 (2007) (discussing standards for imposing vicarious liability).

43. In Title VII harassment claims, employers are afforded an affirmative defense to liability and damages if they prove that they exercised reasonable care to prevent and correct the harassment and that the employee failed to take advantage of internal grievance procedures. Burlington Indus. v. Ellerth, 524 U.S. 742 (1998).

44. Baskette v. Atlanta Center for Reproductive Medicine, 648 S.E.2d 100 (Ga. App. 2008).

45. Broadnax v. Gonzalez, 809 N.E.2d 645 (N.Y. 2004). In contrast, California courts have long allowed mothers to recover for emotional distress arising from injury to the infant during the course of delivery. *See* Burgess v. Superior Ct., 831 P.2d 1197 (Cal. 1992) (recognizing "the unique relationship of mother and child during pregnancy and childbirth").

46. Oswald v. LeGrand, 453 N.W.2d 634 (Iowa 1990).

47. In wrongful birth cases, however, courts have often cited to *Roe v. Wade* and have discussed women's constitutional right to decide whether to terminate a pregnancy. *See* cases discussed in chapter 5.

48. *See* Walker v. Pierce, 560 F.2d 609 (4th Cir. 1977); Cox v. Stanton, 529 F.2d 47 (4th Cir. 1975); Relf v. Weinberger, 372 F. Supp. 1196 (D.D.C. 1974); Madrigal v. Quilligan, D.C. No. CV 75-2057-JWC (C.D. Cal. 1978); Kevin Begos & John Railey, *Sign This or Else . . . A young woman made a hard choice, and life has not been peaceful since*, Winston-Salem Journal, Dec. 9, 2002 (reporting on unsuccessful case of Nial Cox Ramirez); John Railey & Kevin Begos, *"Still Hiding" Woman sterilized at 14 carries a load of shame*, Winston-Salem Journal, Dec. 8, 2002 (reporting on unsuccessful case of Elaine Riddick Jessie).

49. *See* Carlos G. Velez, *The Nonconsenting Sterilization of Mexican Women in Los Angeles* in Twice a Minority: Mexican-American Women 235 (Margarita B. Melville ed. 1980) (discussing trial in Madrigal v. Quilligan).

50. *See* Dorothy Roberts, Killing the Black Body: Race, Reproduction and the Meaning of Liberty 89–98 (Vintage 1997).

51. *See* Johanna Schoen, Choice and Coercion: Birth Control, Sterilization, and Abortion in Public Health and Welfare 75–138 (U. of N. Car. Press 2005).

52. Series of articles in 2002 by Kevin Begos & John Railey, Winston-Salem Journal.

53. John Railey, *"Wicked Silence": State Board began targeting blacks, but few noticed or seemed to care*, Winston-Salem Journal, Dec. 11, 2002.

54. *See* Begos & Railey, *supra* note 48, *Sign This or Else*; Railey & Begos, *supra* note 48, "*Still Hiding.*"

55. *See* House Bill 296, An Act to Provide A Study of Compensation to the Persons Sterilized through the State's Eugenic Sterilization Program (Feb. 21, 2007). The bill was passed by the House, but never taken up in the North Carolina Senate. However, the Speaker of the House has authority to set up the commission. *See* James Romoser, *Nothing done on Womble initiative: His House bill to examine sterilization reparations has not resulted in action*, Winston-Salem Journal, Mar. 10, 2008.

56. Walker v. Pierce, 560 F.2d 609 (4th Cir. 1977).

57. Relf v. Weinberger, 372 F. Supp. 1196 (D.D.C. 1974).

58. Roberts, *supra* note 50, at 95–97.

59. Roberts, *supra* note 50, at 97.

60. Robinson v. Cutchin, 140 F.Supp.2d 488 (D. Md. 2001).

61. Garcia v. Lawrence Hosp., 773 N.Y.S.2d 59 (App.Div.1st Dep't 2004).

62. Johnson v. Jamaica Hosp., 478 N.Y.S.2d 838 (1984) (Court of Appeals).

63. Larsen v. Banner Health System, 81 P.3d 196 (Wyo. 2003).

64. *See* Martha Albertson Fineman, The Autonomy Myth: A Theory of Dependency 188 (2004); Mary Becker, *Care and Feminists*, 17 Wis.Women's L.J. 57 (2002).

65. Harnicher v. University of Utah Medical Center, 962 P.2d 67 (Utah 1998).

66. *See* Andrews v. Keltz, 838 N.Y.S. 2d 363(2007) (no recovery for emotional distress for giving birth to "darker skinned" child when clinic used wrong sperm for IVF procedure). For a discussion of the cases, *see* Leslie Bender, *"To Err Is Human" ART Mixups: A Labor-Based, Relational Proposal*, 9 J. Gender, Race & Just. 443 (2006).

67. William L. Prosser, Law of Torts §54 at 333 (4th ed. 1971).

68. *See* Dulieu v. White & Sons, 2 K.B. 669 (1901); Hambrook v. Stoked Bros., 1 K.B. 141 (1925); Waube v. Warrington, 258 N.W. 497 (Wis. 1935); Amaya v. Home Ice, Fuel & Supply Co., 379 P.2d 513 (Cal. 1963); Dillon v. Legg, 441 P.2d 912 (Cal. 1968); Thing v. La Chusa, 771 P.2d 814 (Cal. 1989).

69. Dillon v. Legg, 441 P.2d 912 (Cal. 1968).

70. *See* Dan B. Dobbs, The Law of Torts at 841–43 (2000) (discussing loss of consortium claims for spousal and parent/child relationships); *id.*at 807–815 (discussing recoverable damages in wrongful death action).

71. Restatement (Third) §47 at 92–93 (Tentative Draft No. 5, April 4, 2007) (Reporters' Note).

72. *Id.* at 82.

73. *See* Thing, 771 P.2d at 814 (recovery denied to mother who was nearby an accident, rushed to the scene, and saw her child's bloody and unconscious body); Marchetti v. Parsons, 638 A.2d 1047 (R.I. 1994) (recovery denied to parents who saw bloodied, immobile child on a stretcher at the hospital).

74. *See e.g.*, Thing, 771 P. 2d at 828 ("the impact of personally observing the injury-producing event . . .distinguishes the plaintiff's resultant emotional distress felt when one learns of the injury or death of a loved one from another, or observes pain and suffering but not the traumatic cause of the injury"). See Martha Chamallas, *The September 11th Victim Compensation Fund: Rethinking the Damages Element in Injury Law*, 71 Tenn. L.Rev. 51, 77–78 (2003) (discussing especially severe effects of "traumatic" versus "normal" loss of a loved one).

75. *See* Richard A. Epstein, Torts §10.15, at 278 (1999) (requirement that plaintiff be a close family member has held "fairly firm over time").

76. Restatement (Third) §47, cmt. e (Tentative Draft No. 5, April 4, 2007).

77. *Compare* Dunphy v. Gregor, 642 A.2d 372 (N.J. 1994); Graves v. Estabrook, 818 A.2d 1255 (N.H. 2003) (allowing claim to fiancée); Lozoya v. Sanchez, 66 P.3d 948 (N.M. 2003) (allowing claim to fiancée); Yovino v. Big Bubba's BBQ, 896 A.2d 161 (Conn. Super. Ct. 2006) (allowing claim to fiancée); Watters v. Walgreen, 967 So.2d 930 (Fla. Dist. Ct. 2007) (allowing claim to stepchildren) *with* Elden v. Sheldon, 758 P.2d 582 (Cal. 1988) (denying

claim to unmarried cohabitant); Smith v. Toney, 862 N.E.2d 656 (Ind. 2007) (denying claim to fiancée); Trobetta v. Conkling, 626 N.E.2d 653 (N.Y. 1993) (denying claim to niece); Grotts v. Zahner, 989 P.2d 415 (Nev. 1999) (denying claim to fiancée); Guzman v. Kirchhoefel, 2005 WL 1684978 (Cal. Dist. Ct. App. 2005) (denying claim to cousin).

78. Guzman v. Kirchhoefel, 2005 WL 1684978 (Cal. Dist. Ct. App. 2005).

79. Dunphy v. Gregor, 642 A.2d 372 (N.J. 1994).

80. Restatement (Third) §47, cmt. e (Tentative Draft No. 5, April 4, 2007) (citing Principles of the Law of Family Dissolution: Analysis and Recommendations §2.03 (c) and Comment *c).*

81. Lozoya v. Sanchez, 66 P.3d 948 (N.M. 2003).

82. Barbara J. Cox, *Alternative Families: Obtaining Traditional Family Benefits through Litigation, Legislation and Collective Bargaining*, 15 Wis. Women's L.J. 93, 133–37 (2000); Cynthia Grant Bowman, *A Feminist Proposal to Bring Back Common Law Marriage*, 75 Or. L. Rev. 709, 764–65 (1996).

83. Such an approach was advocated by Canadian law professor Shauna Van Praagh in a paper prepared for the Law Commission of Canada. *See* Compensation for Relational Harm (July 5, 2001).

84. Currently, wrongful death recovery is governed by statutes, typically naming specific classes of beneficiaries. For nonfatal cases, common law claims for loss of spousal consortium are well established. However, loss of consortium claims are less uniformly recognized for relational injuries to parents or children. *See* Dobbs, *supra* note 70 at 803–05, 841–43 (only minority of states recognize claim for damage to parent/child relationship).

CHAPTER 5

1. *See* Dan B. Dobbs, The Law of Torts 792–94 (2000).

2. *See generally* Jennifer Wriggins, *Genetics, IQ, Determinism, and Torts: The Example of Discovery in Lead Exposure Litigation*, 77 B.U. L. Rev. 1025 (1997).

3. *See e.g.*, Leon Green, *Duties, Risks, Causation Doctrines*, 41 Tex. L. Rev. 42 (1962); Leon Green, *The Causal Relation Issue in Negligence Law*, 60 Mich. L. Rev 543 (1962): Wex S. Malone, *Ruminations on Cause-In-Fact*, 9 Stan. L. Rev. 60 (1956).

4. *See generally* Susan T. Fiske, Handbook of Social Psychology 357 (Daniel T. Gilbert et al. eds., 4th ed. 1998); Neal Feigenson, Legal Blame: How Jurors Think and Talk about Accidents (American Psychological Association 2000).

5. Restatement of the Law (Third) Torts: Liability for Physical Harm, ch. 6 (Proposed Final Draft No.1, April 6, 2005).

6. *Id.* §26.

7. *Id.* cmt. c at 419.

8. *Id.* §31, cmt. a at 638–48. *See also* Dobbs, *supra* note 1, at 464.

9. *Id.* §26, cmt. e at 422.

10. *Id.* §26, cmt. i at 426; *See also* Michael D. Green, *Expert Witnesses and Sufficiency of Evidence in Toxic Substances Litigation: The Legacy of Agent Orange and Bendectin Litigation*, 86 Nw. U. L. Rev. 643, 645 (1992).

11. Restatement (Third) §28, cmt. b at 528 (Proposed Final Draft No.1, April 6, 2005).

12. David W. Robertson, *The Common Sense of Cause in Fact*, 75 Tex. L. Rev. 1765, 1774 (1997).

13. *Id.*

14. *See* Wex S. Malone, *Ruminations on Cause-in-Fact*, 9 Stan. L. Rev. 60, 74 (1956), citing Reynolds v. Texas and Pac. Ry., 37 La. Ann. 694 (La. 1885).

15. Restatement (Third) § 28, cmt. c (1) at 484. (Proposed Final Draft No.1, April 6, 2005).

16. *Id.*

17. *Id.*

18. Wex S. Malone, *Ruminations on Cause-in-Fact*, 9 Stan. L. Rev. 60 (1956).

19. Restatement (Third) §28 at 525 (Proposed Final Draft No.1, April 6, 2005).

20. David W. Robertson, *The Common Sense of Cause in Fact*, 75 Tex. L. Rev. 1765, 1770–71 (1997).

21. *Id.* at 1770.

22. *See generally* Adam Benforado & Jon Hanson, *The Great Attributional Divide: How Divergent Views of Human Behavior Are Shaping Legal Policy*, 57 Emory L.J. 311 (2008).

23. Arthur F. McEvoy, *The Triangle Shirtwaist Factory Fire of 1911: Social Change, Industrial Accidents, and the Evolution of Common-Sense Causality*, 20 Law & Soc. Inquiry 621, 623 (1995).

24. Feigenson, *supra* note 4, at 51.

25. This preference for simple causal explanations has been termed the "preference for monocausality" by cognitive psychologists. *Id.* at 51–52.

26. *See* Susan T. Fiske & Shelley E. Taylor, Social Cognition 67–72 (2d ed. 1991); Fiske, *supra* note 4, 357, 369–70; Feigenson *supra* note 4, at 57–58; Jon Hanson & David Yosifon, *The Situation: An Introduction to the Situational Character, Critical Realism, Power Economics and Deep Capture*, 152 U. Pa. L. Rev. 129, 136 (2003) (discussing "our proclivity to underestimate the role of situational influences, and to overestimate the influence of individual dispositions in explaining people's behavior").

27. Linda Hamilton Krieger, *The Content of Our Categories: A Cognitive Bias Approach to Discrimination and Equal Employment Opportunity*, 47 Stan.L. Rev. 1161 (1995).

28. *Id.* at 1206.

29. *See* Daniel Kahneman & Dale T. Miller, *Norm Theory: Comparing Reality to Its Alternatives*, 93 Psych. Rev. 136, 143 (1986).

30. Lu-in Wang, Discrimination by Default: How Racism Becomes Routine 87 (NYU Press 2006).

31. Ann L. McGill & Ann E. Tenbrunsel, *Mutability and Propensity in Causal Selection*, 79 J. of Personality & Soc. Psych. 677, 679 (2000).

32. Robert A. Prentice & Jonathan J. Koehler, *A Normality Bias in Legal Decision Making*, 88 Cornell L. Rev. 583, 595 (2003). *See also* Christopher W. Williams, Paul R. Lees-Haley, & J. Randall Price, *The Role of Counterfactual Thinking and Causal Attribution in Accident-Related Judgments*, 26 J. of Applied Soc. Psych. 2100 (1996).

33. Richard Delgado, *Rodrigo's Eleventh Chronicle: Emphathy and False Empathy*, 84 Cal. L. Rev. 61, 76 (2003).

34. Wang, *supra* note 30, at 85.

35. Prentice & Koehler, *supra* note 32, at 587.

36. *Id.* at 588.

37. Roe v. Wade, 410 U.S. 113 (1973).

38. *See* Custodio v. Bauer, 251 Cal.App. 2d 303 (1967) (damages for birth of tenth child after negligent sterilization). *See also* West v. Underwood, 40 A.2d 610 (N.J. 1945) (damages for negligent sterilization and cost of subsequent sterilization); Milde v. Leigh, 28 N.W. 2d 530 (1947) (husband entitled to loss of consortium due to negligent sterilization of his wife).

39. Although most courts that have addressed the issue have recognized the claim for wrongful birth, they often disagree about the proper measure of damages. *See* Shelley A. Ryan, *Wrongful Birth: False Representations of Women's Reproductive Lives*, 78 Minn. L. Rev. 857, 865–67 (1994).

40. *See* Centers for Disease Control and Prevention (CDC), U.S. Department of Health and Human Services, *Vaccine Testing*, http://www.cdc.gov/vaccines/pubs/vacc-timeline.htm, Oct. 19, 2006, last visited March 5, 2009.

41. Richard M. Patterson, Lawyers' Medical Cyclopedia of Personal Injuries and Allied Specialties, vol. 5B, §37.11a, at 37–74 (5th ed. 2004).

42. *See* Becker v. Schwartz, 386 N.E.2d 807 (N.Y. 1978); Berman v. Allen, 404 A.2d 8 (N.J. 1979); Azzolino v. Dingfelder, 337 S.E.2d 528 (N.C. 1985); Wilson v. Kuenzl, 751 S.W.2d 741 (Mo. 1988); Atlanta Obstetrics & Gynecology Group v. Abelson, 398 S.E.2d 557 (Ga. 1990).

43. *See* Encyclopedia of Children's Health, *Amniocentesis* (2005) http://www. enotes.com/childrens-health-encyclopedia/amniocentesis (last visited October 24, 2006).

44. *Id.*

45. *Id.*

46. *See* Sara M. Evans, Born for Liberty: A History of Women in America 263–314 (The Free Press 1989); Sara M. Evans, Tidal Wave: How Women Changed America at Century's End 18–60 (The Free Press 2003).

47. *See* Weinberger v. Wiesenfeld, 420 U.S. 636 (1975); Califano v. Goldfarb, 430 U.S. 199 (1977); Wengler v. Druggists Mut.Ins. Co., 446 U.S. 142 (1980).

48. *See* Pregnancy Discrimination Act of 1978, Pub.L. No. 95-555, 92 Stat. 2076 (1978) (codified at 42 U.S.C.§2000e(k) (1982)).

49. Griswold v. Connecticut, 381 U.S. 479 (1965); Eisenstadt v. Baird, 405 U.S. 438 (1972).

50. Eisenstadt v. Baird, 405 U.S. 438, 453 (1972).

51. Gleitman v. Cosgrove, 227 A.2d 698 (N.J. 1967).

52. *See* Atlanta Obstetrics & Gynecology Group v. Abelson, 398 S.E 2d 557 (Ga. 1990); Azzolino v. Dingfelder, 337 S.E.2d 528 (N.C. 1985); Wilson v. Kuenzl, 751 S.W.2d 741 (Mo. 1988).

53. Becker v. Schwartz, 386 N.E.2d 807 (N.Y. 1978).

54. *Id.* at 819. (Wachtler, J., dissenting).

55. *See* Atlanta Obstetrics & Gynecology Group v. Abelson, 398 S.E.2d 557 (Ga. 1990); Azzolino v. Dingfelder, 337 S.E 2d 528 (N.C. 1985); Wilson v. Kuenzl, 751 S.W.2d 741 (Mo. 1988).

56. The first court in the nation to allow a claim for wrongful birth was the Texas Supreme Court in *Jacob v. Theimer*, 519 S W.2d 846 (Tex. 1975).

57. Smith v. Cote, 513 A.2d 341 (N.H. 1986).

58. *See* Dobbs, *supra* note 1, at 794–98 (discussing special damages rules for wrongful birth tort).

59. Reed v. Campagnolo, 630 A.2d 1145 (Md. App. 1993).

60. *See e.g.*, Idaho Code § 5-334 (1991); 424; Minn. Stat. Ann.§ 145.424 (1991).

61. Kingsbury v. Smith, 442 A.2d 1003, 1005–06 (N. H. 1982).

62. *See e.g.*, Rosalind Pollack Petchesky, Abortion and Women's Choice: The State, Sexuality, & Reproductive Freedom 1–18 (Northeastern Univ. Press, rev. ed. 1990).

63. *See e.g.*, Wilson v. Kuenzl, 751 S.W.2d 741, 745 (Mo. 1988) ("The child's handicap is an inexorable result of conception and birth").

64. Azzolino v. Dingfelder, 337 S.E.2d 528, 536 (N.C. 1985) ("[T]he doctor's alleged negligent failure to detect it during prenatal examination cannot be considered a cause of the condition by analogy to those cases in which the doctor has failed to make a timely diagnosis of a curable disease").

65. *See e.g.*, Joan Williams, Unbending Gender: Why Family and Work Conflict and What You Can Do about It 187–93 (Oxford Univ. Press 2000) (discussing the power of the ideology of "domesticity" as an interpretive system); Barbara L. Bernier, *Mothers as Plaintiffs in Prenatal Tort Liability Cases: Recovery for Physical and Emotional Injuries*, 4 Harv. Women's L.J. 43, 55 (1981) (mentioning traditional notion that "mothers are expected to sacrifice their time to child rearing without compensation").

66. *See* Mark S. Dennison, *Landlord's Liability for Lead-Based Paint Hazard in Residential Dwelling*, 35 Am. Jur. Proof of Facts 3d 439, §4 (2008). Some cases have also been brought against paint manufacturers. *See* Hardison v. E.I., Du Pont de Nemours and Co., No. 06CV00606 (Wis Cir. 2006), reported in 11–15 Mealey's Litig. Rep.: Lead 8 (2006). *See generally*, Mark P. Gagliardi, *Stirring up the Debate in Rhode Island: Should Lead Paint Manufacturers Be Held Liable for the Harm Caused by Lead Paint?* 7 Rogers Williams U. L. Rev. 341 (2002) (student comment).

67. CDC, Preventing Lead Poisoning in Young Children 1, 4 (August 2005).

68. CDC, Managing Elevated Blood Lead Levels in Young Children 4, 17 (March 2002).

69. CDC, Using GIS to Assess and Direct Childhood Lead Poisoning Prevention: Guidance for State and Local Childhood Lead Poisoning Prevention Programs 2 (Dec. 2004) ("Children at greatest risk for lead poisoning are those whose families are poor and live in substandard housing built before 1950. These children tend to be African-American or of Hispanic ethnicity").

70. CDC, *Surveillance for Elevated Blood Levels among Children—United States 1997–2001*, 52 Morbidity and Mortality Weekly Report, No. ss-10 at 5 (Sept. 12, 2003).

71. *See* Karen F. Florini et al., Legacy of Lead: America's Continuing Epidemic of Lead Poisoning, app.1, tbl. A-1 (Environmental Defense Fund 1990).

72. James L. Pirkle, *Exposure of the U.S. Population to Lead, 1991–1994*, 106 Envtl.Health Perspectives 11, tbl. 1 (1998) (according to national survey, 11.2% of non-Hispanic blacks had elevated blood lead levels compared to 4.4% of children overall); Debra Brody et al., *Blood Levels in the U.S. Population*, 272 J. Am. Med. Ass'n 277, 279 (1994) (incidence of blood levels of African-American children between one and two years old was 2.5 times higher than among white children).

73. Although there are no published studies revealing the precise percentage of minority plaintiffs in lead paint cases, our conversations with plaintiffs' attorneys and our familiarity with the details of many published cases suggest that the cases track the racial patterns of exposure to lead paint.

74. See e.g., Patterson v. Housing Authority of Birmingham District, No. 2001-2425-RSV (Jefferson County, Jan. 31, 2006), reported in 15-5 Mealey's Litig. Rep.: Lead 7 (2006).

75. CDC, 2005 Report, supra note 67, at 14.

76. *See generally* CDC 2005 Report, *supra* note 67; CDC, Preventing Lead Poisoning in Young Children, Ch. 2 (1991).

77. CDC, 2005 Report, *supra* note 67, at ix.

78. CDC, 1991 Report, *supra* note 76, Ch. 1.

79. In many cases, plaintiffs' attorneys require that the child plaintiff exhibit a blood lead level as high as 30 micrograms per deciliter, well above the CDC's 10 micrograms per deciliter "level of concern." This practice stems from the fact that at lower levels, children are asymptomatic and it is harder to link exposure to cognitive deficits. *See* Daniel F. Penofsky, *Childhood Lead-Based Paint Litigation*, 66 Am.Jur. Trials 47 §155 (2008).

80. La Fountaine v. Franzese, 282 A.D.2d 935, 937 (N.Y. App. Div. 2001).

81. Rosevelie M. Morales, *The New Lead Paint Law of New York*, 15-5 Mealey's Litig. Rep. : Lead 6 (2006).

82. Scott A. Smith, *Turning Lead into Asbestos and Tobacco: Litigation Alchemy Gone Wrong*, 71 Def. Couns. J. 119, 122 (2004).

83. *Id.* at 122 (emphasis added).

84. Sue E. Antell, *Why Evaluate Mothers in Lead Paint Litigation*, 10–11 Mealey's Litig. Rep.:Lead 17 (2001).

85. Helmer v. Draksik, No. 2003-4022 (N.Y. Sup. Ct. 2006) (reported in 15-10 Mealey's Litig. Rep.: Lead 8 (2006)).

86. Daniel F. Penofsky, *supra* note 79, at §200 ("Improper Discovery Attempts").

87. Andon v. 302-304 Mott Street Associates, 731 N.E.2d 589 (N.Y. 2000).

88. Andon v. 302-304 Mott Street Associates, 690 N.Y.S.2d 241, 244 (N.Y. App. Div. 1999).

89. *Id.* citing Jennifer Wriggins, *Genetics, IQ, Determinism, and Torts: The Example of Discovery in Lead Exposure Litigation*, 77 B.U. L. Rev. 1025, 1061 (1997).

90. Anderson v. Seigel, 668 N.Y.S. 2d 1003 (Sup. Ct. 1998).

91. Poole v. Hawkeye Area Comm. Action Program, Inc., 666 N.W.2d 560 (Iowa 2003).

92. Nyugen v. Diversified Lending Services, CA No. 98-7619 (D.C. Super. Ct. June 22, 2000), overruling Campbell v. Bonner, CA No. 92-7771 (D.C. Super. Ct. Jan. 14, 1994) (opinions on file with Jennifer Wriggins).

93. Michael D. Green, *Expert Witnesses and Sufficiency of Evidence in Toxic Substances Litigation: The Legacy of Agent Orange and Bendictin Litigation* , 86 Nw. U. L. Rev. 643, 651 (1992).

94. Fisher v. Powell, No. 00 CVS 2188 (N.C. Sup. Ct. 2002) (finding of fact no.7).

95. Helmer v. Draksik, No.1-2003-4022 (15-10 Mealey's Litig. Rep.: Lead 8 (2006)).

96. *See* Bunch v. Artz, 71 Va. Cir. 358 (Portsmouth 2006) (expert testimony of Lawrence Charnas, M.D., Ph.D).

97. *Id.* at 8.

98. *Id.* at 1.

99. Smith, *supra* note 82, at 122.

100. Susan R. Poulter, *Genetic Testing in Toxic Injury Litigation: The Path to Scientific Certainty or Blind Alley?* 41 Jurimetrics J. 211 (2001).

101. *Id.* at 230.

102. *See e.g.*, Fed. R. Civ. P. 35; Wriggins, *supra* note 2, at 1055–79.

103. Robertson, *supra* note 20, at 1774.

104. Richard J. Herrnstein & Charles Murray, The Bell Curve: Intelligence and Class Structure in American Life (1994).

105. *Id.* at 107.

106. *See* Martha Chamallas, Introduction to Feminist Legal Theory 291–98 (2d ed. 2003).

107. *See* Maxine Baca Zinn, *Family, Race and Poverty in the Eighties*, 14 Signs 856 (1989).

108. *See* Dorothy E. Roberts, *The Value of Black Mothers' Work*, 26 Conn. L. Rev. 871, 872–76 (1994).

109. *See* Martha Albertson Fineman, The Neutered Mother, the Sexual Family and Other Twentieth Century Tragedies 178 (1995) (noting that single-mother families are thought of as "public" families, justifying state intrusion and loss of privacy).

110. *See* Sylvia A. Law, *Ending Welfare as We Know It*, 49 Stan. L. Rev. 471, 482 (1997).

111. Lu-in Wang, *supra* note 30, at 92.

112. *Id.* at 84, citing Richard Delgado, *Rodrigo's Eleventh Chronicle: Empathy and False Empathy*, 84 Cal. L. Rev. 61, 77 (1996).

CHAPTER 6

1. Richard Abel calculated that only 10 percent of scholarly articles published between 2002 and 2004 concerned damages and that no casebook devoted more than 10% of its pages to damages. Richard Abel, *General Damages Are Incoherent, Incalculable, Incommensurable, and Inegalitarian (But Otherwise a Great Idea)*, 55 De Paul L. Rev. 253, 253 (2006).

2. *See* William L. Prosser, Handbook of the Law of Torts (4th ed. 1971); W. Page Keeton et al., Prosser and Keeton on Torts (5th ed. 1984).

3. The latest author of the successor hornbook, Professor Dan Dobbs, has recently devoted several sections to damages. *See* Dan B. Dobbs, The Law of Torts, §§377- 384 at 1047–75 (2000).

4. McMillan v. City of New York, 253 F.R.D. 247 (E.D.N.Y. 2008).

5. *See* Kenneth R. Feinberg, What is Life Worth? The Unprecedented Effort to Compensate the Victims of 9/11, 68–69, 75–77 (2005).

6. *See* Final Rule, September 11th Victim Compensation Fund of 2001, 67 Fed. Reg. 11233-01 (Mar. 13, 2002) (explaining choice of methodology that uses "All Active Male table for all claimants" in order to use "the most generous data available" and not disadvantage families of female or minority victims.)

7. There is a rich body of evidence documenting racial disparities in sentencing in criminal cases, especially in death penalty cases. *See* David C. Baldus et al., Equal Justice and the Death Penalty: A Legal and Empirical Analysis (Northeastern U. Press 1990); U.S. Gen. Acct. Off, U.S. Death Penalty Sentencing, *in* Report to the Senate and House Committees on the Judiciary 5 (1990); Gary D. LaFree, Rape and Criminal Justice: The Social Construction of Sexual Assault 132 (1989); Kimberlé Crenshaw, *Mapping the Margins: Intersectionality, Identity Politics, and Violence against Women of Color*, 43 Stan. L. Rev. 1241, 1269 (1991) (citing Dallas study showing the average prison term for a man convicted of raping a black woman was two years, as compared to five years for the rape of a Latina and ten years for the rape of an Anglo woman).

8. Dobbs, *supra* note 3, §377 at 1047.

9. *See* U.S. Dep't of Justice, Bureau of Justice Stats., NCJ 206240 Bulletin: Tort Trial and Verdicts in Large Counties, 2001.1 (2004) ("About 5% of plaintiff winners in tort trials were awarded punitive damages"); Stephen Daniels & Joanne Martin, *Myth and Reality in Punitive Damages*, 75 Minn. L. Rev. 1, 31 (1990) (punitive damages awarded in 4.9% of cases decided between 1981 and 1985).

10. See John C. P. Goldberg, *Two Conceptions of Tort Damages: Fair v. Full Compensation*, 55 DePaul L. Rev. 435 (2006); Robert L. Rabin, *Pain and Suffering and Beyond: Some Thoughts on Recovery for Intangible Loss*, 55 DePaul L. Rev. 359 (2006).

11. Worklife expectancy is distinct from life expectancy. Worklife expectancy is a statistical measure derived from the past working experience of all people in plaintiff's gender, age, and racial group. It incorporates rates of unemployment, both voluntary and involuntary, as well as expected retirement age. Thus, although women as a group have a longer life expectancy than men, they also have a shorter worklife expectancy.

12. *See generally* Jerome H. Nates et al., Damages in Tort Actions §110.02[2][b] (2007); Childs v. United States, 923 F. Supp. 1570, 1575 (S.D. Ga. 1996) (indicating defendant's expert relied on race-based worklife and earning tables); Michael L. Brookshire, Michael R. Luthy, & Frank L. Slesnick, *Forensic Economists, Their Methods and Estimates of Forecast Variables: A 2003 Survey Study*, 6 Litig. Econ. Rev. 28, 33 (2004) (indicating that some economists still rely on outdated Bureau of Labor Statistic tables, divided by race, gender, and age); Edward M. Foster & Gary R. Skoog, *The Markov Assumption for Worklife Expectancy*, 17 J. of Forensic Econ. 167 (2004) (noting that BLS data establish cohorts divided by sex, age, and either race ("white v. all other") or according to three education-level groupings); Vocational Econometrics Inc. Worklife Expectancy Definitions, *available at* http://www.voecon.com/Worklife/wledefin.html (stating that in constructing worklife tables, "gender is important, given the tendency of women to be more likely to remain home for child rearing") (last visited May 21, 2009).

13. *See* United States v. Bedonie, 317 F.Supp.2d 1285 (D. Utah 2004), *aff'd sub nom* United States v. Serawop, 410 F.3d 656 (10th Cir. 2005).

14. *See e.g.*, Laura Greenberg, *Compensating the Lead Poisoned Child: Proposals for Mitigating Discriminatory Damage Awards*, 28 B. C. Envtl. Aff. L. Rev. 429 (2001); Jennifer B. Wriggins, *Genetics, IQ, Determinism, and Torts: The Example of Discovery in Lead Exposure Litigation*, 77 B.U.L. Rev. 1025 (1997).

15. *See* Parents Involved in Community Schools v. Seattle School Dist. No. 1, 555 U.S. 701 (2007) (invalidating student allocation plan based on race); Palmore v. Sidoti, 466 U.S. 429 (1984) (outlawing consideration of race in child custody decision); Korematsu v. United States, 323 U.S. 214, 214 (1944) (establishing strict scrutiny for race classification); United States v. Virginia, 518 U.S. 515 (1996) (establishing stringent intermediate scrutiny test for gender classifications).

16. 435 U.S. 702 (1978).

17. The ban on the use of gender to determine life expectancy extends only to employer-run retirement and insurance programs. Private insurers, outside the context of employment governed by Title VII antidiscrimination law, have continued to use gender as a basis for setting premiums for automobile and other types of insurance. As of 1995, only Montana had enacted a ban on sex discrimination in private insurance. Private insurers claim they no longer use race-based data in setting insurance rates. *See* Jill Gaulding,

Race, Sex and Genetic Discrimination in Insurance: What's Fair? 80 Cornell L. Rev. 1646, 1659–63 n.59 (1995).

18. *See* McMillan, 253 F.R.D. at 249.

19. 771 F. Supp. 427 (D.D.C. 1991), *rev'd on other grounds*, 28 F. 3d 120 (D.C .Cir. 1994).

20. 139 F. 906 (S.D.N.Y. 1905), *aff'd sub nom.* The Hamilton, 146 F. 724 (2d Cir. 1906), *aff'd sub nom.*, Old Dominion v. SS. Co. v. Gilmore, 207 U.S. 398 (1907).

21. Although all the claimants' awards were reduced, the black claimants suffered the greatest reduction, except for the one white claimant who was proved to be in bad health. *See* The Saginaw and the Hamilton, 139 F. 906, 916 (S.D.N.Y. 1905). *See* Jennifer B. Wriggins, *Whiteness, Equal Treatment, and the Valuation of Injury in Torts 1900–1940* in Fault Lines: Tort Law as Cultural Practice 156 (David M. Engle & Michael McCann eds., Stan. Law Books 2009).

22. For a fuller discussion of the Louisiana case law, *see* Jennifer B. Wriggins, *Damages in Tort Litigation: Thoughts on Race and Remedies, 1865–2007*, 27 Rev. Litig. 50, 52, 57 (2007); Jennifer B. Wriggins, *Torts, Race and the Value of Injury, 1900–1949*, 49 How. L.J. 99, 110–131 (2005).

23. *See* Wheeler Tarpeh-Doe v. United States, 771 F. Supp. 427 (D.D.C. 1991); Reilly v. United States, 665 F. Supp. 976 (D.R.I. 1987); Theodile v. Delmar Systems, Inc. 2007 WL 2491808 at *8 (W.D. La. 2007); United States v. Bedonie, 317 F. Supp.2d 1285 (D. Utah 2004) *aff'd sub nom.*, United States v. Serawop, 505 F.3d 1112 (10th Cir. 2007).

24. Bedonie, 317 F. Supp.2d at 1288.

25. CA 10064/02 Migdal Ins. v. Rim Abu Hanna, [2005] IsrSC, discussed in Eliezer Rivlin, *Thoughts on Referral to Foreign Law, Global Chain-Novel, and Novelty*, 21 Fla.J. In'tl L. 1, 21–28 (2009).

26. *Id.* at 21–22.

27. *See* Shaw (Guardian ad litem of) v. Arnold [1998] B.C. J. 2834 (B.C.S.C, Dec.3, 1998); Tucker (Public Trustee of) v. Asleson [1993] 102 D.L.R (4th) 518 (B. C. A. A. Apr.20, 1993).

28. *See* Walker v. Ritchie, [2003] O.J. 18 (O.S C.J. Jan. 3, 2003) ; Cho v. Cho [2003] 36 R.F. L. (5th) 79 (O.S.C J., Feb. 27, 2003).

29. Walker v. Ritchie [2003] O.J. 18 (O.S C. J. Jan. 3, 2003).

30. *See e.g.*, Gray v. Macklin [2000], 4 C.C.L.T. (3d) 13 at ¶ 197 (O.S C.J Dec.4, 2000); MacCabe v. Westlock Roman Catholic Separate School Dist. No. 110 [1998] 226 A.R. 1 (Alb. Q. B., Oct. 5,1998); Elizabeth Adjin-Tetty, *Replicating and Perpetuating Inequalities in Personal Injury Claims through Female-Specific Contingencies*, 49 McGill L.J. 309, 317-19 (2004) (discussing cases).

31. See Martha Chamallas, *The September 11th Victim Compensation Fund: Rethinking the Damages Element in Injury Law*, 71 Tenn. L. Rev. 51, 69–71 (2003).

32. In contrast, the Israeli Supreme Court has adopted a new version of corrective justice for tort law in which "correction means the restoration of the victim to a just and fair status, safeguarding her normative rights, striving for fair correction of the tort, exceeding the historical dimension of the status quo to which the law wishes to restore the tort victim and looking for its normative aspects." Rivlin, *supra* note 25, at 21–22 (2009) (discussing *Migdal v. Rim Abu Hanna*).

33. See Anthony J. Sebok, *Judge Jack Weinstein's Ruling Barring the Use of Race in Calculating the Expected Lifespan of a Man Seeking Tort Damages: An Isolated Decision or the Beginning of a Legal Revolution?* Findlaw's Writ., Oct. 22, 2008, http://writ.news.findlaw.com/sebok/20081022.html.

34. Feinberg, *supra* note 5, at 74.

35. For an expanded discussion of the difficulties in accurately forecasting future economic losses, *see* Martha Chamallas, *Civil Rights in Ordinary Tort Cases: Race, Gender and the Calculation of Economic Loss*, 38 Loy. L.A. L. Rev. 1435, 1450–52 (2005).

36. *See* Francine D. Blau & Lawrence M. Kahn, *The Gender Pay Gap: Have Women Gone as Far as They Can?* Acad. Of Mgmt. Persp. 7, 21 (2007) ("best guess" is that wages of men and women will continue to converge but probably at a slower pace and that gender pay gap seems unlikely to vanish in the near term). *See also* Francine D. Blau & Lawrence M. Kahn, *The U.S. Gender Pay Gap in the 1990s: Slowing Convergence*, 60 Indus. & Labor Rel. Rev. 45, 45 (2006) (gender pay gap narrowed substantially in 1980s, from 59.7% to 68.7% between 1979 and 1989, but ratio of convergence slowed markedly in the 1990s, rising only 3.5% to 72.2% by 1999).

37. *See e.g.*, Walker v. Ritchie [2003] O.J. No.18 at ¶¶ 134–35 (O.S.C J. Jan.3, 2003).

38. *See* David M. Engel & Michael McCann, *Introduction: Tort Law as Cultural Practice*, in Fault Lines: Tort Law as Cultural Practice at 1–17 (Stan. Law Books 2009).

39. *See e.g.*, Milton C. Regan, Jr., *How Does Law Matter?* 1 Green Bag 265, 272–73 (1998) (explaining "expressive account of law"); Cass R. Sunstein, *The Expressive Function of Law*, 144 U. Pa. L. Rev. 2021 (1996).

40. *See* Martha Chamallas, *The Architecture of Bias: Deep Structures in Tort Law*, 146 U. Pa. L Rev. 463, 486 n.81 (1998) (describing regression analysis indicating that for years 1991, 1992, and 1994, "Catholics were almost one and one-half times more likely than Baptists to have a household income over $25,000").

41. For a general discussion of the public policy exception, *see* Mark A. Rothstein et al., Employment Law §9.9 at 438–43 (3d ed. 2004).

42. *See e.g.*, Michael L. Rustad, *The Closing of Punitive Damages' Iron Cage*, 38 Loy. L. A. L. Rev. 1297, 1356–57 (2005) (discussing disproportionate impact on women of punitive damages reform); Thomas Koenig & Michael L. Rustad, *His and Her Tort Reform: Gender Injustice in Disguise*, 70 Wash. L. Rev. 1, 59 (1995) (in medical malpractice context, women receive two-thirds of the punitive damages awarded); Lucinda M. Finley, *Female Trouble: The Implications of Tort Reform for Women*, 64 Tenn. L. Rev. 847, 866 (1997) (punitive damages have "clustered around contraceptive and cosmetic products, including: IUDs, breast implants; sexual assaults by health care providers; unnecessary reproductive surgery, such as hysterectomies, performed on women without their consent; grossly deficient cosmetic surgery, and abuse or neglect of elderly women in nursing homes").

43. Catherine M. Sharkey, *Unintended Consequences of Medical Malpractice Damage Caps*, 80 N.Y.U. L. Rev. 391, 412–13 (2005).

44. *Id.*

45. *See* Feinberg, *supra* note 5, at 71 (describing outcry of wealthy families when most awards for economic losses were restricted to $231,000 per year).

46. *See* Amanda Edwards, *Medical Malpractice Non-Economic Damage Caps*, 43 Harv. J. on Legis. 213, 216–19 (2006) (discussing history of MICRA).

47. Finley, *supra* note 42, at 851.

48. *See* John Fabian Witt, The Accidental Republic: Crippled Workingmen, Destitute Widows, and the Remaking of American Law 10 (Harv. U. Press 2004) (by the 1920s and 1930s, workers' compensation systems replacing tort law were largely in place).

49. Finley, *supra* note 42, at 858–860.

50. *See e.g.*, Robin West, Caring for Justice 96–99 (NYU Press 1997).

51. *See* Margaret E. Johnson, *"Avoiding Harm Otherwise": Reframing Women Employees' Response to the Harms of Sexual Harassment*, 80 Temp. L. Rev. 743, 765–771 ((2007) (discussing social science studies).

52. Pa. State Police v. Suders, 542 U.S.129 (2004).

53. Finley, *supra* note 42, at 857.

54. Lucinda M. Finley, *The Hidden Victims of Tort Reform: Women, Children and the Elderly*, 53 Emory L.J. 1263, 1284–85, tbls. 1-2 (2004).

55. *Id.* at 1296.

56. *Id.* at 1297.

57. *Id.* at 1299–1300 & tbls. 16-17.

58. *Id.* at 1293.

59. Michael L. Rustad, *Heart of Stone: What Is Revealed about the Attitude of Compassionate Conservatives toward Nursing Home Practices, Tort Reform, and Noneconomic Damages*, 35 N.M. L.Rev. 337 (2005).

60. Terry Carter, *Tort Reform Texas Style: New Laws and Med-Mal Damage Caps Devastate Plaintiff and Defense Firms Alike*, A.B.A. J. October 2006 at 30–31.

61. Data from the University of Texas System Professional Medical Liability Plan, which insures more than 10,000 physicians and medical students, reported a 55 percent decline in new lawsuits from 2002 to 2005. *Id.* at 33.

62. Data on nursing home cases litigated in Florida shows a gender disparity in economic losses even among elderly victims. *See* Finley, *supra* note 54, at 1305–06, tbls. 21-22 (economic damages accounted for only 3.6% of awards for female residents but 40% for male residents).

63. Paul H.Rubin & Joanna M. Shepherd, *The Demographics of Tort Reform*, 4 Rev. of L. & Econ. 591, 592–95 (2008).

64. Joanne Doroshow & Amy Widman, *The Racial Implications of Tort Reform*, 25 Wash. U. J. L.& Pol'y 161, 161–68 (2007).

65. Stephen Daniels & Joanne Martin, *The Texas Two-Step: Evidence on the Link between Damage Caps and Access to the Civil Justice System*, 55 DePaul L. Rev. 635, 654 (2006).

66. *See* Policy Guidance on the Consideration of Arrest Records in Employment Decisions under Title VII of the Civil Rights Act of 1964 (August 23, 2007), available at www.eeoc.gov/policy/docs/arrest_records.html, (use of arrest and conviction records to exclude applicants has disparate impact on African Americans and Hispanics). In March 2009, the unemployment rate for whites was 7.9 percent, compared to 11.4 percent for Hispanics and 13.3 percent for blacks. See U.S. Bureau of Labor Statistics, Employment Situation Summary (April 2009), www.bls.gov/news.release/empsit.nro.htm.

67. Brian J. Glenn, *The Shifting Rhetoric of Insurance Denial*, 34 Law & Soc'y Rev.779, 781 (2000); Regina Austin, *The Insurance Classification Controversy*, 131 U. of Pa. L. Rev. 517 (1983).

68. *See* Sharkey *supra* note 43, at 490–91 (acknowledging that selection bias in the screening of cases might have adverse effects on subgroups that is undetected by data).

69. *See* Frank M. McClellan, *The Dark Side of Tort Reform: Searching for Racial Justice*, 48 Rutgers L. Rev., 761, 776 (1996).

70. F. Patrick Hubbard, *The Nature and Impact of the "Tort Reform" Movement*, 35 Hofstra L. Rev. 437, 493 (2006).

71. See Victor E. Schwartz & Leah Lorber, *Twisting the Purpose of Pain and Suffering Awards: Turning Compensation into "Punishment,"* 54 S. C. L. Rev. 47 (2002).

72. Neil K. Komesar, *Injuries and Institutions: Tort Reform, Tort Theory, and Beyond*, 65 N.Y.U. L. Rev. 23, 58 (1990).

73. Rabin, *supra* note 10, at 361–62.

74. *See also* Roselle L. Wissler, Patricia F. Kuehn, & Michael Saks, *Instructing Jurors on General Damages in Personal Injury Cases: Problems and Possibilities*, 6 Psychol. Pub. Pol'y & L. 712, 736 (2000) (between one-half and three-fourths of variation in awards in noneconomic damages is explained by the seriousness and duration of the injury).

75. For such outlier cases, substantial judicial checks, including postverdict review of awards, limit excessive verdicts. *See* Neil Vidmar, Felicia Gross, & Mary Rose, *Jury Awards for Medical Malpractice and Post-Verdict Adjustments of Those Awards*, 48 De Paul L. Rev. 265, 278–99 (1998); Neil Vidmar, *The Performance of the American Civil Jury: An Empirical Perspective*, 40 Ariz. L. Rev. 849, 893 (1998); Carl T. Bogus, Why Lawsuits Are Good for America: Disciplined Democracy, Big Business, and the Common Good 93 (NYU Press 2001).

76. Abel, *supra* note 1, at 291.

77. Finley, *supra* note 42, at 853.

78. Heidi Li Feldman, *Loss*, 35 N. M. L. Rev. 375 (2005).

79. *Id.* at 376.

80. *Id.* at 384.

81. *See* Sharkey, *supra* note 43, at 429–51. *See also* Joseph H. King, *Pain and Suffering, Noneconomic Damages, and the Goals of Tort Law*, 57 S.M.U. L. Rev.163, 205–06 (2004) (advocating abolition of noneconomic damages and enhancement of economic damages by such recharacterization); Lars Noah, *Comfortably Numb: Medicalizing (and Mitigating) Pain-and-Suffering Damages*, 42 U. Mich. J. L. Reform 431, 437 (2009) ("courts should recast as medical expenses at least some of the sums currently designated as nonpecuniary losses").

Index

Abel, Richard, 180
Abortion: in wrongful birth cases, 128–138
Abraham, Kenneth, 72
Actuarial tables, sex-based, 161. *See also* Gender-based tables
Admiralty, 161–162
AFP blood tests, 130, 133
African American plaintiffs: in false imprisonment case, 52–55; in forced sterilization cases, 105–110; in lead paint poisoning cases, 139–140, 142–144; in wrongful death cases, 57–61, 161
Alternative causation theories, 146–153
Amniocentesis, 129, 132
Andon v. 302–304 Mott Street Associates, 145
Assault, 63, 66
Austin, Regina, 31, 33
Automobile insurance, 70, 71

Baker, Tom, 71
Battery, 38, 63, 66
Bell Curve, The, 150–151
Bender, Leslie, 31
Bernstein, Anita, 194n40
Bias, definitions of. *See* Gender bias; Racial bias
Biracial plaintiffs, and race-based tables, 161
Black-only damage precedents. *See* Segregated precedents
Blood lead levels, 139–140
Bohlen, Francis, 16
Boykin v. Plauche, 59
Boyles v. Kerr, 97
Broadnax v. Gonzalez, 103, 209n45
Bublick, Ellen, 32
But-for test for causation, 121–124
Bystander cases, 10, 47, 113–117, 185; definition of, 93

Calabresi, Judge Guido, 64
Canadian tort cases, 163–164
Caps on noneconomic damages, 2, 6, 170–182; gender impact of, 175–176; impact on children, 176; impact on elderly, 176–177; racial impact of, 177–178
Causal attribution, 4, 120, 124–128, 153
Causation, 119–153. *See also* Causal attribution; General causation; Specific causation
Cause-in-fact, 4, 120–124
City of Los Angeles Dep't of Water & Power v. Manhart, 161
Civil rights claims: for forced sterilization, 105–109; for workplace harassment, 76–82, 85–87
Civil rights principles, 8, 78, 81–86
Coase, Ronald, 14
Cognitive bias, 1, 6, 124–128, 185–186
Cognitive impairments, in lead paint poisoning cases, 138–150
Common carrier doctrine, 49
Compensation-deterrence theory, 17
Compensatory damages: definition of, 157
Consent to sexual encounters, 93, 101
Consolidated Rail Corp. v. Gotshall, 91, 207n11
Contract law. *See* Negligent infliction of emotional distress
Corgan v. Mueling, 99

Corrective justice, 9, 14–15, 64
Counterfactual reasoning, 121–124, 135–136, 150–153
Coverture, doctrine of, 35–36, 69
Criminal conversation claims, 38–39
Critical approach to tort law, 13, 21–29, 33–34
Critical Legal Studies, 16
Critical race theory, 7, 26–28
Critical theory, 15–16
Critical torts scholarship, 13–14, 30–34
Crossover effect, from damage caps, 182
Cultural feminism, 7, 25–26, 93

Dalton, Clare, 74
Damages, 155–182. *See also* Economic damages; Loss of future earning capacity; Noneconomic damages; Survival damages; Wrongful death cases
Danger zone rule, 94, 113
Death telegrams, 95, 104
Delgado, Richard, 30, 127–128
DES cases, 173, 174
Devaluation, 2, 28, 30–33, 36–37, 52–62, 162, 185
Dichotomies. *See* Economic/noneconomic distinction; Physical/emotional distinction
Dignity, harms to, 84–85
Dillon v. Legg, 113–114
Direct victim cases, 94–102; definition of, 93
Discovery requests, in lead paint cases, 144–148
Disparate impact theory, 24, 195n45, 186
Dispositional v. situational explanations, 29, 125, 152
Dobbs, Dan B., 216n3
Domestic violence cases, 68–76; absence of liability insurance in, 70–73; as assault, battery, and false imprisonment, 66; intentional infliction tort, 66–67, 75–76; interspousal immunity, 68–70; joinder rule in, 74; scarcity of tort cases, 67–68; statute of limitations in, 73–74
Down Syndrome, 129, 138
Du Bois, W. E. B., 54
Dugro, Justice Phillip Henry, 53–57
Dunphy v. Gregor, 116
Duty to act reasonably: limitations on, 89; in physical injury cases, 93

Economic damages, 3; definition of, 157; gender-and race-based tables, 158–170
Economic/noneconomic distinction, 157, 171–172, 181, 187
Eggshell plaintiff rule, 112, 121,141
Eisenstadt v. Baird, 131
Ellman, Ira, 75
Emotional distress cases, 66–87, 89–117. *See also* Intentional infliction of emotional distress; Negligent infliction of emotional distress
Equal Employment Opportunity Commission, 65, 67
Equal protection cases, 130

Factual causation. *See* But-for test for causation; Cause-in-fact
False imprisonment, 52–53, 63, 66
Family member exclusion, in homeowners' liability policies, 71–72
Feigenson, Neil, 125
Feinberg, Kenneth, 156, 164
Feldman, Heidi Li, 181
Feminist theories, 7, 46. *See also* Cultural feminism; Intersectional feminism; Liberal feminism; Radical feminism
Finley, Lucinda, 31, 180
Formal equality, 24, 27, 45–46
Fundamental attribution error, 24, 124, 125–126, 137, 152

Gender and racial stereotypes, 4, 48, 50–51, 151–152
Gender-based tables, 5, 7, 158–170
Gender bias, definition of, 23–25
Gender stereotypes, 4, 24, 42, 48, 50–51, 138, 151–152, 185
General causation, 122, 140
General damages, 181
German measles (rubella), 129, 131

Gesell, Judge Gerhardt, 108
Gleitman v. Cosgrove, 131
Goldberg, John, 17, 20
Gonzalez, Justice Alberto, 98
Green, Leon, 20
Green, Michael, 17
Griffin v. Brady, 52–55
Gulf, Colorado & Santa Fe Railway Co. v. Luther, 48
Guzman v. Kirchhoefel, 115

Hanson, Jon, 14, 191n6
Harnicher v. University of Utah Medical Center, 111
Hoffman, Frederick, 162
Holmes, Justice Oliver Wendell, 41, 42, 63–64, 68
Homans v. Boston Elevated Railway, 40
Homeowners' insurance policies, 70–72
Honor culture, 84
Hostile environment harassment, 3, 67, 68, 77–78, 85–86

Impact rule, 9, 40, 42–45
Insurance. *See* Family member exclusion; Homeowners' insurance policies; Intentional acts exclusion; Liability insurance
Intangible loss. *See* Intentional infliction of emotional distress; Negligent infliction of emotional distress; Noneconomic damages.
Intentional acts exclusion, in homeowners' liability policies, 71–73, 97
Intentional infliction of emotional distress, 66–87; definition of, 66; in domestic violence cases, 66–76; in workplace harassment cases, 76–86. *See also* Outrageous conduct
Intentional torts, 38, 63–87. *See also* Assault; Battery; False Imprisonment; Intentional infliction of emotional distress; Slander
Intersectional feminism, 23, 26–27
Interspousal immunity, 23, 68–70, 75
IQ, effect of lead exposure on, 140
IQ testing of mothers, 145–146, 149–151

Israeli Supreme Court, 163

Joinder rule, in domestic violence context, 74

Kamir, Orit, 84
Keeton, Robert, 155
Koehler, Jonathan, 128
Komesar, Neil, 179
Krieger, Linda, 125

Language discrimination claims, 77
Larson, Jane, 31
Law and economics, 7, 14, 64
Lawrence, Charles, 27
Lead paint cases, 4–5, 138–153; African American and Hispanic plaintiffs in, 139–140; alternative causation theories in, 141, 144–153; cognitive impairments, 140–143; discovery requests in, 144–146; IQ testing of mothers in, 144–153; racial and poverty context of, 29, 139–140
Legal Realism, 9, 17, 19–20, 33, 120
Liability insurance, in domestic violence context, 3, 70–72
Liberal feminism, 7, 25
Los Angeles Department of Water and Power v. Manhart, 161
Loss of consortium claims, 35, 116–117
Loss of future earning capacity, 158–159
Louisiana wrongful death study, 57–61, 185; racial differentials in, 61
Lozoya v. Sanchez, 116

MacKinnon, Catharine A., 26, 101
Make-whole principle, 157–158, 168, 169–170
Malone, Wex S., 19, 123
Married Women's Property Acts, 35, 69
McClellan, Frank, 32
McMillan v. City of New York, 156
Medical Injury Compensation Reform Act (MICRA), 171, 175
Medical malpractice cases, 121–122, 128–138
Migdal v. Rim Abu Hanna, 163
Minow, Martha, 55

Miscarriages and stillbirths, 23, 25, 39–40, 45, 47, 103–105
Mishandling of corpses, 95, 104
Mitchell v. Rochester Ry. Co., 197n13
Moral hazard, 72
Mortality tables, 162
Mother/child relationships, 4, 113–116
Multiple cause cases, 10, 139
Multiracial plaintiffs, and race-based tables, 161

Negligence, 63–64, 89–117
Negligent infliction of emotional distress, 3–4, 89–117; bystander cases, 113–117; contract limitation, 95–96; employment discrimination cases, 102; fear-of-disease cases, 94; near-miss cases, 94; reproductive harm cases, 102–112; sexual exploitation cases, 97–102
Nervous shock cases, 9, 36–47
No-fault divorce, 70
Noneconomic damages, 2; caps on, 170–182; definition of, 157; rhetorical significance of, 181
Normality bias, 24, 127–128, 136
Nursing home cases, 176–177

Omission bias, 24, 128, 136
Oswald v. LeGrand, 104
Outrageous conduct, 7, 26, 28, 31, 41–50, 66–67, 75–80, 99, 185. *See* Intentional infliction of emotional distress

Pain and suffering damages, 5, 38, 57, 61,157
Physical/emotional distinction, 2, 36–40, 47, 187
Physical injury or manifestation rule: definition of, 94; in miscarriage cases, 103–104
Pluralist scholars, 196n68
Posner, Judge Richard, 14
Postmodernism, 16
Poulter, Susan, 148
Pound, Roscoe, 63–64, 68
Powers, William, 17
Preemption of tort claims, 80–81
Prentice, Robert, 128
Principles of the Law of Family Dissolution, 75
Privacy, constitutional right to, 131
Progressive approaches to tort law, 191n3
Prosser, William, 16, 42, 83, 155
Proximate cause, 43, 89, 112, 121
Pruitt, Lisa, 83
Public policy tort, 170
Punitive damages: definition of, 157; in Title VII cases, 76
Purcell v. St. Paul City Ry. Co., 43

Rabin, Robert, 17, 179
Race-based tables, 5, 7, 158–170, 187
Race-neutral mortality tables, 162
Race Traits and Tendencies of the American Negro, 162
Racial and ethnic stereotypes, 4, 48, 126, 151–152, 185
Racial bias, definition of, 27–28
Racial devaluation, 2, 32–33, 52–62, 185
Racial harassment cases, 3, 68, 79–80
Racial insult, 30, 48–52; cases brought by whites, 48–52; proposal for tort of, 30
Racially segregated precedents. *See* Segregated precedents
Radical feminism, 7, 26, 101
Rape, 32, 71
Reasonable man standard, 31, 42
Reasonable person standard, 86
Regan, Milton, 19
Relational injury, 89, 113–117
Relf v. Weinberger, 108
Reproductive harm, 4, 6, 102–112. *See also* Miscarriages and stillbirths
Restatement of Torts (Third), 2, 63; cause-in-fact, 121–122, 123; debate over duty in, 89; intentional infliction of emotional distress, 75; negligent infliction of emotional distress, 90, 95, 96, 115; physical/emotional distinction in, 92; physical injury, 93; proximate cause or scope of liability, 121
Roberts, Dorothy, 106, 109, 151

Robertson, David, 19, 122, 124, 127
Robinette, Christopher, 34
Robinson v. Cutchin, 109
Roe v. Wade, 4, 128, 133, 135
Rubella cases, 129, 131
Rustad, Michael, 176

The Saginaw and the Hamilton, 161–162; admiralty damages, 162
Same-sex harassment cases, 65, 77, 81
Schlanger, Margo, 44
Schoen, Johanna, 106
Schwartz, Gary, 17
Scope of liability, 121. *See also* Proximate cause
Segregated precedents, in damages, 58–61
Separate spheres ideology, 36, 43, 45, 48; as linked to race, 42, 48
September 11 Victim Compensation Fund, 5, 156
Sex-based tables. *See* Gender-based tables
Sex stereotypes. *See* Gender stereotypes
Sexual exploitation cases, 2, 4, 97–102
Sexual harassment cases, 3, 68, 71, 76, 81–83, 85–86, 174
Sexual orientation discrimination claims, 77
Sharkey, Catherine, 68, 76, 181–182
Siegel, Reva, 61–62
Slander, 83
Slavery, 27, 35–36, 82
Social and cognitive psychology, 4, 8, 120, 124–128, 134–138
Spade v. Lynn & Boston Railroad, 40
Specific causation, 122, 141
Spector, Justice Rose B., 98
Statutes of limitations, 3, 73–74
Stereotypes, of black women, 51–52, 151–152. *See also* Gender stereotypes; Racial and ethnic stereotypes
Stereotypes, of white women, 42, 48, 50–51. *See also* Gender stereotypes
Sterilization cases, 23, 29, 105–110, 185
Sugarman, Stephen, 75
Survival damages, 57, 59–61

Thomas, Justice Clarence, 91
Title VII of the Civil Rights Act of 1964, 67, 76–77, 80, 82, 85–86, 161
Tort reform, 6, 155, 175–182, 187
Tort theory, 13–34. *See also* Corrective justice; Critical approach to tort law; Law and economics
Toxic tort cases, 122, 146–147. *See also* Lead paint cases

U.S. Constitutional rights, 96–97, 105, 160–161
U.S. v. Bedonie, 160

Victim's perspective, 22, 194n39

Wachtler, Justice Sol, 132, 135, 138
Walker v. Pierce, 106
Walker v. Thompson, 79
Wang, Lu-in, 127, 152
Weinstein, Judge Jack, 155
Welke, Barbara, 45
Wheeler Tarpeh-Doe v. United States, 161
White racial privilege, 37, 48–52
White, G. Edward, 34
Workers' compensation, 58
Workers' compensation exclusivity provision, 80
Worklife expectancy, 159
Workplace harassment, 3, 65, 67–68, 76–86
Wrongful birth cases, 4, 128–138
Wrongful conception cases, 129
Wrongful death cases, 28, 57–61, 103, 117; in admiralty, 161–162. *See also* Survival damages
Wrongful life claims, 132

Young v. Broussard, 59

Zipursky, Benjamin, 191n5

About the Authors

MARTHA CHAMALLAS is the Robert J. Lynn Chair in Law at Moritz College of Law, The Ohio State University, and the author of *Introduction to Feminist Legal Theory*.

JENNIFER B. WRIGGINS is the Sumner T. Bernstein Professor of Law at the University of Maine School of Law.

CPSIA information can be obtained at www.ICGtesting.com
Printed in the USA
LVOW07*2355220816

501425LV00001B/1/P